PRESERVATION HALL

Music from the Heart

PRESERVATION HALL

Music from the Heart

by

William Carter

W. W. Norton & Company
New York   London

Manufacturing by The Courier Group

Printed in the United States of America

First Edition

ISBN 0-393-02915-8

W. W. Norton & Company, Inc.
500 Fifth Avenue, New York, NY 10110
W. W. Norton & Company, Ltd
10 Coptic Street, London WC1A 1PU

1 2 3 4 5 6 7 8 9 0

*Frontispiece: On a typical
night in Preservation Hall the
veteran New Orleans jazzmen
included Louis Nelson
(trombone), Kid Thomas
Valentine (trumpet), Emanuel
Paul (saxophone) and Joe "Kid
Twat" Butler (bass).*

*Page viii: Banjoist-singer
Emanuel Sayles sang from the
heart at Preservation Hall.*

Also by William Carter:
Ghost Towns of the West (1971/1976)
Middle West Country (1975)
Eighteen Nudes (1987)

CONTENTS

ACKNOWLEDGEMENTS

The rich river of New Orleans jazz has fed Western culture so long, now, that it is impossible to say who really created this book. But among those who gave their time directly, thanks go first and foremost to the musicians of Preservation Hall. Some I have known personally for 20 years. The insights gained from people such as Willie and Percy Humphrey, Narvin Kimball, Sing Miller, DeDe and Billie Pierce, Chester Zardis, Jim Robinson, Cie Frazier and Kid Thomas go deeper than the formal interviews I also conducted with several of them.

Working on this book from the mid-1980s onward stimulated me to get to know many more of the musicians, including Louis Nelson, Frank Parker, Kid Sheik Colar, Sadie Peterson, Emanuel Paul, Manny Crusto, James Prevost, Frank Fields, Wendell Brunious, Michael White, Stanley Stephens, Leonard Ferguson and Paul Crawford. Frank Demond, a friend and co-musician since the early 1950s, lent both personal insights and splendid photographs. Further views came from a number of foreign-born musicians who have not only been working on and off at the Hall for many years, but have also been touring with the veterans; among these were Lars Edegran, Barry Martyn, Trevor Richards, Clive Wilson and Jacques Gauthé. Of the New Orleans jazzmen's wives whom I have been fortunate to know over the years, special mention must be made of the help of Alma Barnes, Ora Humphrey and Kathy Edegran.

Managing a jazz institution requires a unique commitment, as this book makes clear. The help of those involved in running Preservation Hall has been indispensable. In absolute first place, of course, was owner-manager Allan Jaffe, who gave generously of his time in countless settings – from cross-country buses and concert halls, to the streets of San Francisco, to the deep recesses of the Hall's voluminous archives, never before opened to a researcher.

Hall staffer Jane Botsford cheerfully diverted many hours from her demanding schedule for my raids on her files and knowledge. Chris Botsford was equally accommodating in matters concerning the road tours and his special relationships with the musicians. Resa Lambert, a stalwart both at the Hall and on the road, was helpful indeed. Sonny Fagart, a knowledgeable part-timer at the Hall, was another plus, as was Speedy Gonzales, who remained part of the Hall scene longer than anyone. Special insights were provided by Bill Sones, who has lovingly driven and cared for the musicians across hundreds of thousands of miles of Greyhound Bus travel. Last, but far from least among the people of Preservation Hall, I certainly must thank Sandra Jaffe, Allan's widow, who took charge after his untimely demise, and after my manuscript was completed. A salute, too, to the Jaffes' two talented sons, Russell and Benjamin.

For anyone researching any aspect of New Orleans music, the Jazz Archive at Tulane University is an invaluable resource. It deserves more foundation support. The Archive's successive curators offered generous assistance, each in his special way. Sequestered in his own archive-like haunts, William Russell conversed with me far into the night, cooked Thanksgiving dinner and critiqued the manuscript with an eagle eye. Richard B. Allen steered me in many unexpectedly fruitful directions, notably toward private papers and writings, and shared his vivid memories and early associations with people and events surrounding the Hall. Curtis Jerde provided an historian's needed perspective and carefully perused the manuscript. Bruce Boyd Raeburn and Alma D. Williams were most helpful in guiding me through the Archive's collection itself.

At the excellent Historic New Orleans Collection, John Lawrence, curator of photography, was kind indeed. And in New York, Alan Lomax, who for many years headed the Library of Congress' folk music department, took time from a tight schedule to give an inspired interview.

Equally indispensable has been the help of unaffiliated individuals who simply love the music and its players. One must at least try to name them. Heading the list is Kelley Edmiston, who volunteered enthusiastically and selflessly on many levels, from interviewing to "gophering," but most especially in paving the way to people who knew her mother, Barbara Reid. Caroline Richmond went far beyond the call of duty in over a year of tough and very caring editorial work on every detail of the book. Pivotal interviews, letters, permissions and other assistance were also provided by Bill Edmiston, Ken Mills, Al Clark, Sue Coil, Jules Cahn, Terry Dash, Dodie and John Simmons, Pat Davies, Nancy Collins, Charlie DeVore, Henry Blackburn, Bob Greene, Sascha Borenstein, Sally Smith Culton, Jerome Cushman, Steve Baffrey, Al Rose, Alden Ashforth, Butch Thompson, Leonard Brackett, Betty Carter, George and Nina Buck, Sue Hall, Shirl and Dick House, Fannie and Harry B. Jaffe, Don Knies, Marty Kaelin, Don Marquis, Mona MacMurray, Michael Smith, Gerry Spiegel, Herbert Friedwald, Robbie and Bunch Schlosser, Charles Stroud, John Paddon, Lulu White, JoAnn Clevenger, Stella Webb, David Young, John Truman, Hugh de Rosayro, Severn Darden, Jack Cooley, Bill Hinson, John Bernard and Tom Bethell. Helpful in other ways were McNeal Breaux, George Smith, Bill Bissonette, Fred Starr, Ray Avery, Joel Gardner, Doggy Hund, Marcel Joly, Bob and Lynn Layman, Ed Marks, Lee Friedlander, Neelan Crawford, Ed Lawless, Gregg Stafford, Tommy Sancton, Jr., Joel Palmer, Jempi de Donder, Walt Sereth, Chrissie Huneke, Haydi Sowerwine, my literary agent – Bob Lescher, and my publisher Alyn Shipton.

An incalculable debt of gratitude goes to my wife, Ulla Morris Carter, who has helped in ways far too numerous to name.

If I have forgotten anyone, it was not by intention.

To my teachers

Introduction

LET IT SHINE

"You got to have soul, man, to do this work."
—pianist and singer Sing Miller

Sitting on a bare bench in the near-darkness, I feel a centering in the heart. In a few minutes the front gate will swing open, letting the crowds pour in. As yet, however, the interior of Preservation Hall is like a nearly vacant stage set. Only a couple of musicians are here. One is tuning his banjo. The other is warming up his trumpet with quiet, long tones. I've said hi to them, and will say hi to the five others as they trickle in. But tonight, for some reason, it's as if I'm saying hi to something inside myself – to a certain feeling I always get when I'm around these wonderful people.

This book is a way of saying thanks to the music that has been an important part of my life for 40 years, to people like owner-manager Allan Jaffe, and to these Preservation Hall musicians who have done so much to deepen my understanding of New Orleans jazz. For well over a quarter century – roughly a third the history of jazz – Preservation Hall has been the single most important factor in re-introducing America, and the world, to the basic style of this nation's most vital and original cultural product.

I wave to the bass player as he takes his place: strong old black fingers carefully testing the gut;

The unabashed joy of authentic New Orleans jazz was summed up by cornetist-singer DeDe Pierce as he performed at Preservation Hall.

wood creaking in complaint to a slightly turned knob. Under the weak overhead bulbs, the faces are like masks, with deeply shadowed eye sockets. The banjo man is strumming chords now, humming to himself, working on what sounds like a new composition.

I have heard them, and so many others, the living and the dead, in so many other settings, at picnics and in Greyhound buses, and in concert halls from Midwestern colleges to New York's prestigious Lincoln Center. But this room is like no other concert hall on earth. Throbbing heart of the operation, the Preservation Hall building is some two hundred years old, and, due to a policy of benign neglect, it looks it. It has become famous for being so unprepossessing and for making its customers either stand in the back or sit on backless benches or – as I saw Jimmy Carter do not so long ago – on the floor.

At the moment a lady waiting in the line along the sidewalk has pressed her pretty face expectantly to a smeared, half-obscured pane of the sagging French doors behind the silent drums. Few realize the smoky smear was added to the glass for a Steve McQueen film shot here in 1965 and that Allan Jaffe avoided removing it afterwards. The old wooden floor, ceiling and walls, with their long-faded pegboard, make for excellent acoustics. It's a room hardly larger than many of the high-ceilinged living rooms here in the historic French Quarter. Dotted around in the crepuscular dimness, gloomy, richly pigmented oil paintings of jazz musicians made in the 50s and 60s serve as a reminder that Preservation Hall evolved in that period out of an art gallery which held occasional pass-the-hat sessions featuring the then forgotten and down-at-the-heels pioneer jazzmen.

Now the drummer and the trombone player – the latter the only white member of tonight's lineup – come in joking and laughing. I myself have played clarinet here on rare occasions, usually just sitting in for a set, and something in the relaxed yet wholly professional manner of these men makes me recall the incomparable warmth of their audiences. So long has Preservation Hall been a tourist "must" in New Orleans that it's hard to realize how thoroughly these musicians were ignored after the music's heyday in the 1920s. This is a town, and a nation, of sharply

The lively tradition of musicians' business cards highlights the functional, adaptive, competitive spirit which has marked New Orleans jazz throughout the century of its existence.

differing opinions, and everyone seems to have their own idea about what Preservation Hall is and means. Visitors often wax sentimental, even mythological, about the place. Some of the buggy drivers on Royal Street have been overheard telling tourists Louis Armstrong was born here (one of the jazz musicians was indeed born in the Hall, and another died here during a performance). But the players themselves are notably concrete and unsentimental. While they are extraordinarily warm and friendly with visitors, their main interest has always been to get good jobs. And that is exactly what Allan Jaffe's skillful management, above all, provided them with.

As the rotund piano man Sing Miller shuffles in, he throws me only a cursory gesture, so I know he's in one of his grumpy moods. I think of how he confided his personal and spiritual pain to me one night, in the dressing room of a huge concert pavilion out on the road. I think of how Sing won that tree-sitting contest in the 1930s, of the paving and hauling work he used to do in lean times when there was only one music job a week or a month. But what I invariably remember about Sing is how moved I am whenever he sings, in that tough-tender way of his, those great spirituals such as *His Eye Is on the Sparrow* or *This Little Light of Mine*.

My mind goes back to a hundred conversations, to a hundred interviews recorded by others, to a jazz history transformed from distant academic knowledge into a vital, living reality through Preservation Hall. What the people will experience here tonight – in fact the gate has opened, they are already flooding in – is but the tip of a much larger iceberg. That tip is the cutting and moving edge. And Willie Humphrey, my favorite living clarinet player, has just come in, wearing his huge Stetson hat and carrying his tiny instrument case all patched and wrapped with plastic tape. Which takes me much further back . . .

* * *

Remembering the Los Angeles of the 1940s and early 1950s, I think of those strange, occasional high palms, poking their lonesome heads into the blue air beginning to grey with smog. And I think of the

Stalwarts Percy Humphrey (left) and Kid Sheik Colar, bandleaders at the Hall for more than 30 years, are shown playing in the Eureka Brass Band, led by Humphrey. From the 20s into the 60s, both paraded through New Orleans' sweltering streets and cemeteries, carrying on a form indispensable to early jazz.

wonderful Kid Ory band. It was the first jazz band that I ever listened to, and it brought a rush of joy which bonded me permanently to the music of New Orleans.

Although several ricky-tick Dixie outfits were grinding away as usual around town, Ory's was the genuine article. Those six or seven mysterious Creole and black men were doing their luminous thing six nights a week at the Beverly Cavern, a dimly lit joint only a few blocks from the wide, silent, leafy, well-clipped, upper-middle-class street where our brick Tudor home was located. I doubt I'm alone among traditional jazz enthusiasts in having felt that, while wandering in an urban desert, one suddenly heard the trumpet call of Truth.

Of course, it was a feeling which blended easily into the idealism of youth. Fabulous baseball or detective figures out of a golden past, such as Lou Gehrig or Sherlock Holmes, were quickly replaced by a galaxy of forgotten New Orleans jazz players of the 1920s. But this was more than hero worship. If my youthful imagination was inflamed by partisan books, cultist magazines and the faded jazz photos I stuck up around the walls of my room, it was the

Old/new star Willie Humphrey, born in 1900, plugged along in relative obscurity for his first 60 years. Then, in the next 30, he earned international acclaim, appearing regularly at the Hall and touring widely with its bands.

music, pure and (deceptively) simple, which really captivated me.

Being about 14, I was only able to go to the Beverly Cavern occasionally – when I could convince my mother to take me there. The music didn't even start until about the time I was supposed to go to bed. Once, I remember listening to the Ory band through the wall from a phone booth in the Chinese restaurant next door. Some of the musicians took their intermissions there, but I was much too awestruck and self-conscious to approach any of those amazing beings who seemed to have dropped into my WASPish world from some other planet.

More often, in my upstairs isolation, I would turn off all the lights in my room, get into bed, glue my ear to the speaker of my little radio, and enter a cocoon of rapture as Ory's weekly radio broadcast came on with tunes such as *Down Among the Sheltering Palms*, his lightning-fast *Tiger Rag* and the inevitable sign-off number, *Without You for an Inspiration Dear*. Only those who heard that famous band, with its powerful rhythm section, its succession of limpid Creole clarinetists, and Ory's rich, rich tone, will know quite what I mean.

At the core of my rapture there was a kind of longing, a craving for something those musicians must have in order to produce such sounds, and which I was somehow missing. Their secret seemed to float over the Hollywood Hills, just like the warm moon beyond my leaded window panes – tantalizingly close, yet unreachably distant.

My collection of old 78 rpm records and some of those new LPs kept expanding. Los Angeles had at least three fine speciality jazz stores around 1950, and I spent a lot of time in them, wheedling owners like Ray Avery and Nesuhi Ertegun into revealing scraps of what seemed their limitless knowledge of the idiom. At Nesuhi's place, the Jazz Man Record Shop, I saw a notice on the bulletin board: a young start-up band was looking for a clarinet player. I knew the instrument, and wanted to play jazz, although I certainly didn't know how. With sweating palms I took a big chance and dialed the number. Before long I was part of an as-yet rather cacophonous but stylistically pure ensemble called the Costa Del Oro Jazz Band. We rehearsed every Friday night in the back room of Ray Avery's Record Roundup.

The rest of the week I would play my records over and over again, clumsily improvising along with them, copying the phrases of the great clarinetist Johnny Dodds as I tried to tease out his inner secrets. In my heart of hearts I felt I was reaching for something that did not really belong to me. What was it about the way the black New Orleans guys played? It was a quality you could recognize but which was not even in the notes, really, let alone in formal musical notation or words of explanation. It was in the music, yet beyond the music.

Looking back, that magnetism seemed some-how related to the shyness that so afflicted me in those years. Behind the jazz and the blues and their folk sources was an uninhibited joy, an emotional honesty, which one longed for amid WASPish constraints. Hiding it, virtually fearing it within oneself, one can nonetheless be powerfully attracted by it when it manifests in something or someone else. I sometimes wonder how many white fans are drawn to black music for the same reason. Integrity of spirit and feeling is one of the American Negro's great musical gifts to the world.

But if it was really a part of myself I was seeking,

A great night at the Hall: visitors typically jamming the intimate, funky room heard earthy strains of (from left) Louis Nelson, Cie Frazier, DeDe Pierce, Chester Zardis, George Lewis and Billie Pierce.

I didn't realize it yet. I was only sure Johnny Dodds possessed that inner release, that sureness and ease, by birthright – and that I didn't. Which meant I would have to work extra hard to come anywhere near capturing it.

Imitation is an excellent way to begin to learn any art form. On the other hand, neo-classicism can also become a cozy trap. A sad aspect of the traditional jazz revival is that a number of its musicians have gone on eating crumbs off the master's table forever, rather than breaking through to their own underlying sources of inspiration.

The real secret of New Orleans music comes in the realization that a man no longer needs to run after it, or try to become it, because he already *is* it. Certainly there is learning to be done in some conventional musical ways. But the essence, formidable to many who lack African roots, is not so much in adding things, tensely filling up every space, forcing, mastering and intending; as in releasing, shedding stiffness, letting go the four-square order, celebrating the accidental and becoming one with the dance. The music creates the player, flowing not from him but through him.

It would be years, yet, before I came anywhere near that kind of comprehension. It would have to await the arrival of the Preservation Hall bands. They would bring into our midst not only their wonderful New Orleans jazz, but something of the social alluvium in which it grows, surrounding it and feeding it – feeding us, listeners and learners alike – until we were drawn into that community of musical feeling, that joyful essence latent in us all.

* * *

For the time being I just beavered away, trying to learn the notes. I played once or twice a week with one band and another all through the 1950s, most of which were taken up by college. For six months in 1955 I left school to make a national tour with Turk Murphy's Jazz Band, a well-known revival group in the San Francisco idiom. It was then that I happened to meet a man who was already a folk hero among traditional jazz buffs, and who would later play an important role around Preservation Hall.

Having begun collecting in 1929, Bill Russell was one of the earliest and most dedicated of traditional jazz record aficionados. He had also co-authored and co-edited a seminal book, *Jazzmen,* which first appeared in 1939. But Russell's most famous contribution was his rehabilitation, promotion and recording of the legendary trumpet player Bunk Johnson. From the 1940s onward, Bunk, and the New Orleans musicians Russell found to play with him, including George Lewis and Jim Robinson, became *the* jazz revival for generations of fans all over the world.

Russell issued records by them and others on a label he called American Music. Recorded in New Orleans by old black men in their undershirts, sitting in rickety chairs in old wooden halls that possessed a beautiful natural resonance, these sides flabbergasted us with their powerful simplicity, their haunting blues feeling, and their amazing purity and drive. For a lot of traditional jazz lovers, Bill Russell was the one who discovered King Tut.

Turk's piano player, Pete Clute, took me to meet Russell one November day while we were playing at the Blue Note in Chicago. Although he was just 50, I thought him quite old – he already had a shock of

PHONE — KID THOMAS   AND   THOMAS VALENTINE
FO 1-1447   FO 1-1447

Kid Thomas' Dixieland Band
MUSIC
FURNISHED FOR ALL OCCASIONS

KID THOMAS,   1132 WAGNER ST.

wild white hair. But there was no doubt of his vigor and dedication. He was living upstairs over a shock absorber factory in a borrowed place which, because of his voluminous files, resembled the stacks of the Library of Congress. He led us on a whirlwind tour of the narrow aisles, talking a blue streak as he yanked down wads of ragtime sheet music to show Pete. For me he played a taped interview with the great Creole clarinetist Omer Simeon. Russell's clothing was so nondescript, and his manner so self-effacing, that, despite my usual reserve, I felt very welcome.

After giving a lot of his time to two musicians still pretty wet behind the ears, he invited us to come back. I promised to do so – little realizing that this would be in New Orleans, where I'd find him living in much the same style, and 30 years later, as I began work on this book. (But then, many of the events around Bill Russell turn out to have time spans on that order.) It was not the last time I would picture "Mr Russell," as the New Orleans musicians respectfully call him, as a kind of medieval monk in his unwavering, zealous purism. Later, someone showed me a letter he had written a couple of years before I met him. For all of Bill's eccentric opinions in other areas, it contains a passage that seems to me to sum up his essential nobility of character:

> Bill Colburn [Russell's close friend] once said, "Music tells a story" – a truth so self-evident and elementary that no intellectual would ever stop to even think so simple a thought. And Bunk said, "When you play music it is like talking from the heart, you don't lie." When he played, every note meant something, not an extra sound or flourish was used.
>
> Maybe some of us, who think so much in the spirit of music, might actually forget that the words we use to talk and write every day also should mean something. They also, at least as much as the notes in music, can and should tell a story. They too should be used to tell the truth.

My last vision of Russell, that November day in Chicago, was of an intense, ascetic figure, huddled in a jacket far too thin against the frigid winds blowing off Lake Michigan. White hair flying, he raced off on an angle of his own, dodging like a halfback through the oncoming rush-hour traffic. We feared for his life. I felt grateful to have been brought a little closer to the heart of jazz.

Bustling night-time crowds along St Peter Street, from the 70s onwards, were a sharp change from the somnolence which had marked the French Quarter in earlier decades.

By 1989 Russell, at 84, was suffering badly from asthma and severe eczema. Yet he was was still to be found almost every night in the entryway of Preservation Hall, a gaunt figure in a seaman's watch cap, obscurely perched on a rickety metal stool under a bare bulb, selling records, petting the cat, and occasionally chatting with somebody who might know him. I still felt grateful.

* * *

Because I lived mainly abroad during the 1960s, I was out of touch with the jazz scene for the better part of that decade. Of Preservation Hall, I knew only that it was some kind of support system for the older black players which had recently been established in New Orleans, and that it had issued a few records.

These were years of rapid change in American life. Not least was the accelerated progress toward greater racial equality. Social and regional distinctions were breaking down, not just because of legal pressures, but as part of the widely rippling social and economic solvent that came to be known as the mass society. National values were shifting. Democratic ideals continued to erode old authoritarian structures. People began dressing more informally, and the distinction between "highbrow" and popular culture began to blur.

Back in the flapper era, jazz had given the sound track to an awakening giant: the sexual revolution. But the ancient Anglo-Saxon mind–body split would not be conquered so easily, and for 40 years pop culture had fought back with saccharine strings and soggy rhythm sections. Now it was rock music's turn to cathect a new generation's broad, deep, sometimes harshly rebellious effort to re-integrate at all levels.

Vernacular arts, such as folk music and jazz, began receiving more serious attention. Until the late 1950s these homegrown forms of expression had tended to be viewed as step-children of the arts, championed only by a few embattled liberals. At Tulane University in New Orleans, an invaluable collection now known as the Jazz Archive was established – a pioneering effort since followed by other universities in support of this uniquely American art form.

The 1960s also brought big changes to the jazz and popular music business. Chasing the young dancers and their disposable incomes, mega-buck promotion poured into rock. Smoke-filled cabarets, such as the one where I had listened to the Ory band, were no longer economically viable. But huge outdoor concerts and jazz festivals – perfect totems of the mass society – climbed a growth curve that was still rising a generation later. The once fiercely fought argument about progress versus regress in jazz – whether it had been true and righteous in the beginning, only to be polluted, first by swing, and finally, unforgivably, by modern and cool; or whether, on the contrary, this ever-increasing technical and harmonic sophistication had spelled steady improvement – gradually gave way to a widely shared acceptance and celebration of all jazz styles, including such once-obscure forms as ragtime and early big-band music. One sign of this was an increasingly diverse and segmented low-budget recording industry.

Preservation Hall was thus born, fortuitously, into a new era of acceptance. Before long, its traveling bands of rugged "New Orleans jazz pioneers" would be billed as an American institution on major media and concert stages around the world.

My first experience of a Preservation Hall band was unforgettable. In the summer of 1969 I went to hear the Billie and DeDe Pierce band at my Alma Mater, Stanford University. A huge tent had been erected next to the Memorial Auditorium for the Summer Music Festival. It was hot and close under the glowing canvas, not just from the July sun and closely packed, rapt listeners, but from the blazing horns and expansive personalities of trumpeter DeDe Pierce and his "gang," as he used to call them.

There was Jim Robinson, laughing and waving his white handkerchief and barking out his forceful, skeletal trombone part as convincingly as he had ever done with the old George Lewis band in the days when I heard them on tour in Hollywood. There was a driving, four-beat rhythm section to confound the flaccidity of half a century of fancy white technicians trying to improve on this music. There was Cie Frazier, with his crisp, parade-style accents, reminding you that jazz drumming begins not in cabarets but in the streets, and pianist-singer Billie Pierce letting no one forget that the old blues begin and end in the heart.

It was the only jazz band I've ever seen that had two basses – incredibly powerful veteran Chester Zardis on string bass, and Preservation Hall's young white owner-manager, Allan Jaffe, on helicon (bass horn). Banjoist Narvin Kimball impressed me with his vocals, with their thread of righteous church-spirituals that had long been weaving their way into New Orleans music. And as for clarinetist Willie Humphrey, this marked the beginning of a long, very important and very personal learning process for me.

That learning might never have occurred if the same band had not kept coming back to Stanford every summer for over 25 years. I got to know them and their music a little better each visit. It was a wonderful band; but it was also more than a band, and what I've learned from them goes beyond music alone.

Initially I had approached jazz with the kind of critical awareness one sees reflected in the work of many jazz writers – as if the performers' every nuance is, or should be, calculated. But this approach derives more from the European fine-arts tradition than from the players' own Afro-American roots. It amounts to trying to justify or comprehend the arti-

Famous in their respective lines of work, powerful bassist Chester Zardis and former US President Jimmy Carter greeted each other at Preservation Hall in 1984.

fact of one culture in terms of another. In fact, and in practice, jazz makes a wonderful bridge between cultures, because of its directness of appeal. But the "revival" musician's knowledge, and his ability to quote a great recorded solo note for note, are like the *New Yorker* critic's impeccable taste and artful descriptions: both are concerned with fulfilling their own value systems, which stress conscious control and cool appraisal, essentially dividing the listener from the music, which misses the point. New Orleans jazzmen do not go about it that way. Neither do their natural audiences, who come for more visceral reasons and pay most of the bills. Communication between the band and them is at the heart of the music.

In other words, jazz is participatory – a dancing music, not a studying music. Instead of being stuck up on a pedestal to be worshiped from afar, the original jazz and its players have always been part of the fabric of life in New Orleans. Hence their down-to-earth ease and spontaneity. While I'd already been a student of traditional jazz for 20 years, it took Preservation Hall to begin to bring this understanding, this feeling for the music's inner naturalness, to my own doorstep.

How was such a teaching transmitted? The spirit enters by many unseen paths. Besides the concerts themselves, there was the way the touring Preservation Hall bands carried so much of their life to California with them. New Orleans players have long been famous for this. Some keep their watches – and their minds – on New Orleans time, no matter where they might be in the world, which is also a nice metaphor for the way they beat out their own distinctive rhythms. (A few, among them Cie Frazier, have been known to wear two watches, leaving one on real, namely Louisiana, time, while compromising with the rest of the world by changing the other to conform to all their comings and goings across made-up zones.)

Every summer, through much of the 1970s, the Billie and DeDe gang would stay for two weeks or more at one of Stanford's sprawling, vacant fraternity houses. It was like a big, extended family. Many of the wives and other relations would follow along on this particular trip, and there were plenty of their children and grandchildren and great-grandchildren who had moved to California who would drop in – not to mention the road managers, themselves from Palo Alto and Stanford, plus us legions of diehard fans and our children, etc., etc. We got to know them all a little better each year, to the point where, if one of us was missing one night, the whole band would be asking about him or her.

Food is a major, continuous issue among all Orleanians. Like the French, they invariably keep their gastronomical meters tuned to the home standard. Buster Holmes would take a break from his well-known French Quarter restaurant (he was later to be franchised around town like some local black Colonel Sanders) and carry unbelievable quantities of special sausages and other elsewhere-unobtainable goodies out on the plane with him, in order to cook red beans and rice, garlic chicken and other hometown specialties for a veritable army of free-loaders. Some of us brought local bands to play for these late-afternoon feasts which preceded the concerts. This or that veteran might sit in with us, or more likely dance with some of the pretty ladies hanging around. The New Orleans jazzmen have always been kind and encouraging about our playing, and we continue to take "jump-up" (impromptu)

Stirred by the hard-to-resist joy of authentic New Orleans jazz, Californians danced amid the picnic hampers at Napa Valley's Mondavi Winery – a scene repeated countless times in the Preservation Hall Bands' three decades of summer tours across the USA.

bands to play them in and out at the gates and baggage areas of San Francisco Airport.

In those years, the entire three weeks in June and July took on the atmosphere of a non-stop New Orleans neighborhood party, replete with sit-in instrument cases and picnic hampers and ice chests, pint bottles concealed in brown bags, and big bowls of plums just picked from the tree at our house – most of it transferred en masse to the backstage of Dinkelspiel Auditorium or wherever else the band was playing that evening. Besides the evening concerts at Stanford and Berkeley and Concord, the band played daytime picnics in lovely settings such as the Mondavi winery in Napa Valley, and at San Francisco's huge, eucalyptus-banked Stern Grove, where in 1989 countless thousands were still turning out to listen to the band, bask in the sun and dance on the grass.

* * *

If all this was a long way from hiding upstairs in my room with my ear glued to the radio, so were the close-in moments of tenderness. I remember one particular evening about 1973, after a concert, sitting

The elemental trombonist Jim Robinson "had all the technique he needed to say what he wanted to say," in the words of the jazz writer Marcel Joly.

near Jim Robinson in the darkened interior of the chartered Greyhound bus. He spoke quietly, his throat choked with pain and love, about how much his recently deceased wife, Pearl, had meant to him. Drifting through memory, such moments amount to a private treasure made all the more precious by the inevitable, steady loss of one after another of these rare souls, with their gentle humor and outrageous kidding, their unbridled anger and warmly interesting tales of days gone by. What Bill Russell had said of their music is true of themselves, all the time, on the emotional level: they don't lie.

Although my way of playing was already pretty well formed, I noticed how it began to change subtly as a result of these influences. Without bothering to ask permission, I began to adopt clarinetist Willie Humphrey, not really as a teacher, but as a kind of spiritual mentor of the hard-to-define inner qualities of New Orleans play.

More than a dozen years later, I can still remember the exact spot on the Bay Bridge, on the way to a concert out at Concord, where Willie began speaking to me about the old days. He told of working the Mississippi riverboats; of once turning down a traveling job with the great Jelly Roll Morton because Jelly had the reputation of getting stranded; of playing different dates in Chicago before 1920 with legendary figures like Freddie Keppard; of a gig with King

Oliver in the colored section of the grandstands at the infamous "Black Sox" World Series. In the fading twilight, with those silver girders whipping past, my sense of being wowed by all this contrasted with a certain calm in Willie's voice. His plain, everyday acceptance of the past and the present, of himself and of me, brought an everyday normalcy to such people and events, to this world of the true knowers, which I had so long thought of as extraordinary, even mythical. He seemed to be showing me that this era and style, which I had once felt to be magically radiant, yet unreachably distant, was just part of the ongoing stream of life and music to which I too, like any decent musician, naturally belonged if I wished, carrying it forward in my time as he had in his.

That secure whatever-it-was in Willie's attitude toward the music was very evident in his playing. Over the years it reached me in an interior way, proving on a deeper level than mere words or notes that there was no more need to battle or strain or be at war with myself, nervously trying to grasp or attain something different than I in fact already was. Within the seamless web of life, jazz came to a man, not as something external or different, but as a gift from the inside, as near as one's own breath. Little by little, as the result of moments like these, I learned to give up trying to force the greats onto some pedestal. To the extent that I stopped aspiring to the music, I could just be it.

* * *

Implicit, too, in New Orleans music, is the recognition that death is part of life. Such unflinching realism, physical and spiritual, comes naturally from the city's Latin heritage. It contrasts with the attitudes long prevalent in our more Anglo-Saxon regions, where death, like passion and intoxication and other affronts to conscious control, was more typically shrouded in embarrassment. To this day, the marching bands which lead the coffins through the sweltering streets from church to cemetery are not only major wellsprings of traditional jazz tunes and style, but active proving grounds for aspiring musicians. Just as Louis Armstrong paid homage to this key part of his own background on his world-

DeDe and Billie Pierce on the road: for the trumpeter and pianist, who had worked the Decatur Street sailors' dives in the 30s, the contagious fun and shared pain were no act.

wide concert tours, so do the Preservation Hall bands, which sometimes go as far as to lead the audience on joyous, parasol-twirling march-dances around the normally staid auditoriums to the tune of *When the Saints Go Marching In*. It's one of many ways in which these musicians are constantly reaching across the footlights to make human contact, to involve us as participants rather than as passive spectators, trying not only to bring us their music but also to involve us in something of the culture from which it springs.

Although he could not join the march because he was blind, trumpeter DeDe Pierce would sing and play his heart out on *The Saints* and on countless others, such as *I Want a Little Girl* and the Creole tune *Eh, La Bas*. He would be led to his place on the stage by one of the other musicians while his wife Billie, who in later years suffered from hip trouble, made her way to the piano with the aid of a walker. When one of the Pierces was singing, the other would make little encouraging comments.

In 1973 DeDe fell seriously ill with cancer of the larynx and related problems. Weakened and thin, he demanded to play the tour anyway. (Unlike the tough commercial booking agencies handling such people as Louis Armstrong, Preservation Hall has always encouraged players to stay aboard as long as they themselves wish to keep playing. Besides being good theater, it does wonders for the oldsters' physical vitality and spirits.) DeDe seemed to save all his strength for the performances, giving ever more of himself the more his resources dwindled. Listeners wondered how anyone could blow that trumpet with such force when he had a plastic tube bending out of the end of his nose, through which he had to be fed. He received daily radiation treatments at Stanford Hospital. When the band continued their tour in the Midwest and East, Percy Humphrey, Willie's brother, had to fly out to replace DeDe, who stayed at our house while he continued his treatments.

Although DeDe was now dying at a faster rate than most of the rest of us, he spent the remaining weeks of the summer giving lessons of one kind or another. He would totter back to the garage room to sit patiently with my teenaged stepson, Jeff Hamilton, who was just learning his first chords of jazz piano. When Jeff felt frustrated, DeDe encouraged him: "That's good, that's good, man," and sang along with him on tunes like *Swanee River* and *St Louis Blues*.

Despite being constantly uncomfortable and often in pain, DeDe was unbelievably good humored. My former wife Betty and I would hear him in his room (it was really the room of Jeff's sister, Jennie), chuckling to himself as if he'd finally seen what a joke life was. Once, when Betty fumbled the feeding procedure and squirted the messy liquid formula all over DeDe and the bed, he laughed uproariously. When he was rushed to the emergency room because he was having trouble getting his breath, the doctor kept thumping him on the back and telling him to cough and say "ninety-nine." DeDe complied by repeating it in different rhythms, such as nine–*ty*-nine, improvising in his wheelchair while the doctor fussed over him, his spirit soaring and refusing to be vanquished by the body.

Every day he would talk with Billie by phone for a long time, laughing and chortling and carrying on. He would ask about each one of the other musicians, how they all were doing, about their health, how the concerts were going. Then he and his wife of almost 40 years, with whom he had performed almost exclusively all that time, would go back to billing and cooing like two young romantic lovers. When she could, Billie came back from the ongoing tour to stay with him for a while. That little room, with its little-girl decor all in yellow, became their love nest.

DeDe never complained about anything. Partly, perhaps, because he had had a very hard life, he had great dignity, great strength. He did not want anyone to be offended by the less attractive inevitabilities of his illness. He kept a bucket by his bed for his coughing and throwing up, and, despite his blindness, he would not allow anyone else to empty it. Carrying the bucket with one hand, he would feel his way to the bathroom with the other. He also insisted on washing his own handkerchiefs and underwear. His cancer treatments were painful and scary, but he took them like a warrior. He spoke well of the doctors and was grateful to all. Mingled with that inner resolve was the sweetness that permeated his playing and his whole life. His replacement, Percy Humphrey, had great respect for DeDe; Percy later told us what a great player he had been, because he had had that soul, that fire and dignity and tenderness, rushing out altogether through his shining horn. Another friend reminded me that DeDe certainly knew fear – he had been terrified at his eye examinations in the 1950s – but he also knew that friends would stand by him.

That fall, DeDe went home to New Orleans. Bill Russell visited him there in the hospital. After DeDe's doctor announced that the cancer had reached a point where he'd never play trumpet again, DeDe told Bill he would switch to playing an old banjo he had at home. "That gives the spirit of the guy, that just didn't give up," said Russell later. "I told DeDe I'd be glad to fix the banjo for him. But it was only a week and he was gone."

It was November. We flew down. I felt humbled, flooded with inner warmth, at Jeff's and my both being invited to play in one of the four street bands that helped the huge crowd accompany DeDe to his final rest. At the Jazz Requiem Mass a band, made up of Willie and Percy and Jim and Narvin and the others, played *Where He Leads Me*. Pianist Sweet Emma Barrett, herself confined to a wheelchair, sang *Just a Closer Walk with Thee*. Psalm 150 was read:

Praise ye the Lord. Praise God in his sanctuary: praise him in the firmament of his power.

Praise him for his mighty acts: praise him according to his excellent greatness.

DeDe Pierce, Napa Valley, California, July 1971

Praise him with the sound of the trumpet: praise him with the psaltery and harp.

Praise him with the timbrel and dance: praise him with stringed instruments and organs.

Praise him upon the loud cymbals: praise him upon the high sounding cymbals.

Let every thing that hath breath praise the Lord. Praise ye the Lord.

In a long article in the *New York Times*, reporter Roy Reed caught something of the flavor of the day:

The band played "When the Saints Go Marching In" in dirge style as the mourners filed out.

As the procession approached the cemetery a knot of angry young men stopped on a curb and stood cursing and threatening violence to each other because of some disagreement that had erupted suddenly in the fatigue of the humid, hot afternoon.

Then one of the bands overtook them playing "What a Friend We Have in Jesus," loud and slow, and the music swept the anger before it into the street and dissipated it, like rain water into a gutter.

The throng surged into the tiny old cemetery and jammed against the high brick tombs while the coffin was buried and the bands continued to play. After the family left, the bands led the crowd in a slow weaving march through the narrow paths between the tombs, the last dirge bouncing hollow off the crumbling bricks.

Finally they reached the gate and entered the open street. There was a pause of perhaps a minute. Then the bands separated and started away in three directions.

Suddenly one of them began to play "When the Saints Go Marching In" in a fast tempo, and the funeral-goers shouted, clapped and laughed and began to dance.

There had been a wake the evening before, and there would be a gathering at Billie and DeDe's humble cottage this night. Simple in some ways, complex in others, the feelings of those few days in New Orleans are still vivid. They seemed to come together in the moment when DeDe was actually laid to rest. Under cloudy, humid skies the teeming crowd had forced us musicians into a tight mass in front of the crypt. I was nearly touching Allan Jaffe's broad back when it suddenly began to shake with grief. Then I realized: not only had these mourners carried DeDe home, but, in another way, he had brought many of us to our true home.

Music for all Occasions
William Russell

William [Bill] Russell (shown above with his adored parakeet, Pretty Baby) was a leading figure in the gradual rediscovery of New Orleans jazz that began about 1940. He was also the "spiritual godfather" of Preservation Hall from 1961 onwards.

At the dawn of this century a new music was born in New Orleans. It was a "good time" music, to make the people happy. Its appeal was so immediate that it soon swept over the whole country and then circled the globe. It was not so much a kind of music as a style of playing. Essentially it was simply a way of "playing a melody with a beat." New Orleans musicians learned to work together to produce the loose, relaxed beat which is so irresistible that one cannot help but dance, or at least sway and pat one's foot to its swing. The easy-going, almost hypnotic rhythm at times seems to run effortlessly by itself. In this style, where the musicians strive to help each other rather than grab the spotlight, it is natural for improvised ensemble choruses to be a feature. Working together harmoniously can generate a feeling of power. The ensembles often build with cumulative effect and surging momentum to thrilling climaxes.

In New Orleans style the melody is always clearly heard. It is never disguised but is sung by the various instruments with a beautiful vocal-like warmth. As one New Orleans trumpeter expressed it, the idea is to "play pretty for all the people." The tune is not obscured by harmonic padding and complicated arrangements, for these musicians know that the secret of true excellence in music, as in life itself, lies in simplicity. New Orleans style has never encouraged the hectic rushing and frantic, hysterical screaming that passes for jazz in many places. Instead, moderate, relaxed tempos to which people can dance or march even in a hot climate are chosen. New Orleans music has always been functional. To this day the business cards of most musicians read "music for all occasions" – not just dances, parties and parades, but for everything from christenings and dedications to funerals.

Part I
The Preserved

Chapter One

THOSE RAGS AND
THEM BLUES

"I hope to do my very best to make you happy."
—clarinetist George Lewis

Preservation Hall means many things to many people: veteran New Orleans jazzmen blowing their hearts out every night in a creaky room in the French Quarter; three bands of these doughty pioneers constantly touring the world; a steady championing of the original style of the 20th century's most distinctive art form; old dreams exploding into fresh life – and sadly faded.

One may well begin with the building. Twice as old as jazz, the weathered edifice which houses Preservation Hall serves to remind us how venerable are the ingredients of this music and its human support system. This interesting St Peter Street structure resembles many of the French Quarter's surviving Creole mansions. Its main wing is a two-story "porte-cochère," or carriage house. Seen from the front, two sets of French doors open onto the street. They are covered with heavy batten-shutters on strap-iron hinges; one set is open when bands are playing inside. The plaster walls are streaked with ancient roses, greens and other pastels long faded into a warm grey composite. On the second level, a wrought-iron "gallery," or balcony, is supported by a row of S-shaped iron brackets. Heavy shutters like

Beloved, cantankerous Sweet Emma Barrett remained one of New Orleans' favorite entertainers all her life. The leg bells were her trademark.

those below cover a row of three French doors, rarely opened in later years except for an occasional album cover photo. Under the lip of the pitched roof, one can see the rippled edge of an earlier one – a flat, round-tiled roof in a style typical of the late 18th century, when New Orleans was still under the influence of Spain.

Visitors enter through a carriageway to the right. Records are sold here, and the passage leads back past the former double parlors – the modest-sized music hall proper – and under lovely sunburst grillwork to a beautiful, flagstoned courtyard. Closed to the public, this patio borders a two-story former "slave quarters," which now houses the musicians' refreshment room, the Preservation Hall offices and remarkable collections of papers and memorabilia. Portions of this service wing include the oldest parts of Preservation Hall – those which survived an 1816 fire that destroyed all the houses along St Peter Street.

Said to have been put up about 1750, the original house also served as a tavern around the time of the War of 1812. The present structure was built after the fire. Designed according to the then-fashionable Creole mode, it was owned by a succession of well-to-do butchers, a "gent's" clothier, a physican, and a tinsmith who had his home and business there until 1905. In the 20th century it was mostly rental property, often occupied by creative artists attracted by the Quarter's bohemian charm. These included the

In the 1860s, a century before becoming Preservation Hall, the building, as shown in the drawing on the left, looked much as it still does. The rear patio and "slave quarters" are pictured in the contemporary photograph on the right. The entire structure had been rebuilt after a fire in 1816 which destroyed more than 60 houses in the French Quarter.

painter Knute Heldner, and two generations of well-known documentary and portrait photographers, Woods "Pops" Whitesell and Dan Leyrer. Mystery writer Erle Stanley Gardner stayed here often, and his fictional character "Gramps Wiggams" is said to have been modeled after Pops Whitesell. The ground floor front, opening directly onto the sidewalk, served as a retail store and an art gallery until the advent of Preservation Hall in 1961.

Maintained with restraint, the old structure not only helps preserve the distinctive character of the Quarter, but frames the music in a way that encourages people to believe in its authenticity and historic value.

* * *

Even more complex and intriguing than those pastels on the Hall's front wall is the rich rainbow of musical and social influences which created the jazz being played there. We can thank the musicians for breathing life into that history, night after night, and for sharing so many of their insights and memories.

Is jazz folk music? "All music is folk music," replied New Orleans' most famous musical son, Louis Armstrong. If that sounded like a conversation stopper, it also expressed Louis' breadth of musical understanding and his universality of appeal. It also says something about the city where jazz was born, and where it continues to be reborn with every

An unexpected visitor joins the sober publicity photo on the St Peter Street sidewalk: (from left) Benjamin Jaffe, Jim Robinson, Cie Frazier, James Prevost, Percy Humphrey, Willie Humphrey, Sing Miller and Narvin Kimball.

generation – indeed, with every note.

Here, Europe and Africa met to form a music which would prove as vital and viable on the world's concert stages as it had at homey dance halls and fish fries. Traditional jazz is "functional" in that it remains cheerfully adaptable to various usages and events. Emphasizing spontaneity, roughness and improvisation, it has never taken itself overly seriously, or implied a split between an ethereal art and the grubby facts of life, in the manner of 19th-century European "art" music. It is functional for the players as well, who can hope to enjoy themselves while they are making money at it, and for whom its benefits have included, for some, escape from the ghetto, and for others, a reaffirmation of traditional family, neighborhood, and spiritual relationships. Jazz is also functional in terms of the whole person, in that it shows its African lineage, where, as LeRoi Jones wrote, it is inconceivable "to make a separation between music, dancing, song, the artifact, and a man's life or his worship of the gods."

On the other hand, New Orleans jazz is not folk music in the sense that folk music loses its meaning and purpose when removed from a certain ethnic context. And it is not functional in the sense that dance jobs or funerals or cornerstone layings, but not today's jazz festivals or commercial recordings or TV spots, are often called "functional" jobs. Like Louis himself, this most American of the arts springs from down-to-earth humanity – and then constantly soars and spreads, in the phrase of a later stylist, Duke Ellington, "beyond category."

When the distiguished folklorist and author Alan Lomax was told that some people thought that folk music is an amateur thing, and that when it becomes professional it becomes commercialized and impure, his reply was unequivocal:

That's a mark of people who think that folk musicians are never paid. Lordy, all folk musicians are supported by their community bounteously. Repeat that. All folk musicians and primitive musicians are supported by their community at a level that Toscanini would be pleased with. Folk music doesn't burst spontaneously out of some amateur. Imagine some spontaneous emotions at a wedding! If daddy doesn't have the right musicians at the wedding, it doesn't go off well, and that applies to Australian aborigines just as much as it does to a Jewish wedding in the Bronx. Remember that. There's nothing naive about music in any of its social settings. It all is very, very complexly regarded by its community. It has to be appropriate, it has to be done the right way, exactly the right way, just as much as grand opera or Bach. . . . People think that all that stuff out there is just purely ad lib. You have to learn it, you have to practice it, to be an apprentice in it, you have to know just what to do, when, just how to do it. Every human music is as subtly adapted to its culture as is our own.

Much of the universality of jazz derived from the breadth of its origins. Right from the beginning, the music spanned wide polarities, tolerated wild paradoxes and inconsistencies. On one level, this is part of the humor and wisdom of life at ground zero in the New Orleans neighborhoods, which have been aptly termed a series of bi-racial urban villages. Cheerfully embracing that atmosphere was also part of the special genius of Preservation Hall. It sometimes meant flying in the face of "normal" business practices – or shattering the expectations of purist jazz fans.

The most commercial of the New Orleans brass bands of the 70s and 80s, the Olympia, led by Harold Dejan, also frequently appeared, with reduced personnel, at Preservation Hall on Sunday nights – among them (from left) Milton Batiste, Lawrence Trotter and Nowell Glass.

Owner-manager Allan Jaffe, who cared deeply and personally about the musicians but was also a shrewd businessman when he wanted to be, took a kind of private delight in keeping the Hall's admission and record prices modest.

Once, during one of the bands' extended tours of the Midwest, the colorful Preservation Hall sticker blew off the side of the Greyhound bus in a blizzard. Within hours an urgent phone call brought two replacement stickers from New Orleans by airfreight. By that time, however, the original excitement had died down, and the new stickers were put away somewhere inside the bus and forgotten for the rest of the trip, which in itself added some fresh fun. Trombonist Frank Demond leaned across the aisle and told a companion, "You've just seen the essence of Preservation Hall."

From the earliest known times, constant
enthusiasm and wide social polarities seem to have
spanned the New Orleans music scene. Here, in
contrast to the rest of the slavery-ridden South,
relatively humane attitudes on racial matters inter-
twined with a passionate love of music, entertainment
and dancing. The city was not a melting pot: among
the earlier generations social and ethnic groupings
remained quite distinct, and the mixing that did go
on later among their descendants was not usually
discussed. But cultural activities, such as the Mardi
Gras parades and music of many sorts, helped to
mediate between the groups. This feeling for music
as a meeting ground still prevails in the city. Implicit
in older jazz, and in the way it is performed, this
bridging/reciprocating function is one reason the

*Enthusiastic participation of
neighborhood folks and "social
and pleasure club" members
alike was always a hallmark of
the brass band processions.*

Right and opposite: The living roots of New Orleans jazz reach deep into the community – and into the shared human experience. On the streets musicians learn to play, not for muted critical approval, but to make people move.

music of Preservation Hall has such wide appeal, in contrast to some later, northern forms which took on implications of class consciousness and separatism.

No one knows how long the Crescent City's love affair with music had been going on before 1792, but by coincidence New Orleans' first public ballroom and its first opera house both opened on the same day of that year – October 4. The ballroom was on Conde Street, and the small opera building was on St Peter, apparently next door to today's Preservation Hall. In the next half century, 80 or more such "official" dancing spots appeared, plus countless local hangouts featuring informal dancing. The exuberant scene has been described by historian Henry Arnold Kmen:

At one end of the scale were ballrooms rife with disorder, thievery, and prostitution, while at the other end were ballrooms such as the Orleans, the St Charles, and the St Louis – unsurpassed anywhere in splendor and decorum. Thus every class and condition of people in New Orleans could find a compatible place to dance. And this was well because already by 1803 when the Americans took possession of the city, dancing was a necessity of life . . .

Travelers from all over Europe and America were struck by the absolute passion for dancing that they observed in this city. As one put it, "in the winter they dance to keep warm, and in the summer they dance to keep cool." . . . There was one tired resident, though, who complained that if the love of dancing in the city became any worse people would never see bed again . . .

For some years prior to 1805 balls had been held ostensibly for the free colored people of New Orleans; but in actuality these affairs were attended by numerous slaves as well as by soldiers, sailors, and other whites.

As for the opera, the little theater on St Peter Street presented 374 performances before yielding to another building on St Philip Street, which gave over 500 performances before it, too, had to make way for a new and larger theater, this time on Orleans Street. All this was going on within the modern-day French Quarter, in a city of only 15,000 people.

As European talent continued to arrive, the New Orleans Opera quickly became the finest in America. By 1835 the city had mushroomed fourfold to 60,000 people. From Haiti, liberated in 1803, freed Blacks arrived in large numbers, bringing their loose-jointed Caribbean culture to the Treme district which borders the French Quarter. With Italians, Germans, and others also pouring in, it is not surprising that the original French-language opera now faced strong competition from new Italian and English companies.

As an example, during one week in 1836, "there were fourteen performances of nine operas. Four companies, two of them unsurpassed in the United States, played in three theaters, one the largest in the country."

The foundation laid by such intense activity and by the loose ethnic chemistry was deep and abiding. New Orleans now possessed a rich musical soil, perhaps the richest in the United States, which would help nurture important new musical and dance forms after the turn of the century.

* * *

Within the European half of the Afro-European genesis of jazz, one other seed was also very potent: the brass marching band. As early as 1838, New Orleans' venerable newspaper *The Picayune* called the city's love affair with brass "a real mania," opining that "our numerous martial bands . . . are perhaps unrivaled on this side of the Atlantic." As Kmen put it, "Any occasion from the laying of a cornerstone to the blessing of a flag was reason enough for a parade. Because of the many nationalities in the city, there was an unusually large number of national holidays on which to parade. Militia companies, fire companies, secret lodges, and other organizations abounded – all with their marching bands." While brass band parades were not peculiar to New Orleans, brass band funeral parades had become a distinctive and well-established local institution by 1808. During one of the city's frequent medical epidemics an observer commented on the "mournful notes of the death march customarily played by full brass bands en route to the grave," followed by "a gay and lightsome air as they returned from the grave."

Up through the Civil War, and on past the turn of the century, the city's varied musical activities all bolstered each other:

The mania for marching in New Orleans fitted perfectly with the love of dancing and the opera. Musicians who came to the city to join one of the theatre orchestras were usually able to augment their incomes by playing in bands and dance orchestras . . .

It was a two-way street: the quality of dancing and marching music in New Orleans was vastly improved by the presence of so many imported musicians; while the money made available by means of these other activities

Spirituals are a vital part of traditional jazz. Sister Gertrude Morgan is shown during the 1950s singing to God in the art gallery, run by Larry Borenstein, which evolved into Preservation Hall.

enabled the theaters to attract the musicians. Since most taught and gave frequent concerts in which they played with their students and with other professional and amateur musicians, the general level of music in New Orleans was significantly raised . . .

Free black Orleanians participated in all this to a surprising degree. Well before 1800 they were dancing at balls of their own, imitating white sophisticates and backwoodsmen alike with such steps as quadrilles, jigs, fandangos and Virginia reels, and playing instruments such as fifes, fiddles, jews-harps and tambourines. Additionally, and significantly for jazz, black drummers and dancers preserved the subtle, powerful rhythms of Africa and the West Indies in open-air celebrations on the levees and at Congo Square (now part of Louis Armstrong Park).

In the theaters, where the Negro's "patronage was needed and sought, he heard the operas and other music of the day"; and "in the ballrooms, he supplied much of the music." One result was that in the early 19th century a lively, improvised black music was already being heard in the city. Even more remarkably, so many free Blacks were taught by French, Italian and German musicians that by the late 1830s they had formed a Negro Philharmonic Society of more than 100 members. New Orleans, with the possible exception of Charleston, was the only city in the South which had a black middle class of significant proportions throughout the 19th century.

But these early foundations of the New Orleans jazz culture were laid amid a moral paradox. If Blacks were allowed greater freedoms here than elsewhere, it was still only a difference of degree; the city had long been a major port for the importation and auctioning of plantation slaves. Although New Orleans had passed into US jurisdiction in 1803, this French, Latin, largely Catholic, laissez-faire culture remained stubbornly itself, tolerating inter-racial marriages and extra-marital unions which produced a prosperous, respectable class of "free Creoles of color." Some of these lived in the Preservation Hall building at one time or another. While the American-ization of the city had begun by the late 18th century, it was not very evident for another 100 years.

Emancipation brought new opportunities for the black musicians even as the painful ironies of segregation were beginning to set in. Negroes were

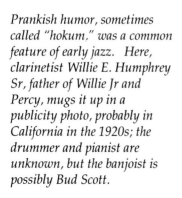

Prankish humor, sometimes called "hokum," was a common feature of early jazz. Here, clarinetist Willie E. Humphrey Sr, father of Willie Jr and Percy, mugs it up in a publicity photo, probably in California in the 1920s; the drummer and pianist are unknown, but the banjoist is possibly Bud Scott.

Sammy Penn (above) and Joe "Twat" Butler (below) sang gag numbers at the Hall and on tour in the 1970s. Butler, who claimed to be a first cousin of Louis Armstrong, specialized in "Big Lunch Blues." His nickname referred to the way the top of his head had looked in the 1920s, when a wide part divided his hair in the middle.

enabled to play in some places previously closed to them, and they also increased their participation in the marching bands. Deeply emotional in its rejoicing and sorrowing, black spiritual music was fed into the brass band repertoire, and thus eventually into jazz, through the funeral processions. These were sponsored by negro fraternal and burial societies. Formerly the province mainly of European groups, this localized welfare network attracted many more Blacks following the abolition of slavery, and still exists today. Many of the bands which marched in the parades also played for advertising functions.

A nationwide craze for minstrel and other road shows soon opened the way for black New Orleans musicians to travel professionally. Around the US generally, in fact, there were a surprisingly large number of professional black musicians during the 19th century. Cornetist Andrew Kimball, an uncle of Preservation Hall mainstay banjoist Narvin Kimball, led a brass band on tour with the Ducournan Bros. Colored Southern Minstrel Company around the turn of the century. In the same tradition, players such as trumpeter Punch Miller and trombonist Worthia "Showboy" Thomas would spend many years on the road with circuses and other tent shows. Later, as senior citizens, they came home and worked regularly at the Hall.

Bits of "hokum" humor appear on the classic jazz recordings of the 1920s, but this lightness of attitude and touch is one of the traditions that tended to be overlooked by later-day "revival" musicians. One of the benefits of Preservation Hall has been to remind us of this long overlapping of jazz with theater and show traditions. Preservation Hallers Kid Thomas, Willie Humphrey, Twat Butler, Jim Robinson, Kid Sheik Colar, Frank Demond and Father Al Lewis have all done little vaudeville routines to help put the show across. Crowd-pleasing antics can, of course, be overdone. Louis Armstrong sometimes belied his true greatness by resorting to tricks like hitting 40 high C's in a row. Within the younger crop of New Orleans brass band players there has been the same unfortunate tendency to blow screamers.

But somehow – perhaps because they came from a more gentlemanly era – the older black New Orleans musicians generally knew how to please their audiences with taste and dignity as a natural extension

A great drummer, though known only locally, Alfred Williams marched with brass bands from the Tuxedo in 1920 to the Eureka in the early 60s. In the 20s he worked with many important jazz bands, including those of Sam Morgan, Manuel Perez and A. J. Piron. He played regularly at Preservation Hall until his death in 1963.

of their own individualistic personalities. The difference between their lighthearted antics during a Preservation Hall concert and a bump-and-grinding Al Hirt, for example, was the same difference in attitude that distinguished their sincere, fresh-sounding notes from the slick arpeggios of generations of straw-hat Dixielanders. In *Call Him George*, a biography of George Lewis, the famous clarinetist who played at the Hall in the last few years of his life, Ann Fairbairn spoke of "his warm, mellow, glowing patina of gentleness that was eventually to reach across the footlights and enmesh the affections of thousands far more securely than the practiced showmanship of his contemporaries." Clarinetist

Willie Humphrey stressed the importance of raising people's spirits and reaching out to make contact:

It means a lot when a rhythm player, during your solo, feels what you're doing and gives it a little lift. It makes you do a little more. I know your public accepts it. Ain't what you doin', you ain't doin' that much you know, but the fella behind you is pushin', and that's what's takin' the audience. But a lot of the guys got wooden heads, they can't see that.

You take a fella, do a whole lot of smilin', all that helps to sell, sells the group. Little actions, little things. You sittin' up there, you playin' deadpan, no smile or nothing, no life or lift – ain't nothing. The music is supposed to be happy music, so you supposed to be happy givin' it. Y'understand? That's been my way of thinkin'. You feel happy, and you look happy, and you try to get the spirit, whatever you doin', try to put it out there with the public. That's my way how this music should be.

You take like [cornetist] Joe Oliver. He used to play, movin' the horn around like that, kind of overbearin' and duhm! duhm! – bump! bump! – drivin' and action, you see? But you sit there dead, and they ain't nothin' to it. Try to get people to tap their foot. Try to shake 'em up a bit: that's what sells. Like [drummer] Paul Barbarin. Paul was good, I'm not saying he wasn't good, but to me his brother [drummer Louis Barbarin] was better. Paul would *sell*. I been knowin' him since way back in 1918. And after he was doin' his solos – that's what Louis Armstrong used to like about him – Louis would get up there, singin' "Dat, dat, dee-dee, dah," and Paul be right there with him. He'd try to push him with them drums. And he'd be smilin', and the people out there be eatin' it up.

* * *

Historian Kmen pointed to a further factor which played a little-noted but crucial role in the gradual formation of jazz during the late 19th century:

There were so many societies, so many parades, so many demands for bands in New Orleans that these bands were seldom large. Most of the time ten or twelve musicians did all the blowing. This meant that the bands were of a size suitable for the larger dance halls. All through the nineteenth century military bands in New Orleans had played for dancing, so it was only natural to hire these bands for dances. But the style of dancing was changing with the cakewalk, turkey trot, and foxtrot replacing the more formal dances of the early period. When a band now played for dancing, it had to play a looser kind of music. Often the brass bands had a string orchestra associated with them to play in smaller places, and frequently bandsmen joined with string players to make a dance orchestra.

Somewhere towards the end of the nineteenth century . . . the music they made became discernibly different from any heard before. Something new, something distinctively American, was being added to the music of the world.

But something else new, something equally jubilant and American, had already arrived. Bubbling out of Sedalia, Missouri, and the river valleys of the Middle West, ragtime was the first product of black America to carve a significant niche in the nation's dominantly white middle-class culture. The demonstrated skill of the black composers of ragtime helped this charming vernacular music counter the malicious racism which had been promulgated by many of the earlier, cruder forms of minstrelsy.

The classic rag was an elegant, urbane, written piano piece. Related to the quadrille, it was polite enough to be played in "nice" parlors (as well as saloons), yet lilting and highly danceable because it was actually a medley of rural, black, syncopated dance tunes. Ragtime style, or "ragging," had for years been infusing the performances of banjo virtuosi, buck dancers, string bands and others; and it would go on influencing countless other popular and classical forms well into the 20th century. Thus, while ragtime proper lasted only from 1895 until 1915, the ragtime style had a far longer and more comprehensive impact on American music – notably jazz.

In New Orleans, piano "professors" like Manuel Manetta and Jelly Roll Morton transformed classic rags into "stomps": referring to a "hotter," more dynamic rhythm, the term apparently comes from the stomping of bare feet in West African-style dancing. But the piano itself – suitable for ladies, an expensive symbol of gentility and heavy to move around – was rarely used in the rough-and-ready New Orleans bands before 1910. In the Crescent City, around the turn of the century, classic ragtime was most often to be heard in the form of transcriptions for instrumental ensembles. A number of the pioneer jazzmen, such as Bunk Johnson, called their groups "ragtime bands."

With the sponsorship of some jazz-loving well-

Ragtime played a special role in the formation of jazz, and a unique outfit, the New Orleans Ragtime Orchestra, was long a special feature at Preservation Hall and around the world. Formed in the 50s and still going strong in the 90s, it was called "captivating and vibrant" by the London "Financial Times," while the "New York Times" said the band "perfectly captured ragtime's grace, stateliness and delightful rhythmic flow." From left: Paul Crawford, John Robichaux, Lionel Ferbos, Walter Payton Jr, Glenn Wilson (substituting for Orange Kellin), Lars Edegran and Bill Russell

wishers, particularly Bill Russell, Bunk would become a dominant figure in the "jazz revival" 40 years later. And with Russell's more-than-able assistance on violin, a stellar group called the New Orleans Ragtime Orchestra would for over 20 years give concerts at Preservation Hall, as well as appearing on film tracks and in concerts around the US and Europe. Led by Swedish-born pianist Lars Edegran, the appealing group re-created the true flavor of a New Orleans society orchestra of the 1910-1920 era, mingling rags with popular songs, marches, cakewalks, waltzes and blues – all in a "ragging" style which set this group apart from similar ones elsewhere by emphasizing the zesty tone and individualism of each player.

Yet ragtime was still a parlor enthusiasm, as it were – an emotionally restrained art, performed by respectably trained reading musicians clever enough to throw in a bit of razzamatazz for effect. Ragtime played an indispensable role in the formation of jazz by introducing its lilting cross-rhythms, its melodic lines and its compositional structure to the eclectic music of New Orleans. But the deeper dimension of jazz – its richer, subtler black essence – entered from another angle.

It says something about the ripeness and maturity of
New Orleans' multi-ethnic experience that two
musical streams as fundamentally different as the
African and European were here so profoundly
merged. Much of the forward-driving energy of the
new music came from the polar tension between the
differing traditions. The European emphasizes the
regular and rational, the controllable and predictable;
the African, the off-beat and off-balance, the accidental
and circumstantial. Take the matter of melody:
although New Orleans jazz is primarily an improvised
music, a constant sense of the melody is also extremely
important. Exposing the basic melody clearly,
repeatedly and beautifully is the most fundamental
obligation of the trumpet player, who is generally the
bandleader. Rather than do this in a monotonous

The prototype of the Hall's image as a place for redoubtable veterans was ancient, spirited, frequently photographed Henry "Booker T." Glass (above and left). Born in New Orleans in 1888, Booker T. performed from 1908 in the city's leading brass and dance bands until his death at the age of 92. (His son Nowell Glass, also a drummer, is pictured on page 32.)

way, however, he constantly rephrases and syncopates it, changing the attack and the emphasis, charging the music with momentum and unpredictability by means of a continual tension against a steady ground beat laid down by bass, banjo (or guitar) and drums.

Talk with any Preservation Hall jazzman about how to play the music, and the matter of tone will often leap to center stage. It's an individual thing, not a matter of conforming to a predetermined standard as in a swing band or symphony orchestra. Listen, and you'll hear every nuance between European cleanness and African "dirtyness." Leaving aside such matters as reeds, mouthpieces, and the problems of teeth and lips associated with advancing age, the whole concept of tone means different things to different people. In jazz, just as in conversation, how you speak to someone is inseparable from what you are telling them. A good way to grasp this is to compare the recordings of some of the reed players who appeared at Preservation Hall – Albert Burbank, John Casimir, Willie Humphrey, Paul Barnes, George Lewis, Raymond Burke, Captain John Handy, Emanuel Paul. Each had a distinct musical personality, much of it attributable to "tone." The harmonic and thematic simplicity of traditional jazz helped permit a vast, expressive complexity of tone and rhythm. And these were precisely the more negroid elements. Musicologist Ernest Borneman gave this description of the role of tone in African music:

When we want to stress a word, we raise our voice – that is to say, we go up in pitch. But in those African languages where a change of pitch on any given syllable may alter the meaning of the entire word, you are left with only one device to emphasize your point: timbre. You can alter the tone color, the voice production, the vibrato of the syllable you wish to stress. This combination of pitch and timbre in African language is what the philologists call "significant tone." It has had the most profound effect on the history of American Negro music . . .

While the whole European tradition strives for regularity – of pitch, of time, of timbre and of vibrato – the African tradition strives precisely for the negation of these elements. In language, the African tradition aims at circumlocution rather than at exact definition. The direct statement is considered crude and unimaginative; the veiling of all contents in ever-changing paraphrases is considered the criterion of intelligence and personality. In music, the same tendency towards obliquity and ellipsis is noticeable: no note is attacked straight; the voice or instrument always approaches it from above or below, plays around the implied pitch without ever remaining on it for any length of time, and departs from it without ever having committed itself to a single meaning. The timbre is veiled and paraphrased by constantly changing vibrato, tremolo and overtone effects. The timing and accentuation, finally, are not stated, but implied or suggested. The musician challenges himself to find and hold his orientation while denying or withholding all signposts.

In jazz, as in literature, tone has much to do with the attitude of the artist to his audience and to himself. Take the trombone. Shouting, extroverted, gut-level players like Jim Robinson and Louis Nelson made their points clearly and without qualification. Reflection and conscious control intervened in the tone of more inward musicians like Preston Jackson or "Frog" Joseph, and in that of younger men who crafted their styles in the survey-course world of the "revival" period – such as Frank Demond and Freddy Lonzo. For all its variety, tone in New Orleans derives from dancing and other forms of social participation between the players and listeners. It is therefore supposed to betoken respect, including respect for the eardrums (even if it sometimes misses this target).

Nowhere is tone more important than in achieving the full expressive power of the blues. Blues is the song of an impacted culture-within-a-culture, the quality most obviously missing from sterile imitations like "Doo-wapa-doo" Dixie; it is what every successful black bandleader in New Orleans has always known his black audiences most wanted to hear. Again, the African background:

European and American visitors to Africa have often been puzzled by what they perceived as an African fondness for muddying perfectly clean sounds. African musicians will attach pieces of tin sheeting to the heads of drums or the necks of stringed instruments in order to get a noisy, rattling buzz. When confronted with a wooden flute, which naturally produces a relatively pure tone, they will sing or hum while they play. And their solo singing makes use of an extravagant variety of tonal effects, from grainy falsetto shrieks to affected hoarseness, throaty growls, and gutteral grunting. This preference for what western

The soul and fire of the postwar traditional jazz revival was summed up in the famous style of clarinetist George Lewis (below). He emanated quiet discipline, loved playing hymns and remained close to his deeply spiritual mother, Alice Zeno (above), who had a decisive influence on his character.

musicology tells us are impure sounds has always been evident in black American music, from the rasp in so much folk, blues, and popular singing – think of Mahalia Jackson, or James Brown – to the gut-bucket sounds of early New Orleans jazz trumpeters, who sometimes played into brass spitoons or crammed homemade mutes made out of kazoos into the bells of their horns.

The blues is better understood by hearing a single gumbo-rich phrase from the throat and fingers of pianist Billie Pierce or her sister, Sadie Colar, or any of the other Preservation Hall singers, than by reading definitions. Still, it's worth pointing out the technical essentials. The third and seventh tones of the scale, and sometimes the fifth, are partially flatted. (Pianists, being technically unable to do this, may instead associate the neighboring half-tones in various ways.) And, as a song form, the blues typically occupies twelve bars, taken relatively slowly, in three lines, of which the second repeats the first.

Despite early attacks on the blues as immoral and dirty from some sectors of the rising black middle class, there has long been musical cross-influence between blues and spirituals, and often, in blues lyrics, a mingling of the sacred and profane. The well-known gospel singer Mahalia Jackson offers a good example. Thus the creative tension between value systems – propriety and orderliness on the one hand, and life's messier realities and uncertainties on the other. The classic blues stanzas deal mainly with relations between the sexes. But a creative singer may also comment about any detail of everyday life, as did Preservation Hall pianist-vocalist Sing Miller during the 70s when he threw in a verse about the gas shortage. While the origins of the term remain shrouded in the dim centuries of slavery, "blue" suggests a melancholy or depressed mood; and in a now-obsolete English usage "blueman" means "Negro."

Unlike the free coloreds of New Orleans, plantation slaves were largely barred from playing musical intruments, particularly drums and horns, for fear that these could signal insurrections. The human voice and clapped hands became, then, their instruments of last resort. So it was from the rural South that the blues came. Originally a pure folk phenomenon, the "country" blues continued for several generations following Emancipation. They were gradually shaped and professionalized in the

"Short bands" – trios and quartets – were often featured in the early 60s as an economy measure (from left): Punch Miller, John Joseph, George Lewis and Emanuel Sayles.

"tonks" and other "low-life" institutions of the towns, and through a fledgling phonograph industry that quickly discovered a huge market in "race records."

In New Orleans the "Delta" blues brought in by country musicians were filtered through urban musical currents, especially jazz. During the hard years of the 30s, for instance, these jazzy blues were well represented by the piano-trumpet duo of Billie and DeDe Pierce, often accompanied by clarinetist George Lewis and drummer Albert Jiles, who played together in the low dives along Decatur Street to a mixed bag of sailors and dock workers. "Was them people rough?" ex-Floridian Billie later said to a questioner in the Preservation Hall carriageway; "I cain't say. I was rough right along with 'em."

In the formative years of jazz the darker, rougher, brassier, looser, more blues-oriented and instinctive players tended to come from "uptown," whereas the more refined and literate players, including the Creoles, came from the older "downtown" sections nearer the French Quarter. This distinction has sometimes been oversimplified; there was, in fact, a great deal of mixing and cross-influence. Willie Humphrey recounted his own experience:

The musicians that lived below Canal Street considered themselves better musicians. [George] Baquet and [Lorenzo] Tio were ahead of me – they were great. Course they had good musicians from uptown. That's where I'm from – uptown. My [clarinetist] father lived uptown, and others. But they just considered they were better musicians down in the Creole part of town.

Lorenzo Tio was a better clarinet player than Alphonse Picou, and Charley McCurdy was a better musician than either one of 'em. They had others around there but those were the good guys, the big names.

A whole lot of guys were professional musicians. They could sit in the pit and play. It makes a difference when you can read the music and when you can't read.

I had a pretty good reputation because I was playing with all them bands and I was sitting in with the guys that played the [written] music, so that meant a whole lot. With all the bands. I used to go out and catch the shows, the circuses and go sit there and play with the circus band. And they'd play top music. My granddaddy [James B. Humphrey, a famous music professor] taught us all that kind of music. My granddaddy was very dutiful; he made a fair musician out of me. I should have been a hundred times better than I am 'cause I used to get my lessons every day.

My mother was a Creole. I didn't consider myself a Creole. My father lived in California. After the District [Storyville] closed, he had a job in California. He stayed out there. When he came back, he went out again. He was on the road a lot, playing with shows and circuses. My father had nothing to do with us after my Mama died. She was real young. My grandmama raised us.

A player like Willie – musically literate, blessed with a fine ear, and an entertainer, yet hard-toned, bluesy and offbeat – fused many influences.

Although Orleanians of all classes and backgrounds had heard some kind of early jazz well before World War I, their musical preferences tended to mirror their social differences. The guitarist, banjoist and author Danny Barker remembered, "All these musicians played for different types of people. In fact there was a caste system within the Negroes themselves. The Catholics liked Creole music, which was refined, and the Protestants were closer to the blues shouting and the spirituals and screaming to the skies and the Lord. All the bands had a particular section of society where they entertained . . . and particular halls where they played."

Dr Leonard Bechet, brother of the great soprano saxophonist and clarinetist Sidney Bechet, put it this way:

A person have to go through all that rough stuff like Sidney went through to play music like him. You have to play with all varieties of people. Some of the Creole musicians didn't like the idea of mixing up with the – well, with the rougher class, and so they never went too far. You see, Picou – Picou's a very good clarinet, but he ain't hot. That's because he wouldn't mix so much.

You have to play real hard when you play for Negroes. You got to go some, if you want to avoid their criticism. You got to come up to their mark, you understand? If you do, you get that drive. Bolden had it. Bunk had it. Manuel Perez, the best ragtime Creole trumpet, he didn't have it.

See, these hot people they play like they killing themselves, you understand? That's the kind of effort that Louis Armstrong and Freddie Keppard put in there . . .

When the settled Creole folks first heard this jazz, they passed the opinion that it sounded like the rough Negro element. In other words, they had the same kind of feeling that some white people have, who don't understand jazz and don't want to understand it. But, after they heard it so long, they began to creep right close to it and enjoy it. That's why I think this jazz music helps to get this misunderstanding between the races straightened out. You creep close to hear the music and, automatically, you creep close to other people. You know?

A normally soft-spoken man like clarinetist George Lewis could become indignant when he came up against the idea that a lighter shade of skin made one musician better than another (even though he himself looked down on musicians he thought were not neat and clean). Of Manuel Perez, the famous black Creole trumpeter, George said:

I heard him play but never played with him, because there was a prejudice among them people – segregation.

A morning mood in the 700 block of St Peter Street recalls a neighborly feeling long predating the night-time revelry of the late 20th century. Portions of the Hall itself are twice as old as jazz.

Some of those Creole bands wouldn't hire a man whose hair wasn't silky. And some of the halls wouldn't accept you in there. There was one on Robertson Street like that, Jeunes Amis Hall. You wasn't accepted there. And they would look at you hard if you was playing in that band. I don't say Manuel Perez ever segregated anybody I know of. But everybody in his band was light-skinned, you know.

The black Creoles had themselves been made to feel the pinch of segregation quite acutely. A proud, cultivated, Catholic caste who spoke a French patois, they suffered a painful decline in socio-economic status, which began in the Antebellum period and was accentuated by the backlash following Emancipation. An 1894 Louisiana law stated that a person with any negro blood was to be considered a Negro. Struggling to distinguish themselves from the rougher, Protestant hymn-shouting types, the Creoles gained a reputation for aloofness and defensive superiority of the sort sometimes attributed to the famous pianist, composer and bandleader Jelly Roll Morton. As late as the 1950s they were sometimes forced to stand up on buses because, regarded as neither white nor black, they were refused seating in both sections. Who could blame such a people for struggling to maintain their pride?

A true Creole, Peter Bocage played a lighter, sweeter, more lilting and technically correct trumpet and violin than the "ratty" black uptown school. His credits included the old Superior Orchestra with Bunk Johnson; a decade with Armand Piron, the top New Orleans society orchestra of the 20s; his own Creole Serenaders from 1928 on; and the latter-day Love–Jiles Ragtime Orchestra. Bocage was a regular at the Hall until his death in 1967.

Quite a few Creoles, including Jelly Roll's family, had Haitian roots. Predominantly artisans and tradesmen, they left an indelible mark on the buildings and society of the Seventh Ward. And with their "Spanish tinge" rhythms, their graceful embellishments, and charming dialect songs such as "Eh, La Bas!," the Creoles were an indispensible part of the rich cultural amalgam feeding into early jazz.

At least two important Preservation Hall players, trumpeter Peter Bocage and banjoist-singer George Guesnon, came directly from this class. Both were well-trained musicians, looked up to by others. When, for a brief period in the early 60s, the bandleaders at the Hall held regular meetings to coordinate policy, Bocage was made the "leader of the leaders." And "Creole George" Guesnon was sometimes sought out as an authority or "professor" to settle musical differences of opinion. Bocage and Guesnon were both known, however, for attitudes that tended to cause problematical relationships.

In the manner of his old friend Jelly Roll, Guesnon was a natural balladeer. His fertile imagination, poetic speech rhythms and romantic grandiloquence were oddly blended with a love of funky, low-life details. He said he had been raised as an altar boy in a strict Catholic family, but that once he got a taste of the jazz life and the red light district, he had become "a black sheep." Like so many New Orleans musicians, he grew up with a trade to fall back on if necessary: "My father was a plasterer, my uncle a bricklayer, and to think of being anything else but one of those trades was out of the question. So I put my ukelele in a box out of sight and went to work as a plasterer's apprentice with my father."

In later years Guesnon still practiced assiduously, complained about more primitive players, suffered from delusions of persecution, and, as Bill Russell put it, "quit music often, and quit the Hall oftener." It was somehow typical that he changed his birthday to conform to an incorrect date given on the liner notes of a record, because once that happens that's what everybody thinks, so it has to be the truth. Competition is very much a part of the New Orleans jazz tradition, but George was not above giving credit where he felt it was due:

One night I told Jelly [Roll Morton], "I've heard rumors that they had a cat in New Orleans that could cut you." He said, "You don't have to tell me; his name was Tony Jackson. Man, you know something? Have you ever had a cat to worry you with an instrument?" I said, "Sure I had a cat in New Orleans named Narvin Kimball. That's the only cat that worried me with a banjo, and he played all that stuff southpaw." Jelly said, "Well, Tony was the only cat that worried me with a piano. Everything that I used to do, I just never did feel positive that he wasn't doing it a little bit better."

Very much in the Jelly Roll pattern, as well, was the Creole's sense of a golden era in the past, *vis-à-vis* a declined present. The long, dry period Guesnon referred to was an underlying reason for the formation of Preservation Hall:

Maybe you don't know yet, but this year I put up my banjo and guitar never to play them again. No need for a lot of details. Al Hirt gets $8,500 a week, Pete Fountain the same and Audio Fidelity records came all the way to New Orleans to give the Dukes of Dixieland a banquet and to present them with a check for $100,000 for royalties on records. All this, while the true creators of this art form are reduced to the status of playing for nickels and dimes picked up from the passers-by on the streets. I'm no complainer, neither am I angry over this, but it's just a little more than I'm able to take.

There was a time when I played a seven-hour job for $1.50 a man, but then it was a way of life. I could accept that and always there was that dream that someday we would get ours. Every dog was supposed to have his day and that kept one struggling, moving on and taking as an everyday norm every heartache and hardship possible. Now in the end we wind up with the dry bones, that and nothing more. It's only a fool that beats his head on the iron walls of impossibility, and I can clearly see now that it was all a hoax, we were never meant to get anything out of jazz, past, present, or future. From now on I'll just listen to my records (thank God I could get that far) and on them I'll find one consolation, that even though they got all the money, at least I could carve the pants off any banjo player in New Orleans when it came to playing jazz.

GEORGE GUESNON
MUSICIAN AND
(TEACHER OF STRING INSTRUMENTS)

HOME ADDRESS   PRIVATE LESSONS BY
1012 N. ROMAN ST.   APPOINTMENT
NEW ORLEANS. LA.   PHONE CR. 6628

MUSIC FURNISHED FOR ALL OCCASIONS

Behind Guesnon's frustration lay the fact that, despite generally cordial relations between the black and white musicians themselves, a firm barrier prevented their working together until the advent of the civil rights era and Preservation Hall. There were separate black and white musicians' unions, with separate pay scales and jurisdictions. Although black bands were always able to perform professionally for white audiences, the white jazzmen, with their good connections and fancy, programmed sound, were long accustomed to getting the best-paying gigs. When a black band played in a strip joint, a curtain was put up between the runway and the band so that black eyes could not see the white "disrobing artists." And black bands playing in white hotels or private homes were not allowed to eat there, but had to order their food from colored restaurants and gulp it down in the kitchen or hallway.

The amazing thing, as Preservation Hall bassist Papa John Joseph later said, was that, "We didn't think so much about segregation in the old days, that great old time; not so much as the young generation does nowadays." In truth, most black jazzmen felt glad just to be at those hotels and parties. As compared with the bleak outlook for most of their neighbors during the Jim Crow era, musicians enjoyed careers that offered at least the hope of relative freedom, advancement and professional camaraderie. Barbara Reid, who had been friendly with many of the New Orleans players for years and helped to found Preservation Hall, noted during the civil rights era that "All the current published mass media makes much issue and to-do about the feeling of late musicians and singers having felt 'Jim Crowed.' Very few in my experience have felt this way. Mostly they

A patio session behind the carriageway in the early 60s included George Lewis (left) and George Guesnon, of whom the drummer Alex Bigard said, "He works hard and fills a band with fire, heart and drive. In my book he's the greatest, the perfect chord master and the only guy I've ever known down here in New Orleans who could take a solo on anything in any key."

just shrugged when confronted with such a situation, or else it didn't exist for them. They were too busy being what they were, with some few exceptions."

The music itself opens the heart. There is the long New Orleans tradition of music and other cultural activities, such as Mardi Gras, mediating between social groups. And for all its longterm problems and interminable little bickerings, the Cresent City has always had a friendlier, more gentle and languorous atmosphere than the more tumultous towns of the North. It was the kind of place where all sorts of groups, from Italians and Germans, to Greeks and Jews, to the tough residents of the "Irish Channel," had long known their own niche and maintained a jaunty pride of neighborhood and family status.

Still, the paradoxes go on. As late as the 1980s, one of Preservation Hall's outstanding young black regulars enjoyed happy relationships with all his neighbors in a middle-class section – including the white man next door, who, however, refused to speak to the musician's wife because she was white.

The dedicated cornetist Johnny Wiggs (born John Wigginton Hyman) not only played and recorded from the 20s onwards but taught many musicians, brought others back from retirement, co-founded the New Orleans Jazz Club and taught architectural drawing in New Orleans high schools for 25 years. Influenced by both white and black styles, he appeared often at the Hall from 1965 to 1967.

While most jazz scholars have believed that the white jazzmen learned by listening to the black pioneers, at least one, Al Rose, held to a mixed-parentage thesis, citing the fact that the earliest known jazz band, that of Jack Laine in the 1890s, was mixed (the Jim Crow rules had presumably not yet been enforced). More usual are the reminiscences of both black and white musicians who tell how the Whites hung around places where the Blacks were playing and "picked up on it," but that the Blacks were not allowed to go learn from the Whites, whether or not they might have wanted to.

In fact, music was everywhere in New Orleans in the years preceding World War I – in the air, outdoors and in, spilling out of windows and doorways . No one can say exactly how an oral tradition like the blues found its way into jazz, but Johnny Wiggs, a white cornetist who played often at Preservation Hall in the 1960s, offered a rare glimpse of how they were transmitted to a future jazzman. In the following summary of his interview, which is preserved at Tulane University's Jazz Archive, the description of the horns may be open to question – but not the blues spirit:

Johnny Wiggs feels that the bottle men played a very influential part in his early musical life. The bottle man collected bottles. He went around blowing on his horn and gave the children miniature dolls, furniture and candy in trade for bottles. The horns were about three feet long and made of tin. They had a brass reed soldered on, then a wooden mouthpiece. These colored men removed the wooden mouthpiece and "humored" the double brass reed with their mouths like a clarinet player humors his reed to get various intonations and pitches.

Johnny feels they were likely the most gifted people in the world for the blues. All the bottle men played beautiful blues. They were all over town. One could hear them several blocks away. When you heard them, you ran to the shed to get your bottles ready. Johnny later heard that sound in Negro trumpet players. He calls it the "bending of notes."

Johnny Wiggs also remembers the street criers, especially the blackberry women. The blackberry women brought their children with them and sold blackberries. They picked the berries all over as there was much wilderness in New Orleans then (1907-08).

Johnny had already heard Joe Oliver and others of his style by 1917, at dances at the Tulane gym. He will never forget the feelings he had when he first heard that band. It reminded him of the Negroid music he had heard early in life – the bottle men, washerwomen, and others. Joe Oliver could bend or stretch the notes half a tone or more. Oliver had a dirty tone which Louis Armstrong almost copied to perfection when he first arrived in New York. Since then, Armstrong has gotten away from it – it puts too much strain on a person's lip. Oliver held his mute halfway in the cornet bell, working the mute in and out with his hand to help bend notes.

Oliver was a supercilious Negro and took nothing from anyone. He was the "big boy" in music in New Orleans and knew it – he had all the jobs sewed up. When someone asked for the title of a tune Oliver played, he would say, "Who Struck John?" [a musicians' codeword for a tune made up on the spot] no matter what the real title was. He had one cock-eye. He was cute as hell, and mean. It was surely fun to watch him. He was the boss.

Like many of the jazz pioneers, Joe Oliver had middle-class aspirations and attitudes. Louis

Tuning up in the storeroom over the music hall (above), 87-year-old Papa John Joseph re-echoed sounds dating back to the very birth of jazz around the turn of the century. He had begun his career playing with the "first man" of this most American of art forms – the legendary Buddy Bolden. Opposite: Papa John outside the room where he would play his final note.

Armstrong, on the other hand, came from the wrong side of the tracks. That the Oliver band played in the brothel district of Storyville, as well as at society gigs and at dances in the Tulane gym, shows the wide social functionalism of early jazz. Although the importance of that famous district has often been over-emphasized, Louis left us an account of one slum-dweller's early musical inspiration:

I was just a youngster who loved that horn of King Oliver's. I would delight delivering an order of stone coal to the prostitute who used to hustle in her crib right next to Pete Lala's cabaret, just so's I could hear King Oliver play. I was too young to go into Pete Lala's at the time, and I'd just stand there in that lady's crib listening to King Oliver. And I'm all in a daze. I'd stand there listening to King Oliver beat out one of those good old good ones like "Panama" or "High Society." My, what a punch that man had.

All of a sudden it would dawn on the lady that I was still in her crib, very silent while she hustle those tricks, and she'd say, "What's the matter with you, boy? Why are you still there standing so quiet? This is no place to daydream, I've got my work to do." So I'd go home very pleased and happy that I did at least hear my idol blow a couple of numbers that really gassed me no end.

A generation earlier, another legendary trumpeter, Buddy Bolden, often cited as the first real jazzman and bandleader, was known to wait until late at night, after the "nice" people had gone home, before playing the really low-down, dirty blues associated with the honky-tonks. Bassist Papa John Joseph remembered Bolden quite well. "Buddy Bolden is the first man that ever played a blues for dancin'," he told Bill Russell and co-researcher Richard B. Allen in a 1950s interview. "Professor Holmes hired him to play a parade in Lutcher. That man say he couldn't understand how a man could play that much trumpet and couldn't read." Papa John described the rivalry between Bolden's rougher "uptown" style and the more polished bands such as that of John Robichaux: "Buddy Bolden outplayed Robichaux' band in a way, 'cause they used to play them blues. Robichaux had a real reading band. But Buddy Bolden, nobody read in his band, and he used to kill Robichaux anywhere he went for colored. Them blues. Colored halls. Pretty much all his jobs was colored."

Although Bolden was about Papa John's age (both are believed to have been born in 1877), that almost mythic "first man of jazz" quit playing in 1907. Beset by mental problems, Bolden was institutionalized and died obscurely in 1931. Papa John's finale was more dramatic. At Preservation Hall, shortly before midnight on January 22, 1965, he and the Punch Miller band had just finished a spirited rendition of *When the Saints Go Marching In*. Amid rousing applause, the 87-year-old bassist turned to pianist Dolly Adams and said, "That piece just about did me in." With that, he collapsed and died.

As they say in the music business, Papa John had paid a lot of dues through many hard years, between the time jazz began and the advent of Preservation Hall. It is to those hard middle years, leading directly to the Hall's founding, that we now turn.

Sing Miller

Sunburst of the Soul
An Interview with Alan Lomax

The noted ethnomusicologist Alan Lomax was a friend of Preservation Hall almost from its inception. The following is taken from an interview he gave after attending a Preservation Hall concert at New York's Avery Fisher Hall:

America's is the richest of all musical cultures. Everybody came here; everybody brought their music. And for a long while we were all ashamed of being Americans, and each one of us was ashamed of our own background, including the people of New Orleans. They are just beginning to accept it.

Music is made with your whole body, and with your whole life history, and with everything that you know. And if New Orleans music stops being made in New Orleans, it will no longer be the same music.

What happened was that for many reasons jazz became a non-respectable, non-profitable thing to do. There was a gap for a long time. Suddenly, Allan Jaffe and some other revival people began to fill that gap, and now the young people are coming back in, and we're seeing some new music. The best way to work with culture is with models. When a culture has a good model, it has a keel which keeps the whole boat steady. And Preservation Hall has emerged as a model for jazz. It's re-established the great old model of jazz. One of the real musical revolutions happened in New Orleans. It was like the invention of theater in Greece. And now it's re-established and moving again at its very root. The last of the great participants are in the ship, guiding it. And *sometimes* you hear that peak of excellence. It's only in the actual emergence, that peak of excellence, that the thing becomes alive.

Early jazz is probably America's most important cultural contribution. It was a magical fusion of many very big traditions: the tradition of concert music in Europe, the greatest of the African traditions, and the tremendous inventions of all the American frontiers, and England, the blues, spirituals – all fused, so that a new kind of music emerged. Basically, it was counterpoint in polyrhythm. No music had ever been so complex. European composers were absolutely amazed. They had been doing counterpoint, but suddenly here were these people doing counterpoint in polyrhythm, and all the parts were being improvised jointly. With virtuosic control of the tone, and with everybody singing through the instrument rather than playing notes from music – singing their own song which was contra to the other song. It was polyrhythmically organized, and improvised at the same time, using the concert instruments of Europe. There had never been anything like this.

The jazz tradition emerged from the city, from how an American city was organized, with its particular character-istics, its democratic, multifarious qualities. Jazz came from a typical American town, with its corruption and everything else, and it somehow reflects all that. It's easy-going, and complex, and direct, and confident, and cocky, and it's "everything's going to turn out all right in spite of the fact that it's pretty sordid as well." That's the mood of the American city, and jazz really captures that mood.

Jazz is a merging of Africa and Europe. That's been said many times. I'm not saying anything new here, but my emphasis is different. Europeans have a whole different approach to music, and to conversation, and to organizing human interaction, than Africans have. The fundamental African invention is the overlap. If you were an African, you would be talking at the same time that I'm talking, and not interrupting me. This overlapping is the basic aspect of African music. It works in the melody and the harmony and the rhythmic parts and the orchestration and the voicing. We forget that Africans have a musical culture that goes back 50,000 years! It's the *first* musical culture, probably. And they have come over here: they're missionaries in our continent. We're learning from them, step by painful step.

In the New World people took the song form, the coupled dance, the contradance, the European orchestra – and they molded it to Blacks in their own style, with the overlapping, polyrhythmic, parallel harmony, filling the holes, breaking systems. In the Caribbean it happened in a different way. In New Orleans these sophisticated people, these African Frenchmen, got hold of those European instruments with the valves and the frets and proceeded to play them with a new approach to orchestration – with winds in polyrhythmic relationship to rhythm. That's an African orchestra. There's no European orchestra that plays that way. In New Orleans they studied European counterpoint, and they had the whole African tradition available to them. They put it together, and out of it came the most complicated music that the human species has ever produced. Africa plus Europe: the African love, and the Euro-pean subtleties and gentleness – the positive together with the positive.

Now, understand: it's not like each person was improvising something enormously big! He was just being himself, his small little self.

Like Sing Miller tonight. The first note he sang, I began to cry. That first note of Sing's made me burst into tears. This little, humble, crushed-looking man was in great big Avery Fisher Hall, and he knew it. And the first note he formed was as beautiful as a garden of flowers. It was a sunburst of the soul.

Chapter Two

SURVIVAL

*"I'm thankful that I was one of them that kept barrelin'
and fightin' to keep it alive in our humble way."*
—trumpeter and leader Percy Humphrey

In a 1984 interview the well-known folklorist Alan Lomax observed, "Preservation Hall isn't for 'preservation.' It's so that a certain dynamic can continue to flow into the society." Three-and-a-half years later this was quoted to the Hall's owner-manager, Allan Jaffe. He summoned his remaining meagre energy to reply, in a voice weakened by painful cancer treatments, "The musicians don't care about 'preservation.' They care about keeping the things alive that made the music great."

But keeping themselves alive was the first order. New Orleans jazzmen walk around on the ground like anybody else – not on a cushion of esthetic niceties, or in clouds of nostalgia about a fabled past. Jaffe understood this very well. The music, and the things that made it great, could only survive among the survivors. Decades of hardship, struggle and loss had passed before anyone realized or cared how many, and how much, still remained.

A kind of mini-tradition developed among some of the New Orleans jazzmen: they were proud to be part of a band that opened up a job in a new spot, and none liked to be among the last to play a job before it closed down. Competition and cooperation were

Ready for challenge, Percy Humphrey had long known the hard art of endurance when he acted as leader of the foremost Preservation Hall band in the 70s, 80s and 90s.

another of the polarities within which this music lived. Those long, mostly lean years leading up to Preservation Hall did much to shape the attitudes of the players – their professionalism on the road, for instance, at ages when few others contemplate grueling one-nighter tours for months on end. It had taken plenty of courage to maintain a stubborn commitment to a music which, in each era, most rational people believed had just about died out. That it did not die, as other styles came and went, was testimony not only to the durability of the players, but also to the joyful essence of the music – those permanent, humane qualities that made it great.

* * *

Although Papa John Joseph had his roots in the very earliest, formative period of jazz, very few other Preservation Hall players did. Most of the best known among them grew up with the music played in New Orleans in the dozen or more years following World War I. This was the era known in the North as the "Jazz Age," when the lively, rebellious-sounding new music was taking America and Europe by storm. Because well-paying jobs had suddenly opened up in such places as California, New York and Chicago, as well as on the Mississippi and Ohio riverboats, New Orleans saw an outmigration of many of its greatest jazzmen – people such as King Oliver, Louis Armstrong, Jelly Roll Morton, Kid Ory and Johnny Dodds. However, contrary to widespread assumptions, many other fine players either remained in New Orleans (e.g., Albert Burbank, Emile Barnes) or kept coming and going as the jobs dictated (Willie Humphrey, Polo Barnes). Still others established solid careers elsewhere, yet returned to New Orleans and worked at Preservation Hall in their later years (Emanuel Sayles, Punch Miller).

In contrast to the flood of jazz records pouring out of Chicago and elsewhere during the 1920s and 1930s, there was only meagre documentation of the music which continued to be played and developed in New Orleans during these decades. The reasons were more economic than musical. The recording and talent industries were being developed in the North, while New Orleans was enduring a long decline brought on by the loss of river commerce to

The hard-driving, florid style of alto saxophonist Captain John Handy managed to shatter the "moldy fig" bias against the use of his instrument in traditional jazz when he was featured by Preservation Hall at home and abroad during the 60s. Born in 1900, he had first played several instruments in a family band, then specialized on clarinet with many of the leading New Orleans names of the 20s. In 1928 Handy took up sax, touring widely, and he continued to play both reed instruments in brass bands. In 1970 he appeared at the Newport Jazz Festival. He passed away in January 1971.

the railroads and accentuated by cultural isolation from the US mainstream. This very provincialism helped shield the hometown players and preserve their old-style dancing jazz from trendy "improvements" until after World War II.

Although no commercial recordings of black jazz bands were made in the city during the 30s, a few fine sides did appear during the 20s. These included performers who would later become well known at Preservation Hall, and they illustrate some important features of the music.

The early New Orleans recordings showed the wide spectrum between the more literate and trained musicians, with their carefully organized arrangements, and the "rough-and-ready" school. Generally speaking, it was the former who landed the best out-of-town jobs and who were able to adapt themselves to newer styles such as swing. But, as the years went along, the music played in New Orleans by jazz and brass bands alike tended to change in the other direction – becoming looser, rougher, more spontaneous and "African." The old musical culture from which the teaching "professors" had come was gradually thinning out. The Creoles were in decline, and country Blacks continued to pour into the city as a part of the longterm national urbanization process. In the years after World War I, future Preservation Hallers arrived from such outlying Louisiana villages as Deer Range (trombonist Jim Robinson), Reserve (trumpeter Kid Thomas Valentine), Thibodaux (trombonist Louis Nelson), Raceland (trumpeter Punch Miller), Madisonville (trumpeter Ernie Cagnolatti) and Donaldsonville (banjoist Emanuel Sayles).

As compared with the bands of today, each of the groups which recorded in New Orleans in the 1920s had its own fresh, distinctive sound. Classic jazz was still on the cutting edge of popular entertainment. The influence of roadshow traditions and ragtime was still evident in the styles of individual players, and in the structures of tunes like *Red Man Blues* and *Bogalusa Strut*. No one knew when, where or how the national jazz craze would end, but the participants were determined to mine it for all it was worth. Emanuel Sayles, later a leading Preservation Hall banjoist and singer, remembered that "You had to be smart enough to change as the music came out."

Future Preservation Hallers in the Original Tuxedo Orchestra, c.1928, included Matthews, Salvant, Kimball and Foster; from left: Bill Matthews, Guy Kelly, Papa Celestin, Jeanette Salvant [Kimball], Narvin Kimball, John Thomas, Chinee Foster, Joe Rouzon, Simon Marrero and Clarence Hall.

Rehearsals were much more common than now, and instrumentations were rapidly evolving: saxophones and pianos were added, for example, and the drum kit expanded, while the violin and second cornet were disappearing. In contrast to the narrower habits of the revival bands after World War II, jazz scholar John Joyce pointed out that "Very little was fixed or standard about New Orleans jazz during its formative years . . . its individual bands . . . freely adapted their size and make-up, style and repertoire to fit a particular social or recreational occasion."

Over a dozen musicians who later played at the Hall worked with Papa Celestin and Bebe Ridgely's Tuxedo band, which specialized in society gigs and actually became two bands following a split. Others also performed under Sidney Desvigne, who through most of the 1920s led a band on the riverboat *Island Queen*, plying between New Orleans and Cincinnati. Desvigne later formed a large and successful swing orchestra. Other "polite" bands of the time furnishing plenty of jobs included groups under A.J. Piron, John

Robichaux, Peter Bocage and Fate Marable. Still others were put together by those well-known steamer magnates, the Streckfus Brothers.

Smaller, hotter, "purer" jazz bands, in which many other future Preservation Hallers also played, but which, alas, never recorded, included those of the legendary trumpet greats Buddy Petit, Chris Kelly and Kid Rena. (Rena did record, but only briefly, and well past his prime.) One of the longest surviving Preservation Hall stalwarts, bassist Chester Zardis, remained proud of his association with these groups, as well as of his work with the large swing bands that played on the Mississippi riverboats.

In 1929 the Jones–Collins Astoria Hot Eight cut four exciting sides which showed the best of both worlds: the black heat, drive and blues sense combined with clever breaks and first-rate solos, all subsumed under careful but not over-elaborate arrangements. Banjoist Emanuel Sayles and pianist Joe Robichaux, both leading figures at Preservation Hall 30 years later, were key members of this band, which worked regularly at the Astoria Ballroom on South Rampart Street and sounded not unlike some of the great Jelly Roll Morton groups.

Another fine New Orleans outfit of the "organized" sort was Louis Dumaine's Jazzola Eight. In 1927 it made four sides of its own, plus two more accompanying singer Genevieve Davis. The rarest treasure on the Dumaine recordings is the beautiful playing of trombonist Earl Humphrey. The middle brother of Preservation Hall stars Willie and Percy Humphrey, Earl also played occasionally at the Hall until his death in 1971. Although some say Earl was the greatest of all New Orleans trombonists, his only recordings are these, plus a few others made long after he had passed his prime.

By contrast, a rough-and-ready style was commited to wax in 1927 by the famous Sam Morgan band. Its joyful forward momentum was so unique that it must be heard to be appreciated. The rhythm section laid down simple block chords on an unvarying four beats to the bar, while the horns blazed away in constant ensemble with a naive, irresistible charm. Trombonist Jim Robinson, a central figure in the traditional jazz "revival" of the 1940s and 1950s, and thereafter at Preservation Hall, cut his teeth in this band. He stayed in it for ten years, until it broke up in 1933. Banjoist Creole George Guesnon also played with the Morgan band, although not on the recording. Both remembered how Morgan would rehearse his rhythm section separately, spanking a slapstick at them until they got a perfectly even tempo. Church-going Baptist country folks, the three Morgan brothers (Sam and Ike, cornets; and Andrew, clarinet and tenor, who also played later at the Hall) never played hymns at dances, but did so on the recording date at the request of the producers. (A fourth musical brother, Al, reputedly one of the greatest of all New Orleans bass players, was not on the recording.) The Morgan group's versions of *Sing On*, *Down by the Riverside*, and *Over in the Gloryland* became the first hymns ever recorded by a jazz band. This foreshadowed the revival period after 1940, when *When the Saints Go Marching In*, *Just a Closer Walk with Thee* and other jazz-hymns would become extravagantly popular.

* * *

If the struggle to survive has seldom been easy for any jazz musician, this was particularly true for black Orleanians from the later 20s to the early 60s. In a thousand stories they would tell you: I played a job, I had a lousy payday, and I was out looking for the next job. Some worked fairly reliable, routine road circuits for certain periods. Others went out on the road full of hope, time and again, only to return with empty pockets – as did Jim Robinson with the Sam Morgan band, the Bunk Johnson band, the George Lewis band. Some quit; some fell under the shadow of alcoholism; many died before their time. But others, such as banjoist Narvin Kimball, went on working nights as well as days for years on end, learning, as he put it, to "sleep fast."

Rarely recounted in the histories are the stories of jazzmen trying to keep a middle-class family together; of the telegrams reaching them somewhere out on the road saying their wife was sick or their baby was just born; of their deep wish to provide a better education, a better start, for their children than they had. Some of the wives worked in whatever menial jobs they could find: a few were musicians themselves; others made do as best they could within the family and neighborhood support systems. Family

A rare early photo of a "hot" New Orleans group traveling out of town shows Buddy Petit's Jazz Band in Mandeville, Louisiana, in 1920 (from left): Leon René, Eddie "Face-O" Woods, George Washington, Petit, Buddy Manaday, Edmond Hall and Chester Zardis, who was still playing at Preservation Hall 70 years later.

stability and size varied as much as did class and background.

Clarinetist Willie Humphrey said he worked hard all his life trying to find a way to play for a living. He fell back on trucking or teaching music (at 50 cents a lesson) when he had to. His wife, Ora, remembered that he'd go out playing on the boats and in St Louis for four or five months at a time during the Depression. And when he was home:

He had a truck. He'd put on his clothes to sell wood and coal. He'd say, "Well, I'm goin' out now, I'm the coal man." Come back around one o'clock and put his other clothes on: now he was a teacher, a musician. He'd put a dollar on the mantel at night, that was his food for the next day. We used to call it "My Blue Heaven," a very small house. We stayed there until we had three children. I never complained about it. I had one dress I could put on when I'd go out. We weren't hungry, that's one thing. My children, they all grew up and had a good education and everything, it'll come back on 'em. I have four – three boys and a girl. Dione's oldest daughter got a scholarship to Xavier College, and she has one boy in medical school.

Willie Humphrey acknowledged that New Orleans jazzmen were a stubbornly independent lot.

*Belting out "The Saints,"
Percy Humphrey led a touring
band in the early 70s that
included (from left) Dave
Oxley, Sing Miller and Albert
Burbank.*

Yet they were also part of a social network long
accustomed to reciprocal obligations – people helping
each other out. It was a special blend, nicely expressed
in the music with its voices at once brashly individual
and sensitively interdependent. A paradox hard to
fathom for northern city dwellers lacking a feel for
the Latin background or southern paternalism, this
feeling imbues the local survival system, and it would
later become part of the atmosphere around Preservation Hall. A noted local psychiatrist observed
that the city, with its closely knit families and clans,
its climate of tolerance and acceptance, and its unify-
ing rituals, "gives unusual opportunities both to be
yourself and to belong to a group." As the black poet

Tom Dent put it, in describing a New Orleans street parade, "the entire crowd of his people carried away into unity of motion, singleness of purpose, individuality of motion; second line is everybody's thing together and everybody's thing for themselves" [see inset page 290]. The wisdom of the paradox emerged constantly, and at odd moments – as when Willie talked about favors (his "granddaddy" being a highly respected and influential music teacher):

My granddaddy was a man who never liked for no favors. 'Cause when people do a whole lot of favors they look for something. So, I'm like that. I don't like for nobody to do no whole lot of favors for me. Now, I cater to doctors and lawyers. I do favors for them. I don't do no favors for them, but I look to them to be reasonable, that's what I'm speaking about. You got to depend on your doctor.

Unlike the "country" players, the Humphreys were relatively versatile reading musicians whose professional skills helped them ride the waves of changing styles and market demands. Percy and Willie first played together as children in their grandfather's band at a Memorial Day service at Chalmette Cemetery in 1911. Thereafter, the taciturn Percy followed a somewhat different course than did his more flamboyant older brother. Canny and tough-minded, Percy stuck it out at home. "You hang onto what you have," he said later. Percy did some trucking with Willie, sold insurance for 30 years, and took whatever grinding local music jobs were available.

The hours were long. There were times when Percy played from eight at night until eight in the morning without a break. "I used to sit up there many nights with my eyes closed, playing. Not brisk like I should, but I'd be playing. After I'd done that for maybe half an hour, if you tired and sleepy and you commence setting, them eyes look like you're in a trance. But you're working." The grandfatherly trumpeter liked to recall incidents such as the time, at the end of a long evening, when a redneck employer laid a pistol on a table and said there just wasn't enough money to pay the band the agreed-on pittance. Percy told the man he guessed he'd just have to use that gun, because they weren't leaving without their money. The man paid.

Willie Humphrey between numbers at the Hall

Originally "breakin' time on drums," Percy became a bandleading trumpeter in 1925 because he got tired of leaders always trying to heap blame on the drummer. In the 20s and 30s he played in pit bands and at parties, at the Masonic Temple, the Astor Roof and other nightspots, including the Alamo Dance Hall, which doubled as a bookie joint by day. A mainstay during the Depression were the "jitney" halls, where the male customers paid five or ten cents a dance to dance with the hostesses. The girls kept half. To help them keep their turnover high, the band never took breaks, and played as many as 50 tunes an hour. Often, Percy would count off the next tune before the last one had even finished. "Papa had a big stack of music, and I knew I had a pretty good reading outfit. All I had to do was select what numbers I wanted to use. You had to have plenty of music, because every dance was no more than two choruses or maybe three."

Jitney musicians were paid 15 dollars a week for seven nights. Even at those rates, Percy remembered, "your friends be trying to steal the job for twelve dollars." To keep body and soul together, and to make sure he had something else when each job ended (sometimes abruptly), "I always kept two or three jobs going at the same time." A key part of this was his work with the marching brass bands, particularly the well-disciplined Eureka:

Man, we used to wear them numbers out, them old hard marches like *Under the Double Eagle*. We'd been parading out there since eight in the morning, and at two in the evening [bandleader] Wilson called them old hard numbers.

I played them funerals for a dollar, them parades four or five hours a day. It wasn't enough money to get the uniform. We used to wear white duck pants and white shirt, and I tell you we weren't getting enough out of it to pay your laundry bill. Every Sunday everybody out there, nice and clean, spic and span and what-not. Working the poor wives and mothers and aunts and everybody to death [doing the washing and ironing], but we loved it. Didn't know what it was to say no. We didn't *not* want to play.

It depended who was the organization and who we were playing for. If it were a strict church member and being buried by a society we'd play *The Saints* and keep it straight as possible. Not too much jazz, just hymns we'd play or marches or whatnot. Now if it was what we call a "rounder" or corner bum or something like that, well, we'd

Connecting with an old friend before a gig at New Orleans' Jazz and Heritage Festival in 1984 (above), Willie Humphrey showed his love for jaunty fedoras and lively human contact.

turn loose everything we had. But the band stayed in key, and they stayed in harmony with what they were doing. They got bands out here, man, they don't know what harmony is. Everybody going his way, spreading out, everybody wants to be noticed, everybody wants to be heard. To me it's not music, not the kind I'm accustomed to.

Percy Humphrey remembered that, by the early 1930s, the kind of old-time jazz later restored to popularity in the Preservation Hall era was already being laughed at as corny:

[Reedman John] Handy used to make fun of [cornetist] Tom Albert. 'Waw, waw, who's that Papa Tom?' Well, these other guys 'round here now trying to play just like Papa Tom was playing . . .

Certain musicians wanted to know, "Why you gonna have rehearsals? Why do you rehearse so much and the jobs are so far in between?" I tell 'em, "See, I'm expecting it to pay off some day. I may not live to see it, or may not get the breaks, but we keep on rehearsing, and we keep on the way we're going, playing a job once in a while, just what

we're doing may come back. And the youngsters, people younger than we are, they'll probably reap the benefit of it. We may be too old to work, but by trying to keep it alive, and keepin' it alive, keepin' it before the public, somebody going to benefit by it." And some of those guys that said, "Man, what am I gonna come to your rehearsals for?" – we kept it going until it caught on, and now many of us making a few dollars out of it. If we hadn't continued fighting to keep it alive, the rock-and-rollers would've had it, and the whole lot of us doing this traditional jazz would have to hang them horns up.

But it survives, and a few of those progressive jazz people have come over to help us keep it alive, and I'm thankful that I was one of them that kept barrelin' and fightin' to keep it alive in our humble way.

In such circumstances New Orleans musicians learned to be tough, not sentimental. Although sweet and friendly, they knew long since that being folk

The work of the front-line triumvirate of brother hornmen Percy and Willie Humphrey (opposite) and Earl Humphrey (right) stemmed from the teaching of their grandfather, James Brown Humphrey, who played a unique role in the earliest years of jazz. That "fair-skinned Negro with red hair," as the authors Berry, Foose and Jones told it, in "Up from the Cradle of Jazz" (1986), "starting about 1887, boarded the train each week, wearing a swallow-tailed coat and carrying a cornet case and music sheets in a satchel. The professor had many New Orleans pupils who entered the ranks of early jazz; he is also said to have taught whites. Most students on his weekly tour of the plantation belt – 25 miles either way from the city – were illiterate workers who lived in shacks behind the sugar and cotton fields along the river . . . Humphrey by 1890 was a rare commodity, a black man who lived off his talents as an artist. He played all instruments, directed bands and orchestras, and became a catalyst sending rural blacks into urban jazz ensembles."

heroes cannot, as Sweet Emma Barrett used to say, be cashed at the A & P. Hence their resentment at being sketched or taped without permission – records have been issued for which they were never paid, and postcards and paintings of them have long been offered for sale around the French Quarter without their consent. They are little affected by either publicity or condescension. But the long, hard years taught musicians like Percy Humphrey to be very careful about money: for example, to work only for a guaranteed wage, never for a share of the gate. The growl in his firm lead horn seemed to spring directly from life's "school of hard knocks."

In 1986 a part-time trumpeter, Bruce Dexter, was introduced to Percy as one who had played a lot of traditional jazz in the postwar California revival period. Percy's comments were as stacatto as his horn: "You still got your own teeth?" "Yeah." "You can play." On another occasion, referring to a young trumpeter from overseas who, after a few months in New Orleans, stormed home in a huff because he was not sufficiently appreciated, Percy remarked drily, "There's plenty of work. *If* you're not choosy."

His aunts called him "Butch," and some of the other musicians continued to do so into the 1980s. During World War II he unloaded boxcars for the war effort by day while playing jobs at night – he had too many children to be drafted – and on Hiroshima Day Percy had to beg the man on duty to unlock the gate so he could go work his "gig."

Appreciating such a past helped enlarge the present. One night in 1985, somewhere in the Middle West, Percy could be observed on the stage of a huge concert hall, with those elegant, subtly authoritative little finger gestures of his, doing his funny routine on *Tiger Rag*. An hour later, the felt-hatted, pear-shaped figure in the black overcoat, false teeth firmly glued in place despite recent lip blisters, toting the diminutive horn case all covered with red plastic repair tape, stepped carefully across the crisp snow in front of the Greyhound's blinding headlights toward

Down-home gigs helped traditional musicians keep body and soul together during the Depression and long after. Cultural isolation had the beneficial effect of helping preserve older, simpler jazz styles. The trombonist is Eddie Morris, the band that of Kid Clayton, playing a picnic in 1956.

LABOR DAY NITE
★DANCE★
At Newly Enlarged and Decorated
GYPSY TEA ROOM
ST. ANN and VILLERE STREETS
MON., SEPT. 3rd · 9 P.M 'TIL ?
MUSIC BY

SIDNEY DESVIGNE'S ORCH.
ADMISSION . . . . $1.00 TAX INCLUDED
MAKE TABLE RESERVATIONS NOW ! !

Lush swing bands of the 30s, including that of Sidney Desvigne, followed national trends and provided steady work around New Orleans and on riverboats to players able to meet their professional requirements.

a softly glowing open doorway – the home of the university president, where Percy and his men were the guests of honor.

* * *

For many years the Humphreys shared the limelight as the leading figures in the prime touring band from Preservation Hall. More typical of the average player to be heard at 726 St Peter Street on any given evening was tenor saxophonist Emanuel Paul, who passed away in 1988. A mainstay of the Kid Thomas band from 1943, Paul's memories showed that the need to "sleep fast" was not confined to the Depression:

Across the river? I done pretty good there [three nights a week at Speck's Moulin Rouge with Thomas]. The hours were so long – till three o'clock in the morning. Eight to three. And I was working [days] at the naval supply on 14th Avenue and the River. I'd bring my horn and my clothes, and when I'd get through working, I'd change my clothes. Got the ferry right there at Napoleon [Avenue]. Just as I'd cross the river, I'd get on the levee and they had a restaurant there. I'd eat my sandwich, and after that I'd catch my bus and go on to Specks.

Not much sleep. I used to be late to work at times. I used to sew sacks of beans, rice, flour, things like that, and stack them out for the Navy. It was a pretty good job, but they weren't paying nothing. Fifty cents an hour. I had to have something.

I played with different bands during the daytime. Parades, funerals, anything they want. Sometime I played a funeral as low as three dollars. All that hot sun and walking. Specially across the river, 'cause it's like that in the country. Could see, in the summertime, that heat sticking up like little needles in the asphalt as you walk. Your feet would be boiling hot . . .

Thomas go downtown and buy that tune. And I had to transpose the music. Read from the piano [score]. Seldom got anything for the band, 'cause he couldn't read it. I'd practice at home and learn it, and go there and play it. The rest of them'd catch on. Joe James'd do the same thing on the piano. He couldn't read. He already knew the chords, but didn't change in the right place at times. And Thomas would go to [music professor] Manetta. He'd play along with Manetta. Manetta'd play it on the trumpet. He'd catch it that way. All of them new tunes, he'd catch.

Although a good reader, Paul, like Thomas, was a self-taught musician, lacking the advantages of having grown up in a musical family. Born in 1904, he first played violin, then banjo for twelve years, then the saxophones – much of this having to do with the sheer availability of the expensive instruments, which were alternately lent to him, bought by him, stolen from him, pawned, reclaimed and demanded by the available jobs. Like many others, he played in the local, federally sponsored Works Progress Administration (WPA) band in the 30s. In the same era Paul turned down two offers to play in Chicago, preferring to hang onto his jobs at home. Forty years later, under the Preservation Hall aegis, he would tour extensively with Thomas. These tours included a State Department-coordinated visit to the Soviet Union in 1979 – work that left him relatively comfortable in his sunset years. But the early memories remained indelible:

> The deacon and the preacher started me to playing the music, and then they kicked me out because I was playing dances and picnics. Baptist church. I say they didn't like a musician in the church and I figured, who's going to blow the trumpet on the last day? Where is he going to be? In Heaven, isn't it? That sound going come down from Heaven from that trumpet blower. Why you want to put me out of there? You going to put him out of Heaven?
>
> That's where the jazz come from in the old days, following the wagons. About six men in the wagon. When I was ten years old, they'd take me out to watch the wagon and the horse. They'd be playing for a wedding. We'd take a horse and ride around the grounds and enjoy ourselves. They played good music. Waltzes, old time music, two-step, one-step. It was jazz.
>
> I used to hear bands for blocks and blocks. Went to the cemetery sometime. In the old days there would be band rehearsals all over town on Sunday.
>
> 'Good old days?' Hard time days. They wasn't good for me, not all of them. Bad, tough coming up.

*   *   *

In those hard old 30s, bassist Papa John Joseph ran an impromptu message service-cum-booking agency for his musical friends out of his barbershop. Others found meagre work through similarly imaginative means. Part of the problem for the natural, but untutored, musicians was that they could not or would not play in the the slicker, fashionable mode

*Emanuel Paul typified
Preservation Hall sidemen in
the breadth of his experience
from the 20s on, but was
atypical in that he played tenor
sax, usually associated with
later styles. In brass bands he
furthered the shift away from
baritone horns to saxophones,
his final choruses breaking
from the strict parts into
cascading arpeggios reminis-
cent of his jazz phrases.*

then being laid down by sophisticated dance
orchestras in places like Harlem and Kansas City. It
would be decades, yet, before any significant portion
of America's dominant, urbanizing middle-class –
the nation's primary music market – slackened their
preoccupation with progress, glitzy modernity and
the future, and began to seek values linked to a more
straight-from-the-heart, rough-and-ready past.

Although it has often been assumed that the
simpler kind of old jazz – the approach of most of the
Preservation Hall bands – was the way the music had
sounded in the "pure" days of the 20s and before, that
assumption is half-true at best. The jazz played in
New Orleans before the "diaspora" of its musicians
was a varied, complex, developing amalgam of
influences, fusing the work of primitive and polished
players alike. But from the late 1920s on, with many
of the more skillful musicians having departed for

better jobs elsewhere, and with the main national trends moving the music in smoother, fancier, more Europeanized, less "African" directions, the jazz of the relatively isolated black New Orleans neighborhoods tended in the opposite direction – toward greater roughness, looseness and simplicity.

The contrast between the more literate early jazz and rougher later variants would be echoed at Preservation Hall. Compare the relatively graceful, refined piano work of a Jeanette Kimball, who appeared on some of the most important jazz recordings made in New Orleans during the 20s, with Sing Miller's heavier, bluesier, Fats Domino-like, rocking soul sound.

While bands such as those of Duke Ellington and Benny Goodman and Cab Calloway were riding the shiny rails of an urbanizing America, future Preservation Hallers like Kid Thomas and DeDe Pierce lived on the fringes of a southern community whose old sophistication had faded. New Orleans' newer musical energies were rural-based. Throughout the Depression and war years, hymn-shouting Protestants and Delta blues men continued arriving in New Orleans from the country. Long on spirit but short on technique, they infused jazz bands and brass bands alike with unbridled heat, a deep

The proud decorum of the old processional bands matched the solemnity of the many occasions for which they were hired (from left): Albert Warner, John Casimir, Showboy Thomas and Wilbert Tillman all appeared at Preservation Hall.

spiritual strain, and gut-level blues feeling. From similar influences came a new form – rhythm and blues – which was born in New Orleans but quickly exploited elsewhere, much as the original jazz had been. Quite a few of the younger future Preservation Hallers cut their teeth in the rhythm-and-blues movement of the 40s and 50s.

At the same time, the older-style local dance halls were islands in time within a city which had never truly been part of the US mainstream. Still functional, if only marginally, the music being played in them by men like the haunting clarinetist Albert Burbank, or the hard-driving bassist Slow Drag Pavageau, was being conserved and protected by a kind of purity in isolation. This lean kind of conservation would pay off later for the relative few who survived long enough. During the 1930s, reduced to playing only an occasional parade in what might have been his prime years, Jim Robinson went to work on the docks as a stevedore. So did George Lewis. Both would live to hear their simple, emphatic phrases imitated all over the world, from the 60s onward, by young white enthusiasts. But who could have guessed such an outcome? For decades, the very insularity that was protecting this earthy cultural product was also killing it.

The so-called "revival" – the very gradual, somewhat periodic, but enduring resurgence of interest in traditional jazz from the 40s onward – was a product not of New Orleans, but of the North, of California, of Europe and even of Australia. For most of the diehard fans and many of the younger musicians, the guiding attitudes behind the revival tended to be idealistic and non-commercial. Claims that traditional jazz was important (a) as a fine-art form and (b) as authentic folk expression, while representing different strands of the Euro-American value cluster, were usually put forward as one. But such attitudes toward the music were rarely, if ever, displayed by Orleanians themselves, who viewed the hometown product as nothing special, or, if they were musicians, as a potential source of jobs. Preservation Hall was invented and run by transplanted northerners. But their policy was to hire only musicians who lived in New Orleans. Thus the Hall involved peculiar blendings of northern idealism and local pragmatism. Although French Quarter denizens, students, teachers and the like patronized the Hall in its earliest years, it was not long before New Orleans residents came there only infrequently, whereas out-of-towners would cheerfully wait in long lines to get in.

* * *

One of the earliest to write glowingly of traditional jazz was the Swiss conductor Ernest Ansermet. In 1919, after hearing a performance by New Orleans' Sidney Bechet and the Southern Syncopated Orchestra, he was moved to publish a long magazine article praising Bechet's artistry and stressing the music's African and spiritual influences. Ansermet was enough of an artist himself to cut through the judgmental habit of Puritan societies to the simple truth of the music – its uninhibited joy:

> I couldn't say if these artists make it a duty to be sincere, if they are penetrated by the idea that they have a "mission" to fulfill, if they are convinced of the "nobility" of their task, if they have that holy "audacity" and that sacred "valor" which our code of musical morals requires of our European musicians, nor indeed if they are animated by any "idea" whatsoever. But I can see they have a very keen sense of the music they love, and a pleasure in making it which they communicate to the hearer with irresistible force – a pleasure which pushes them to outdo themselves all the time, to constantly enrich and refine their medium. They play generally without notes, and even when they have some, it only serves to indicate the general line, for there are very few numbers I have heard them execute twice with exactly the same effects. I imagine that, knowing the voice attributed to them in the harmonic ensemble, and conscious of the role their instrument is to play, they can let themselves go, in a certain direction and within certain limits, as their heart desires. They are so entirely possessed by the music they play, that they can't stop themselves from dancing inwardly to it in such a way that their playing is a real show.

Forty years later, in 1959, on the eve of his own death – and of the birth of Preservation Hall – Bechet, one of the few true geniuses New Orleans jazz has produced, had this to say about the music he loved:

> A man, he's got all kinds of things in him and the music wants to talk to all of him. The music is everything that it wants to say to a man. Some of it came up from jokes and

The size and style of brass bands varied with the event – and era. Included on this warm day in the 50s were (from left) Jim Robinson, Wilbert Tillman, Andy Anderson and Emile Knox.

some of it came up from sorrow, but all of it has a man's feelings in it. How that came about, that's my real story. The music has come a long way, and it's time for it now to come out from around a corner; it's got to come up and cross the street. If I could believe it would do that, I wouldn't worry. For me, all there is to life aside from the music, it's not the things you'd expect people to say. All I want is to eat, sleep, and don't worry. Don't worry, that's the big thing. And that's what's holding back the music from this step it has to take. It's still worried. It's still not sure of itself. It's still in the shade, and it's time it just stood up and crossed the street to the sunny side.

But that's not yet. It won't happen yet. It has a way to go, and I'm not ready to say what that way is. All I say is, it's my people. The worry has to be gotten out of them and then it will be gotten out of the music . . .

Back in New Orleans when I was young, back there before all this personality stuff, all this radio and contracts and "attraction" – the music, it was free. It was all different then . . . There were always people out listening to us play. Wherever there was music, a whole lot of people would be there. And those people, they were just natural to the music. The music, it was all they needed. They weren't there to ask for "attractions."

And that left the music to be itself. It could have a good time; it was free to. And that spirit there was to it, that was a wonderful thing, there was a happiness in it. It was there to be enjoyed, a whole lot of spirit.

"Functional" jobs have always taken traditional jazz bands to strange settings. Here, on September 23, 1961 (from left), Sammy Penn, Kid Thomas, Twat Butler, Louis Nelson and Emanuel Paul played for the opening of a gas station at 2900 Gentilly Boulevard, New Orleans.

Spirit and enjoyment: surely these are the beginning and end of jazz. But over such a seemingly simple subject, fierce moralistic arguments had raged in those 40 years among jazz critics of every stripe, arguments often more descriptive of their own and society's tensions than of the music itself. Not until the new ethic of enjoyment which accompanied the "greening" and "rainbowing" of America did the righteousness subside. Was it by happy chance or destiny that, just as Preservation Hall came into being, middle-class Americans were starting to relax and act more like Orleanians? Dancing on the grass at a huge outdoor concert of the Humphrey band in San Francisco, amid picnic hampers and wine bottles and a conga line of twisting bodies, a young man of the 80s exclaimed, "This is just a big family reunion!"

* * *

Among the steps on the way to that reunion were a series of recordings made in New Orleans, particularly those done by Bill Russell over a ten-year period starting in 1942. Three years earlier, on a tip from Louis Armstrong, Russell had discovered a long-forgotten New Orleans trumpeter, Bunk Johnson, who had been one of Louis' teachers, and who was now working on a plantation in New Iberia, Louisiana. Russell helped this doughty oldster in bib overalls to get a new set of teeth. Eventually, with the help of a couple of other aficionados, Russell brought Bunk to New Orleans and recorded him.

More recordings and performance tours followed. Bunk Johnson became the patron saint of a small but impassioned coterie of true believers who thumped scripture-like books and magazines and preached that the old jazz was noble and all subsequent styles heresy. Between the lines, as there had often been in jazz appreciation circles, were liberal feelings about society's victimization of black artists who were really unsung heroes, and about the commercial exploitation and corruption of their once-pure music, such as had happened when the entertainment industry got hold of Louis Armstrong.

This was not the view of the old-style musicians themselves. Their approach, with few exceptions, was not to criticize the US mainstream or separate themselves from it, but to continue to try to win its acceptance, hoping for more work in the competitive but friendly atmosphere in which the music had originally flourished. In a sidewise reference to the more primitive jazzmen who had become the darlings of the revival fans, George Guesnon said of the Crawford–Ferguson Night Owls, a technically accomplished all-white group which performed briefly at Preservation Hall in the early 60s and for ten years thereafter on the riverboats: "They ain't no stevedores, but they can play."

Musicians, in other words, are interested in music, not social theories. Bill Russell was a musician, and that was always his approach. Despite his scrupulous research and discerning taste, he never, for upwards of half a century, wanted to be called either a historian or a critic. Least of all did he wish to be viewed as a patriarch or shaper of the jazz revival movement which took so much of its impetus from his recordings. Living and breathing a spirit of truth in simplicity, however, Russell seemed to have been sent straight from central casting for the part.

At times Preservation Hall seemed to benefit from a similar mystique: an assumption that something quasi-holy was going on within those patinated walls – the preservation of an untouchably pure form handed down from a golden age. Closer to ground-level reality is the fact that jazz styles have always been evolving, in New Orleans as elsewhere. The players have always been looking for jobs, and whoever shows up on a recording or on a bandstand on a particular night is often as much a matter of

The haunting horn of Albert Burbank graced some landmark recordings made by Bill Russell in the 1940s. The gentlemanly clarinetist later became a regular at the Hall and on tour.

availability and fluky chance as of golden ideals.

Russell's aims had been as clear and unpretentious as the man himself. "My only idea was to hear some good music," he explained. "I wasn't trying to re-create any old-time bands. I just wanted to record Bunk and get an idea how he played, how he sounded. I've had the criticism so often that I put the band together for Bunk, that I picked the men and told him who to use, and tried to create the 1900 sound." Devotees of the George Lewis band, which Lewis maintained had *originally* been his band, but which seems to have been created for Bunk and then to have survived him to become world-famous in its own right, rarely stopped to consider the fact that some of its key members had not been Russell's or Bunk's first choices. Both would have preferred a guitar to a banjo, for one thing, but no guitarist was available at the moment. As a result, the forceful, unvarying four-beat sound of banjoist Lawrence Marrero became the trademark and *sine qua non* for generations of "trad" bands from London to Osaka.

Thus, in the meandering ways of history, Russell's dedication unintentionally helped seed the long-term rebirth of the early jazz styles heard at Preservation Hall. During its first two decades, the Hall drew mainly on a core population of black musicians who had been found, recorded and interviewed by researchers, beginning with Russell, during the 40s and 50s. But these were increasingly supplanted by players of more mixed lineage.

Contributing to the timeless charm of the sides Russell issued on his American Music (AM) label, with its straightforward graphics and fine clear photographs, was the happy irony that the local recording studios of the day refused to record Negroes. So, instead, Russell recorded them with a single microphone in some wonderful old social halls. Although Russell would have preferred less echo, many listeners have felt that those resonant woods and cavernous, humid spaces provided an ideal sonority for the stripped-down, spacious sounds which seemed to evoke days beyond recall.

* * *

Having toured widely in the 50s, the George Lewis band was the only one to come under the Preservation Hall aegis, from 1961 onward, with an established international reputation. As would prove true at the Hall, it was not only the music itself, but also Lewis' musicians' personal warmth and accessibility, that brought many new devotees into the traditional jazz fold.

Other prominent names in the postwar revival of traditional jazz were the Kid Ory band, which worked and recorded regularly in California from the 40s into the 60s; an entourage of musicians around Sidney Bechet, who was living largely in France; the San Francisco jazz upsurge spearheaded by Lu Watters, Turk Murphy and Bob Scobey; Louis Armstrong's famous small band of polished soloists, the All Stars; and a floating population of important Orleanians, such as the Creole clarinetists Omer Simeon, Albert Nicholas and Barney Bigard, who added their florid colorations to innumerable bands of mixed quality and style heard in cabarets from Manhattan and the Chicago Loop to Bourbon Street and Hollywood Boulevard. Traditional jazz media appearances were pioneered by the radio shows of Rudi Blesh, Orson Welles and others. Los Angeles' frenzied Dixieland Jubilees started in the late 40s; of greater longterm impact were the nation's first jazz festivals, appearing in the mid-50s.

The impassioned, biting sound of clarinetist Emile Barnes made him a favorite of buffs, who treasure his relatively few recordings. Milé's active career ran for 58 years – from 1908 to 1966.

The term "Dixieland" had come into wide use following the electrifying success of the first jazz recordings, which were made by the Original Dixieland Jazz Band in 1917. A white group from New Orleans, the ODJB toured widely and took America and Europe by storm. "Dixieland" usually refers to an emotionally shallow, razzamatazz style favored by glib technicians, banjo-thwacking fraternity boys, and pizza parlor entertainers in red-and-white blazers and straw hats. Represented in the 80s by such outfits as the Dukes of Dixieland and Pete Fountain, with "that happy Dixie two-beat," it blends vaguely into the sentimental image of New Orleans jazz which had begun to soak into the national psyche by the late 40s: sin-soaked Storyville, red-garter girls on ironwork balconies, bittersweet darkies strumming on riverboats, and an undiscovered great young horn man from the wrong side of the tracks. More to the point, Narvin Kimball said that Dixielanders played faster tempos and missed the real feeling of the blues. Reedman Polo Barnes put it this way:

When I left Los Angeles and came back home to New Orleans, I was really surprised to find how many of the musicians had actually forgotten the differences between the two. Dixieland music was taken from traditional New Orleans jazz, but New Orleans jazz actually didn't have any name.

Dixieland is the style of the white boys, because, to tell the facts, they just never could understand that beat, that parade beat. I don't know if they wanted something of their own. These people are southern and everything is "The South" and Dixieland is "The South." But we weren't interested in the South, we were more interested in just New Orleans. That Dixieland music, too, they were more interested in showing themselves. It's a real show, like clowns, whereas in traditional New Orleans music they was more interested in making you play, making you dance. They'd play with so much feeling that even a little baby in your arms would jump like that to that music!

In truth, there was, from the earliest times, less difference between white and black jazz in New Orleans than was often the case elsewhere. Harmonious relations prevailed, and the early generations of Whites learned directly from the pioneers. Dixielanders, many of Italian extraction, tended to go their own way and find relatively better jobs than the traditionalists: prominent names included Sharkey Bonano, Tony Almerico and Irving Fazola among the Whites, and Papa Celestin, Octave Crosby and Thomas Jefferson among the Blacks. Closer in spirit to the players in whom Bill Russell was interested were a handful of Whites who showed a deep affinity for the emotional values of black music. Players like the clarinetist Raymond Burke, the cornetist Johnny Wiggs, the bassist Chink Martin and the clarinetist Harry Shields all played at Preservation Hall in the 60s. Burke was a mainstay at the Hall and on tour until his death in 1986. Possessed of a warm, rich tone and subtle ear, he ran a little collectibles shop by day. The personable clarinetist agreed with some listeners in voicing his consternation at the harsh loudness of some of the drummers, banjoists and trumpeters with whom he had to play.

In the postwar years, virtually all these musicians found some jazz work in cabarets around the French Quarter, which remained a quiet, quaint, somewhat bohemian multi-ethnic and affordable residential section. However, segregation laws, separate unions and the expectations of white customers still prevented white and black musicians from appearing together. Forerunners of today's raucous tourist traps, the jazz joints had a surface sizzle but were generally depressing places – an important factor in the minds of more idealistic listeners who would

The subtle unorthodoxy of Raymond Burke's warm, reedy style was best appreciated close up. A long career as a leader and sideman (as well as a dealer in strange collectibles) associated him with an unusually wide range of pure and Dixieland style bands; yet Raymond remained, in all things, sweetly himself.

lend their support to the Preservation Hall idea. Insiders hung around the Quarter but preferred to attend outlying funeral processions and the last of the neighborhood jazz dance halls, which were gradually closing during the 50s.

George Lewis' drummer, Joe Watkins, commented: "Any of them clubs on Bourbon Street, when we get away from there and play where people could dance, I noticed a big change in your spirit." The painter Jack Cooley, having spent most of his life in the Quarter, remembered, "Those operators of Bourbon Street joints were sleazy, crude, mafioso types. They didn't pay those old musicians their due. Those were just niggers the people from up north wanted to see."

*   *   *

During the 1950s, jazz lovers from out of town were becoming something of a sub-species around New Orleans. Some of these – along with New Orleans aristocrat Dr Edmond Souchon – made recordings which remain valuable documents of a fading era. A few sessions were done live in the commercial black dance halls still operating. Dave Wyckoff and Alden Ashforth made historic recordings distributed over the years on specialty labels including AM, Folkways and Pax. In January 1961, a few months before Preservation Hall formally opened, Herb Friedwald came to town and made an important and extensive series of recordings for Riverside Records. Friedwald had become enthralled with dance-hall ensemble jazz and the audience rapport that went with it. Like a number of others, he regretted the subsequent influence of concert tours, Bourbon Street and Preservation Hall in moving the music toward solo-oriented, tourist-pleasing routines. Nonetheless, the wide national distribution of Friedwald's often excellent Riversides helped give impetus to Preservation Hall.

Basking in the sunset glow of the old music in the last of its "natural" settings, the buffs and intellectuals were a fresh ingredient in the ever-evolving sociology of jazz audiences. Since all music is folk music, and all folks are folk, the seasoned professionals handled the worshipers and experts as deftly as they would later handle the tourists. Richard B. Allen, for many years curator of the Jazz Archive at Tulane, enjoyed recalling what happened one night at one of the last surviving dance halls:

A folklorist from Baton Rouge, and an English trumpeter named Joe Lyde, and I were all sitting at a table, having a ball, listening to the Kid Thomas band at Speck's Moulin Rouge. It was the kind of night when all the people are out dancing. The deputy sheriff who's assigned to make sure nobody else raids the gambling game is there, but he's gotten so drunk he's dancing with the waitress, and nobody cares what's going on. But right in front of the band is this long table. And all these serious jazz fans, these real music lovers, are there. Joe Lyde described them as "stony-faced jazz critics," which just fit perfectly. And we just about fell out laughing because Thomas looks at 'em, points his trumpet straight at 'em, and plays, *Smile, Darn You, Smile!*

Around the USA and Europe in these years, a handful of traditional jazz record stores became nerve centers for what was going on locally. Fans fondly remember Jazz Man and Ray Avery's in Los Angeles, Commodore in New York, Groove in Chicago and Dobell's in London. For New Orleans it was

Slow Drag Pavageau, born in New Orleans in 1888, got his nickname as a noted dancer. Only later, when aged about 39, did he take up string bass. From 1943 until his death in 1969 he was world renowned as the pounding, slapping, four-to-the-bar heartbeat of the Bunk Johnson and George Lewis ensembles. In his last decade he appeared both at the Hall and as the fancily bedecked Grand Marshal who paraded at the head of brass bands.

successively Blackstone's at 439 Baronne, operated by Oren and Henry Blackstone (Richard B. Allen was later a managing partner), the Jazz Record Center at 706 Bourbon, and finally a shop opened by Bill Russell at 600 Chartres after he moved down from Chicago in 1956. Later, Russell moved his shop to the 700 block of St Peter Street, just opposite the art gallery which, in 1961, would become Preservation Hall. Eventually, the Hall itself, particularly its carriageway and the sidewalk in front, would inherit this role as the headquarters where everyone met to find out what was going on in town.

One enthusiast, Charles Stroud, remembered how, in the 50s, rumors, such as "Burbank's sitting in for Picou!" would circulate. Jazz lovers would go rushing all over town, sometimes until four in the morning, looking for music. A future prominent jazz cornetist from Minneapolis, Charlie DeVore, praised Bill Russell for selflessly helping out in a thousand small ways:

In his shop Bill had a little blackboard and people would pop in and read it to see what parades are on Sunday, and is Thomas still playing across the river, and are Billie and DeDe at Luthjen's this weekend. I personally could never get over the fact that as practically a total stranger he had taken me under his wing and introduced me to all those musicians. Bill loved all those musicians, and he still does. But he is not a romanticist at all; he has one of the most brilliant objective minds that I ever encountered. It is just amazing the fields of interest he has been involved in. He is a great human being.

He always had a birthday list, and he would send birthday cards to people. When George Lewis was on the road a lot, he would stop by and get flowers for George's grandmother. She was a remarkable woman; she didn't have any electricity in her place, and Bill would take me up to meet her and take flowers to her every time. If someone was sick, we would go around and visit them. I met Wooden Joe [Nicholas] that way. Joe was sick, and even though he wasn't feeling well Bill asked him to demonstrate his mute so I could see how he did the mute stuff.

It was a great experience. I was just a young kid who didn't know what to do with my life, and I said, "This is it for me," and I started playing the cornet. The other musicians were wonderful and great to know, but Bill was the intermediary, the person who made it all possible, so that eventually they came to trust me like they did Bill. I owe everything to Bill. I don't think he realizes, and he probably wouldn't care anyway. I revere him like a father or grandfather.

Despite the intense interest of such devotees, the music and the musicians were in sharp decline. No amount of documentation or assistance could reverse the economic trends in which a popular art must ultimately earn its keep or die. By a lucky chance, insularity from the national mainstream had for 50 years protected the earthy, soulful sounds of players like Wooden Joe and Emile Barnes from the influence of more slippery technicians of the sort favored by the mass entertainment industry. Now, however, the neighborhood "cultural wetlands" were gradually getting absorbed into the national mainstream. Players whose styles had been shaped by local standards, and their own sincerity, found themselves high and dry.

Tulane and the local New Orleans Jazz Club both sponsored what events they could. Although Willie Humphrey, for example, sometimes made gratis appearances to help things along, at this point neither he nor Percy really believed the old music would make a meaningful comeback. Experienced troupers like Willie and drummer Paul Barbarin were teaching music by day at the Grunewald School of Music, and playing on and off at night, mostly on Bourbon Street. Such gigs were not easy to get or hold. Occasional recording jobs meant some temporary pocket money for a few; taped interviews, academically respectable, brought a few dollars more. Richard B. Allen, who was trying to help however he could, said later, "Some folklorist might say hooray, but I've seen a musician like bassist Albert Glenny, who played with Buddy Bolden, literally starving."

Year by year, more of the veterans were dying, and none of the younger black players, who were naturally hoping for professional and social advancement, were interested in playing the older style. Yet what was shrugged off locally was acquiring ever more significance from afar. Painstaking dis-cographies of New Orleans music were undertaken by Europeans, particularly. In places like Australia and Ohio, Los Angeles and London, clutches of middle-class revival musicians were struggling to sound like old black men from impacted New Orleans neighborhoods.

But was the living essence of jazz about to be severed at its roots? That was how the situation looked to many observers. Bill Russell, who had moved to New Orleans simply because he liked to listen to its jazz, told an interviewer, "Whereas this city used to be full of music, old musicians say the city seems like a cemetery, it's so dead." This impression was borne out by that of a young Englishman, Barry Martyn. Later a well-known bandleader and drum-mer, he first arrived in New Orleans in 1960:

It was the worst period in New Orleans music. Some of the musicians were dying just because if they couldn't play, they had no more reason to live. There just wasn't any music to hear. I was in town for about three weeks before I heard a note of music played. People gravitated to Bill Russell's store on St Peter because there was nothing else to do. I used to go every night without fail.

The founder of the highly regarded Young Tuxedo Brass Band, John Casimir blew his E-flat and B-flat clarinets at the Hall and on the streets with a high-pitched wail that is well remembered by trumpeter Charlie DeVore: "At the funerals Casimir's clarinet was so moving I could never get through one of those things: I would break down and cry like a baby. One time the band was right in front of the house when they brought the casket out, and Casimir was playing this real mournful hymn. The widow had a white hand-kerchief, and she was waving it to Casimir and saying, 'Goodbye George, goodbye George,' and Casimir was playing some wailing stuff. It was so moving it just tore me up."

One Sunday afternoon, before I'd heard any New Orleans music, we were just sitting in there talking, and here came this racket. It wasn't exactly like the three stooges, but you can't imagine how quiet the street was then, and we heard this singing and loud talking. I recognized Kid Howard – and I couldn't believe it. I'd seen him in '59 when he played trumpet with the George Lewis band in England. But Howard had gotten so sick, he was so small, like a Biafran refugee, that his collar fit him like a horse's collar. The other two characters were [trumpeters] Kid Sheik and Punch Miller. Slow Drag was there, too [Alcide "Slow Drag" Pavageau, bassist with the Lewis band]. They were all pretty drunk, and they came in. Slow Drag started monkeying around with a guitar. The three others were passing this trumpet around between them, taking choruses on the "St Louis Blues." Howard couldn't even blow, so he stood up and sang a chorus. That was the first New Orleans music I heard, and it seemed monumental because there was nothing else.

Nothing else? Not exactly. The seed of something was already growing quietly, just across the street.

Polo Barnes

That Was a Wonderful Life
Polo Barnes and his Diaries

No musician ever came to Preservation Hall with more solid credentials than Paul "Polo" Barnes. Born in New Orleans in 1901, his was a highly musical family; on his mother's side the Fraziers and the Marreros each contributed important names to the annals of traditional jazz. At the age of six Polo began the way a lot of other future reedmen did – on a ten-cent tin fife. Then, inspired by his older brother Emile, he taught himself to play clarinet. When he was about 17, the saxophone was just beginning to appear. By working long hours in the family mattress factory, he was able to buy himself an alto in 1919. After a few lessons from Lorenzo Tio Sr, he quickly became known as one of the city's outstanding jazz saxophonists. He was an "always helpful and modest man," wrote Alan Barrell, with "a flair for arranging, a patient approach to organizing and a deep, deep love of the music."

Polo founded a group called the Original Diamond Band, including his cousins Cie Frazier and Lawrence and Eddie Marrero. From 1919 to 1922 he had a job with the hot, well-established Kid Rena band (which included another cousin, Simon Marrero, on bass). In 1923 he joined the Original Tuxedo Orchestra, which, along with the group led by A. J. Piron, was New Orleans' leading society jazz ensemble. During this period Polo composed and recorded *My Josephine*, and in 1927, when he heard the record in Chicago, King Oliver sent for him to join a band that included such prominent musicians as Kid Ory, Red Allen, Barney Bigard, Omer Simeon, Paul Barbarin and Luis Russell. Polo Barnes' career alongside such major figures of the "classic" jazz era in the North placed him among the small minority of musicians who survived to become regulars at Preservation Hall. Polo's intermittent stints with Oliver carried right through his last, desperate tours at the bottom of the Depression. He also toured with Jelly Roll Morton in 1928–9. Even if Barnes had done nothing else, his beautiful soprano sax solo on Morton's recording of *Deep Creek Blues* would have earned him a niche in jazz history.

Between road engagements Polo returned to New Orleans, where he worked with many different groups. He joined the US Navy in 1942 and spent the war years playing in navy bands and taking advanced clarinet lessons from a former conservatory teacher. Always an eager learner, he attended barber college in 1948 and cooking school in 1949–50. After playing with Papa Celestin's re-formed Tuxedo Band from 1946 to 1951, he moved to Los Angeles in 1952 and retired from music for five years.

Polo moved back to New Orleans in 1959 and quickly became musically active again, almost exclusively on clarinet. Then, in 1961, he was called back to California to work at Disneyland in the Young Men from New Orleans, which included veterans such as Johnny St Cyr, Harvey Brooks and, briefly, Kid Ory. Polo hung onto the seasonal Disneyland job until 1964, when he finally returned to New Orleans to stay. There he became a mainstay at Preservation and Dixieland halls, primarily with the Percy Humphrey and Kid Thomas bands. He made a few overseas appearances in the 1960s and 70s, but failing health forced him to retire before his death in 1981.

If Polo Barnes' career was proto-typical for a professional New Orleans jazzman, in one way it was unique: he kept a daily diary. While whole sections of it – including the Morton years – were unfortunately lost, enough remains to reveal some of the usually overlooked, and often grim, ground-level realities of the life of a jazz musician. Here, for

example, is a log of the King Oliver band's jobs for the first two weeks of March 1935. Dates are listed on the left, each musician's pay on the right; "N" signifies a negro audience, "W" a white one, and "B" a radio broadcast.

1   Gadsden, Ala. N .50
3   Columbus, Ga.(Liberty Theater) N .25
4   Columbus, Ga.(Army camp) B N 3.00
5   Moultrie, Ga. N 1.00
6   St Augustine, Ga. N 1.50
7   Daytona Beach N 3.00
8   Lakeland N 2.00
9   Tampa N 1.00
11   St Petersburg N 2.00
12   Sanford N 1.50
13   Melbourne N 1.00
14   Melbourne N 1.00
15   West Palm Beach N 3.00
16   Vero Beach (Fireman's Ball) W 3.53

Forty years later, in 1975, Polo earned $3,177.50 for 82 appearances at Preservation Hall, or $38.75 per night, plus $9,005.00 on tour – a total of $12,182.50. Of course, expenses had risen a lot, but not that much. One of the nicest features of the Hall is that it has provided many musicians with this kind of added support, with dignity, at a time of their lives when they were otherwise at their most vulnerable.

Rarely written about, but often crucial during the lean years, was the supporting role played by many jazz-men's wives. "I always kept a job and I always kept our nose above water," reminisced Alma Barnes. She was perched on the edge of their big bed in the typical clapboard house on black, lower-middle-class South Roman Street. "We had a hard time, I'm tellin' you. But he never complained to me and I never complained. We always said to each other, 'Well, maybe tomorrow will be better.' That was a wonderful life. I don't think there's another man on earth like him, with his sweet ways." Alma continued, "He was always happy when he played music. I don't care where he played it. He really loved playing music. He used to play the most beautiful melodies, old waltzes and things. Just be sitting in that back yard, under that tree, and everybody be sitting on the steps like they spellbound."

Sometimes Polo would bring people home from Preservation Hall at two in the morning. Alma would fry them an oyster sandwich on French bread with all the trimmings. One friend, Mona MacMurray, remembered that "their home was always open to everyone. There was an almost constant stream of house guests – musicians, photographers, writers from overseas, friends and fans from other cities in the United States. And to so many friends here in New Orleans, a quick visit to 'Daddy Paul and Alma' always gave the spirit a lift."

Polo was a gentle person, with a soft way of spinning out clarinet phrases that wove through gaps in the louder brass ensembles and lent the band a subtle swing. His warm personal dignity shone through a long, appreciative letter written to Sandra Jaffe from his Disneyland job. "Hello Sandra Dear," it begins, "Gee but it made me feel so good to get a hearing from you and Allan." Polo went on for several pages telling about the big night of September 30, 1961, when Louis Armstrong was featured with their band on a barge, coordinating with four other bands in a steamboat, 400 girls singing *The Saints*, massive fireworks, dancing, etc. – the whole thing lasting from 8 p.m. until 5.30 a.m.

Polo's diaries expressed the tough, base-line reality that was always closer than the glossy PR photos to musicians' actual lives. By 1960 his journals reflected

renewed musical activity in New Orleans and at Disneyland. The following entries, however, show that the 1950s were as rough for Polo as they were for many other New Orleans jazzmen – an important background factor in the Hall's establishment. All who have enjoyed this music should be grateful to these pioneers for their courage, endurance and manly restraint:

Jan. 13, 1953. Rain. Go to social security office. Told to return at 2.30. Interview and advised to go to commercial office for employment in music. Return home and mail letter to Labiches in New Orleans for raincoat and steam iron.

Jan. 16. Go to California Employment Office, 1400 Hill St. Sent on job at restaurant at 5728 Santa Fe Ave. Start working as dishwasher from 4 PM to 12 PM. Salary $6 a day and 2 meals. Come home after work and have liver and onions for supper.

Jan. 18. Go to church today (Hope Lutheran). Put clothes to soak. Alma cook dinner at her work at Betty's Taco Den. We have dinner over there.

Jan. 19. Received iron and raincoat from Labiches today. Mail prayer to Dorothy in New Orleans. Go to J&K Restaurant, mop & work hard today last day. Discharged for their old employee who want to return to work.

Feb. 10. Polo start work (sub.) at Western Elementary School at 54 St. & Western. Mr. Fox is head custodian.

Feb. 11. Go to work earlier today to get ideas from Mr. Fox. PTA meet today. Eat hamburger at Western & 54th. Sleep in boiler room. Get cigarettes. Come home in car with Mr. & Mrs. Fox. Eat supper that Alma cook for us at Betty's. Go to trade school. Kid Gavalan KO's Chuck David in 9th Round.

Feb. 13. Go back to work today. Teachers are nice. Give Polo Valentine cake – work late today. Mr. Fox notify Polo that his status has been promoted from sub to relief custodian. Polo very happy. Alma cook spaghetti and chicken at Betty's – cut her hand.

Mar. 19. Work at Benjamin Franklin High School. Clean brass door knobs. Mr. Crandall tells Polo to wash vulgar writings from walls outside of buildings and cut grasses on sidewalks.

Apr. 7. Polo cook red beans. Feeling was hurted by Oliver saying nigger. Polo asks Oliver not to say that again in his company. Oliver's feeling hurted.

Apr. 11. Go and file application for local membership in Local 47 (white). Pay dues for rest of 1953 ($9). Go to Nickels music store, buy clarinet & sax reeds. Go to May's store for credit (unsuccessful). Get 1/2 doz sox @ 1.50 ($9) from Bullocks. Get shoes from repair shop.

Apr. 13. Polo wash clothes and cook

Polo Barnes with drummer Louis Barbarin

white beans. Alma starts concession at Melody Room 8852 Sunset strip. Sweep at school today. Alma work at Betty's Taco Den at night.

Apr. 19. Go to church. Alma put on chicken before going to work. Go to show Bway nr 7th see Elisabeth Taylor in "Girl Who Had Too Much." Go to Sidney Flueger's house and play clarinet and sax.

May 13. Alma work at Betty's today & Ciro's at night. See Christine Jorgansen & Walter Winchell (columnist). Kid Howard & Jim Crow Robinson visit Polo & have cabbage dinner with him. Polo work at school. Alma get home at 2:45 AM.

Jul. 1. Polo & Mr. Dean finish washing and spotting walls on new bungalows. Start on lavatories. We started to mop today but head custodian wants us to finish wood work. Dusting.

Oct. 8. Polo finds new method of sweeping. Finish early. Take Alma, Kenneth, Dot & children in cab to Merlin's Restaurant. Lawrence Marrero visit Polo. Merlin & Polo go to Beverly Cavern to meet Geo Lewis & his band. Dorothy cook mustard greens. Polo give Betty $65 for 1 mo. rent.

Jan. 28, 1954. Pocket wallet missing. Polo mail income tax return. Alma cook pork & beans.

Feb. 18. Polo & Alma go to lawyer, get release on wage attachment.

Nov. 16. Polo go to classes at Venice High. Start work late. Polo & Mr. Dean listen to former President Truman speak over radio to clear himself of charges. Polo go for Alma at Taco Den.

Nov. 19. At school Polo did swell job in record time.

Nov. 22. Polo's birthday. Go to church (Hope Luth.). Get 1 qt. of wine from Sam. Alma cook spring chicken & spaghetti. Polo read, rest for his Birthday. Go to Taco Den Restaurant for Alma.

Luthjen's

Those Marvelous Dance Halls
Prelude to Preservation

After World War I, jazz spread rapidly from its birthplace in New Orleans to the rest of the nation – indeed, to the entire world. Because many of the city's most talented musicians moved away as well, the notion became widespread that New Orleans had been denuded of good jazzmen. Yet quite a few musicians remained, and as late as the 1950s pure New Orleans jazz could still be heard, on a more or less regular basis, in rickety dance halls scattered around inconspicuous areas of town. In 1955 Barbara Reid, later one of the guiding lights in the formation of Preservation Hall, published the following account, under the title "Back o' Town," for a short-lived avant-garde literary magazine called "Climax."

Everyone who comes to New Orleans hears jazz. Walk down Bourbon Street and you can't help yourself; good, bad and indifferent. There are names known all over the world and names known only to jazz fanatics. But for the visitor who wants to see some real New Orleans color and hear an entirely different type of music, we suggest a little beer garden at the corner of Marais and Almonaster, named Luthjens.

It's a strange little place that looks as though it might be almost too tired to stand. During the week the dance hall is closed but on Friday, Saturday and Sunday a four-piece band keeps the place packed. There are streamers, gaudy lights, soggy tablecloths and wonderful music. Luthjens has been known for some years among the musicians as the "Old Folks Home" because of its steady popularity with the people of the neighborhood. Most of these people have been spending their nights out at this establishment since they themselves were young.

One is advised not to stand or dance too closely to the bandstand because of Harrison Brazely's powerful trombone. It extends an awesome distance past the railing. Signs all around the wall warn against jitterbugging; but we might suggest you beware what we term "The Cajun Stomp." The Kitty is passed occasionally. No request is ignored and even the most boring of top tunes is made enjoyable by the band. Only beer or soft drinks may be had. Visitors and celebrities may expect to be treated with indifference. Regular neighborhood customers have been found to be a paying proposition.

Mama Lou's

There was a time in the childhood of jazz when the Lake Pontchartrain shore was speckled with dance halls built out over the water. There are plenty of Orleanians who still remember weekends at Milneburg, West End or Spanish Fort, and the seafood, dancing and music.

In this historical area there is still one dance hall out over the lake that provides for the public as it did years ago. If you are willing to make a five-mile drive from the edge of town, park by the side of a narrow dark road with crickets and frogs, embark on a wooden walk which is lined with swamp weeds some ten feet tall, cross a mound of railroad tracks still in use and continue approximately three city blocks along a very sketchy pier with the waves of the lake swishing beneath, an unusual treat awaits you. For, on Saturday nights only, Mama Lou provides one of the most uninhibited bands in the city.

Mama Lou keeps a close eye on her customers, and when the hall starts rocking (literally) too much, she sees to it that a subdued blues calms things down a bit. Estimates on Mama Lou's age are in the late eighties. Nevertheless, if the mood takes her she joins in the dances. The lighting is glaring and the decor is NOT modern. There are granite-top tables to permit the full indulgence of boiled crabs which are excellent.

The band cheerfully plays all requests but exceed themselves on the more standard and archaic New Orleans numbers: numbers like *Careless Love Blues*, *Corrina* and *Bill Bailey*.

Watch your step on the bridge – some of the boards are missing.

Happy Landing

Of the many places in and around New Orleans devoted to dispensing authentic jazz in combination with dancing and the inevitable seafood for the entire family's consumption, an establishment known as Happy Landing has long held a top rating. It seems that one of the prime requirements in providing this type of pleasure consists of having a somewhat sinister appearing building located in an almost inaccessible spot. In this respect Happy Landing is typical, and also in making the difficult venture worthwhile.

On Saturday nights five colored gentlemen well along in years play blues, stomps and rags for an audience ranging in age from those who toddle to those who totter; all equally appreciative. Happy Landing is located opposite the New Orleans Airport on Little Woods Road on the lakefront. The whole family is welcome and everybody dances, including the small children.

These musicians, and the people they play for, emphasize the important fact that New Orleans jazz is healthy and something for the entire family to enjoy; it disproves the theory that jazz has to hide in grimy dark bistros with members of the narcotics squad breathing in eager anticipation.

102

Luthjens Burns

In a suitably gothic, if tragic, finale to the era that was, Luthjen's dance hall was gutted by fire on January 30, 1960. An article in the magazine of the New Orleans Jazz Club memorialized its passing with a feeling of grateful remembrance.

A flimsily constructed building which had proven a bastion against the inroads of more "progressive" music is suddenly a thing of the past. On Saturday morning, January 30th, 1960, "Luthjens" beer parlor and dance hall, located at 1200 Franklin Avenue in New Orleans, was gutted by fire, taking the lives of Mrs. Clementine Luthjens (age 81) and her son Jules (age 50), the proprietors.

Mrs. Luthjens was a semi-invalid, spending much of her time in a wheel-chair. Occasionally she used crutches when she wished to move around the business part of the establishment. Her son tended bar. The two occupied the back apartment of the tar-paper covered building. They were last seen alive by Edward Grunblatt, a son-in-law of the deceased woman, at 2 a.m. He had been tending bar, and closed up at that time.

For many years (nobody knows exactly how many), this humble little downtown bistro has been steadfast in employing only the oldest, most authentic of the remaining Negro jazzmen. Usually only two or three nights a week was a "live" band employed. The rest of the week customers had to settle for jukebox music. But on weekends, the old place roared.

It was run in an oldtime, informal manner. No shennanigans or excessively exuberant monkeyshines were tolerated. It was a "family place" – that's what the Luthjens wanted to keep it. Patrons usually consisted of entire families. This might include a mother

and dad and several "kids." Frequently two or three unescorted ladies would comprise a party. They, too, were welcome. Often a lonesome male would come in to drink and to listen, and possibly get in a dance or two. Nobody raised an eyebrow if two girls danced together. There was no offense if some very sweet fat lady got up from her table and meandered over to yours – even if your wife was with you. She would break the ice by saying, "I see you are not dancing with your old man. Mind if he drags me around for this one?" Occasionally, a lone bachelor – feeling the impact of the music and the beer at the same time – would wander off into a not-too-congested corner, and start a little dance of his own – all alone!

Most of the patrons were in shirt-sleeves. Any number of the balding, rotund male customers wore suspenders. The most popular dances requested: the two-step, the one-step and the waltz. A small bandstand at one end of the room was elevated about two feet off the floor.

It would be impossible to enumerate each and every famous jazz band who played there. The list would be interminable. Those we were fortunate enough to hear "in the flesh" at one time or another were of national caliber, and even internationally known. The everlasting pair – DeDe and Billie Pierce – seem to have been sort of "housemen" for Luthjens, for they played there very often. George Lewis did a long stint also, with varying accompanists and sidemen. Often, visitors from out of town were even more fascinated by the customers than they were by the music.

The whole place was a page taken from over a quarter of a century ago. Luthjens will be mighty hard to replace. We doubt very seriously if it ever will be.

The perennial duo of DeDe and Billie Pierce played regularly in Luthjen's Dance Hall in the 1959s. In later decades they appeared under the Preservation Hall aegis, both in New Orleans and on tour.

Thomas Valentine at Specks' Moulin Rouge

Richard B. Allen

Another who helped at Preservation Hall in its first years was Richard B. Allen. His 1972 liner notes for an album by trumpeter Kid Thomas' band evoked an old-fashioned joyousness approaching extinction in the new era of mass entertainment:

Until the late 1950s there were many dance halls across the Mississippi from New Orleans. A string of communities line the west bank of the river: Algiers, McDonoghville, Gretna, Harvey, Marrero, Westwego and Bridge City. Kid Thomas has been an Algerene since shortly after World War I, but he did most of his playing during the 50s in Marrero and Westwego dance halls. On

Saturday nights it was the custom over there to gamble, to dance and to get drunk. The halls somehow gave the impression of converted barns. They were huge old buildings with a bar, a dance floor, a bandstand, some rickety old tables and some hard chairs. Often there was a card and dice table with a bright light hung low over it.

The place where Kid Thomas' band did most of its work was Speck's Moulin Rouge in Marrero. He had been there since World War II and had built up a regular following. The building itself looked even older than it actually was since it was built of used lumber during that war. The bandstand was in the rear. The musicians looked relaxed as they sat behind the music stands and Thomas' assorted mutes. There was a small kitty for tips and a sign in the rear advertising "Kid Thomas Swing Band."

Everybody had fun. Their motto was "Let joy be unrefined," to quote an old-time Chicagoan. I never saw a fight there. Perhaps this was because Specks Rodriguez, the owner, hired a deputy sheriff for the night, but I don't think so. He was usually too busy dancing with a waitress to head off any trouble. We were there for beer, whisky, dancing and the barrel-house music. Drinks were cheap. The band played waltzes, one steps, rhumbas (which some local musicians refer to as "rumbles") and fox trots. The management frowned on jitterbugging and other acrobatics in many New Orleans dance halls, but this wasn't so at the Moulin Rouge. There was one couple who did the wildest Apache dance this side of Marseilles. Many, if not most, of the people were Louisiana French.

At a table next to the bandstand an old, crippled, bald-headed fiddler sawed away, barely making a sound since he used a comb as a mute. Thomas says he could not play the fiddle, but he really could tune it. This is an especially novel idea for a New Orleans musician. Specks Rodriguez, himself, played the fiddle and encouraged anyone to sit in, even if only on Jew's harp.

Looking back on those Saturday nights, I think the band had the best time of all. Kid Thomas always gets his kicks. I can't forget him grinning as he put down his slapstick and picked up a glass to mute his trumpet, driving down the last choruses of *Panama*, while "Smiling Sammy" Penn choked his cymbal as he chewed his cigar. Joe James, then Thomas' pianist, must have been accident prone. Like the fiddler, he often hobbled in on crutches, but this didn't hurt his time. The words of his *Stingaree Blues* would have us roaring with laughter. In fact, Kid Twat Butler, Sammy Penn and Kid Thomas sang good-humored blues also.

Kid Thomas liked to play numbers that the people want, whether they are old standards or the latest hits. He would buy a few pieces of sheet music every week and stuff them into his ever-present suitcase. If the dancers clapped hard enough after a tune, the band played it again, and the shaking started on the spot.

You saw the same faces on the bandstand over and over. Thomas never fired anyone. His band stuck together, and they pulled together. It did not matter what kind of music his men had played or with what kind of band they had worked. They all fell into that rough-house groove, and they fit the group. The strength and warmth of Kid Thomas' personality helped. The men in the band and the people on the dance floor were country men together.

When I step off the Algiers Ferry, I feel like the clock has been turned back to a happier, calmer and friendlier time.

Bandleader Kid Thomas wows the crowds with drummer Alonzo Stewart and clarinetist Albert Burbank, California, early 70s.

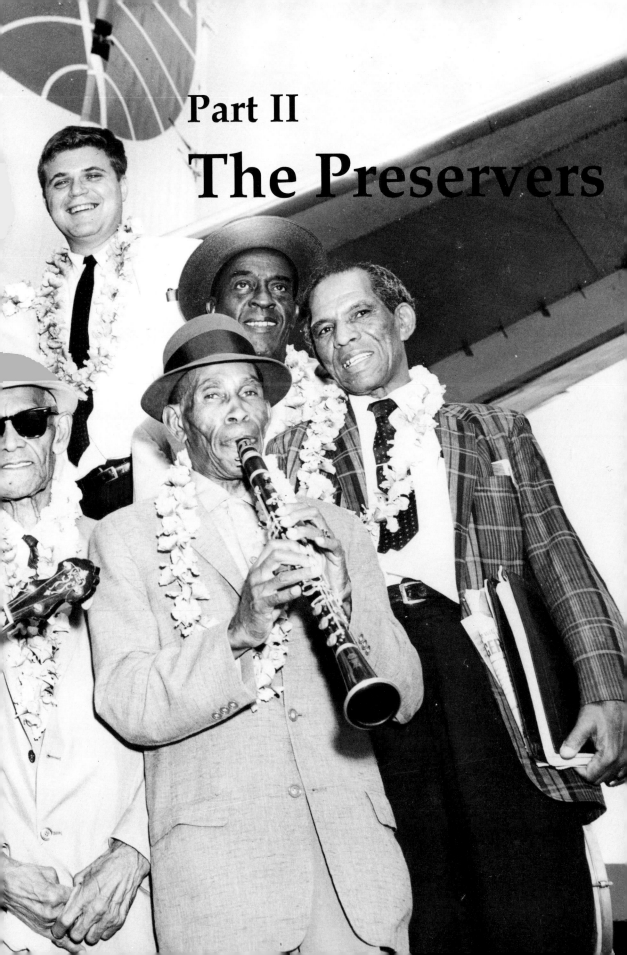

Part II
The Preservers

Chapter Three

MR LARRY'S ART STORE

"People played, people kept coming in,
and Larry was watching, watching . . ."
—*drummer Leonard Ferguson*

Across the street from Bill Russell's record shop was a gallery called Associated Artists. The man who owned it seemed about as different from Russell as one could imagine. Yet the two would remain friends for decades, their destinies inextricably mingled in the gradual coming together of Preservation Hall. If Russell was the Hall's spiritual godfather, E. Lorenz Borenstein was its practical founder.

By all accounts Borenstein was as fascinating a character as one could hope to encounter. Opinions on him range from revulsion to monumental respect. A number of French Quarter denizens involved in two areas of his special interest – art and real estate – saw him as a "svengali," "the worst thing that ever happened to the French Quarter." Allan Jaffe knew Borenstein as well or better than anyone. While far from approving of everything Borenstein did, Jaffe felt that the people who disliked him were those who knew the least about him. Another close friend concurred, adding that people liked Borenstein best one-on-one, for he was a wonderful conversationalist; but that, when a third person appeared, he often reverted to belligerent sarcasm.

Photographed sitting here behind singer and banjoist Emanuel Sayles, and under one of the paintings commissioned by himself, Larry Borenstein was a strong-willed, enigmatic entrepreneur whose pass-the-hat jazz sessions led, with some odd twists and turns, to Preservation Hall.

Associated Artists, the gallery which later became Preservation Hall, looked as quiet as the French Quarter in the 1950s generally was. Discernible in the doorway is art dealer Borenstein, whose wide-ranging interests included a passion for unadorned folk expression -- including New Orleans music.

Borenstein was not given to saying please and thank-you. Yet countless people attested to his benevolence, which he took pains to conceal. Others replied that he enjoyed playing the role of benevolent dictator. Fiercely independent musicians like George Guesnon, Louis Nelson and Kid Thomas, who were nobody's fools, all praised him warmly. Jaffe's wife, Sandra, was friendly with him. And Jane Botsford, Jaffe's close assistant for many years, declared flatly: "Larry was a great man." The continuing controversy seemed a perfect example of those factional disputes that, as the historian, jazz clarinetist and Oberlin University President Frederick Starr pointed out, Orleanians will go to any lengths to keep alive.

For all their evident differences, Larry Borenstein and Bill Russell had some important things in common. Both were discerning collectors – Russell of records, interviews, instruments and countless other items relating to jazz and New Orleans;

Borenstein of stamps, coins, pre-Columbian artifacts, rare books, paintings, foreign currencies, real estate and almost anything else he thought (usually rightly) would rise in value. Borenstein loved the thrill of finding a nugget among the slag, then showing it off and merchandizing it. In some ways, this was what Preservation Hall was all about. Both Russell and Borenstein were utter individualists, rebels from their differing Midwestern backgrounds: brilliant eccentrics driven to follow their own very different stars without the least worry of what anyone else might think — which, more than anything else, may have been what made them respect each other.

But where Russell was ascetically self-denying and self-effacing, often tending to the needs of everyone except himself, Borenstein appeared hugely self-indulgent. Under a rumpled pork-pie hat, his squat, thickly bespectacled figure was commonly seen strutting around the French Quarter in a T-shirt which exposed, defiantly, the wavelike rolls of his gut. Underscoring his anti-establishment image, he bought dozens of those T-shirts at a time, had his maid wash them for two days until they were "washed out," and kept stacks of them at home, in his various offices and wherever else he was hanging his hat. He liked to frighten competitors and tenant-victims by halting along the narrow sidewalks to draw a bead, with his thumb, on a historic building across the street which he might or might not be thinking of acquiring for what he called "my portfolio."

Larry Borenstein's instinct for intrinsic value went well beyond the mundane. An artist friend, John Truman, said that he had "an uncanny instinct for the difference between pot-boiler art and drawings and paintings that had a certain quality," that most of their discussions were abstract and intellectual, and that he possessed a sweeping and exact knowledge of geopolitics, philosophy, history and the history of art. "Like myself, Larry inclined to a certain cynicism. We were both atheists. He was a liberal. The man was controversial. He was a connoisseur. He loved jazz, and that was his relaxation. He didn't get involved in intellectual discussion of how somebody's horn sounded; he just enjoyed it." But did he have a good understanding of the music? Knowledgeable people, including Bill Russell and pianist-bandleader Lars Edegran, said he did.

Born in Milwaukee in 1919, E. Lorenz Borenstein was apparently a grand-nephew of the Russian revolutionary Leon Trotsky, whose real name, like that of Borenstein's ancestral family, was Bronstein. His father and mother had emigrated from somewhere near the Ukraine and met in Wisconsin. The elder Borenstein, who had once played baritone horn in a Russian army band in Latvia, was a merchant and an investor, as well as a rabbi.

At the tender age of 13, the day after his Bar Mitzvah, Larry Borenstein left home and took a job at the Chicago World's Fair, telling fortunes in the role of "Prince Cairo" in a sideshow called "Streets of Paris." Next, he landed a position as assistant to the famous illusionist Dunninger ("I received his thought waves," Borenstein later explained, refusing to divulge whatever other techniques were involved). Thereafter Borenstein went on tour with a carnival, giving lectures in a sideshow called "Mysteries of Life." Privately, he called this exhibition "The Pickled Punks" because it consisted of fetuses, of various ages and deformities, preserved in formaldehyde. (The show's highlight was a two-headed unborn baby – only one of its heads was made of latex.) By the age of 18 Borenstein was ready to apply his business experience to the peddling of magazine subscriptions. Later, he would be quite proud of a magazine article written about him by journalist and author Tom Bethell, which included this description of his activities during that period:

Earthy paintings of the old musicians, made during the transition period from art gallery to jazz hall, remained a distinctive feature of its dimly lit walls. This double portrait by Noel Rockmore shows trumpeter Punch Miller with trombonist Louis Nelson.

Circa 1960, emerging artists were encouraged to draw and paint the venerable musicians – the kind of thing the players would not find time for in the much busier decades to come. Here, Joan Farmer sketches Kid Thomas Valentine.

Larry did very nicely touring in Oklahoma and Texas during the fall and summer of '37; he introduced a notable innovation – towing a rack of bikes behind his station wagon. Kids he had hired would ride up on the bikes to suburban front doors soliciting subscriptions, creating the illusion they were hometown kids from next door. Borenstein cleared about $15,000 in nine months, "phenomenal for the Depression," he allows. "I've made money at almost everything I've done," he candidly admits.

He put himself through Marquette University with the proceeds, majoring in philosophy, worked for the *Milwaukee Sentinel* at the same time, and after that he was a reporter for the *Toledo Blade*. Borenstein was working for the American Vacation Association and was heading for Florida when he first arrived in New Orleans. The Association was employing him to help stimulate winter tourism in the South. On the night Borenstein arrived in New Orleans, Dec. 7, 1941, Pearl Harbor was attacked. His boss advised the war wouldn't last more than two or three months and to stick around and make some contacts in New Orleans. Borenstein stayed for more than 30 years. "The war knocked hell out of the travel business anyway," he commented.

Borenstein and Russell would not meet until 1952, when Russell asked Borenstein's advice on finding an apartment. Russell's account of Borenstein's early years in the city, while conflicting at some points with Bethell's, helps round out the picture of the multi-faceted entrepreneur:

Larry did so many things in his life. He was a chess expert, he did these stunts of playing several games at once. He had the eye of a guitar expert and a violin expert. He

Attending an impromptu jazz-gospel rehearsal and/or recording session in the soon-to-be Preservation Hall are (from left) William Russell, Kid Thomas Valentine, Barbara Reid, Kelley Edmiston, George Guesnon, Sister Pitts [or Williams], Sister Williams [or Pitts], Sister Idell Williams and Brother George Boone.

had that kind of mind, and that kind of photographic memory. He was a stamp expert of course. Somebody told him unless a person had made a couple hundred thousand by the time they were 40, they weren't a success. He made that twice and lost it both times, the first time in currency when they devalued the pound and the second time when he got a divorce from his first wife.

Anyway, about 1941 he thought he was going to be drafted. He came to New Orleans just to have a last fling. He went down Royal Street and went into the De Forest Book Shop. He gets into one of the boxes, and there's a lot of old English documents there. Each one had a blue stamp on it, one of the very early stamps worth a lot of money, and they were all ten cents apiece or so. So he tells the kid who worked there, "I'll take the whole box." It was worth hundreds, maybe a couple thousand dollars. "Is that all you got?" "Yes sir." So the next day he goes back, and the box is filled up again. He took the box but said, "I want to see the boss." So he had to go over to a warehouse on Tchoupitoulas Street, and there were big Chinese tea crates, all full of those documents. He didn't have the money to buy them, but he knew a stamp dealer and a museum man who were delighted to put up all the money and give Larry one-third interest without his making one cent of the investment. He was giving the other guys the chance to buy documents and stamps worth many dollars each for fifteen cents each, and Larry made enough on that to buy his first house. That's the kind of story Larry could tell.

Borenstein never did have to go into the army. He first worked for a pawnbroker on South Rampart, then opened a succession of his own shops in the French Quarter selling stamps, coins, foreign currencies, books and the like. But the deep devaluation of sterling caught him with a massive margin position in British pounds, which wiped him out completely. Struggling to recover, he decided to open an art gallery on a minimum of capital. On July 20, 1954, he leased 726 St Peter Street. (He later offered to buy the building, but the owner always refused to sell it to him.) By 1955, spirituals, blues and jazz were being played casually at the gallery, which some musicians called "Mr Larry's Art Store." Borenstein later described these sessions as the origins of Preservation Hall:

I am a music lover whose taste ranges from the popular to the esoteric and back again. New Orleans jazz is one of my favorite kinds of music. Through the war years and afterwards, I bought all the jazz records, read all the jazz books and listened to all the live jazz I could.

In 1952 I moved my gallery to 726 St Peter Street. This is next door to Pat O'Brien's famous night club, and I found that to do much business I had to stay open at night. That circumstance interfered with my going out to hear music. Billie and DeDe Pierce were playing at Luthjen's on Almonaster Street, and Kid Thomas was at the Moulin Rouge in Marrero, and Kid Howard was at Fump and Manny's in the Irish Channel. But I couldn't get to hear any of them, because ordinarily by the time I closed my gallery and got over to the music hall the band would be packing up its instruments. So I bought an old piano and invited the musicians to come to the gallery. I supplied beer and passed a kitty. These sessions – called "rehearsals" to avoid union trouble – were closed; only people I knew or who seemed seriously interested were invited. If music got under way without prearrangement, I would telephone friends to pass the word and ensure an audience. Usually the musicians divided a few dollars; sometimes, when some generous out-of-towner worked his way in, the rewards were better. . . . The layout of the gallery was such that the large double doors opening into the street made it easy for passers-by to drop in.

Punch Miller, back from his long years on the road, started coming around frequently with a pick-up band.

Punch usually had with him Eddie Morris on trombone, Simon Fraser on piano, Steve Angrum on clarinet, Ricard Alexis on bass and Bill Bagley on drums. However, personnel varied often as usually the band was assembled with almost no notice and might be anywhere from four to eight pieces. Before long Kid Thomas and his band were coming by regularly, usually for Sunday afternoon "rehearsal" sessions. As other bands got wind of this arrangement, the gallery became a frequent host for sessions and "rehearsals." Billie and DeDe Pierce began coming in also, then Willie Pajaud, Danny Barker, Lemon Nash, Kid Sheik, and as the roster of musicians expanded so did the audiences. No order in schedule, though, so the music was sometimes great and sometimes plain awful. One night the band would be made up of three trumpets, a trombone and a drummer – the next might find it heavy on the rhythm section and short on wind.

Kid Thomas had a "rehearsal" every Thursday night, and on Sundays Noon Johnson often stopped by with his trio. Piano "professors" Stormy Weatherly, John Smith and Isidore Washington often dropped in, as did busking guitarists, banjoists and harmonica virtuosos. Often impromptu sessions got underway because Lemon Nash dropped in to say "hello" and just happened to have his ukelele with him.

As interest in the music grew, so did resistance. Neighbors who found they could live comfortably with Pat O'Brien's music found ours something to complain about. The police calls became a constant source of apprehension. On two or three occasions the police sent the paddy wagon and jailed everybody. The bands frequently included both white and Negro musicians, and it was simpler to charge them with "disturbing the peace" than with breaking down segregation barriers.

These were changing times in New Orleans and the mood was reflected in night court. A certain judge managed to combine the judicial dignity of a kangaroo court and the philosophy of lynch law with the humor of Milton Berle. An archconservative, the judge was outraged at any racial mixing. One night in 1957 Kid Thomas and several musicians, white and colored, stood before him. In stern tones the judge delivered a lecture. "We don't want Yankees coming to New Orleans mixing cream with our coffee." He went on to say that Thomas Valentine was well liked by decent folks in nearby Algiers and also appreciated as a "good yard boy." People thought well of him for giving cornet lessons to West Bank kids, and if he would remember his place in the future and not get "uppity," the judge would let him go this time.

The sessions grew in popularity, and so I moved my gallery to an address next door, and after that the old

Entertaining in the back corner of the art gallery (and possibly promoting Goebel's beer) is a trio favored by Borenstein in the 50s (from left): Noon Johnson (bazooka), Lawrence "Sam" Rankins (guitar) and Harrison Verrett (banjo).

building was used exclusively for music. This was the birth of Preservation Hall. Incidentally, no attempt was made, then or since, to fancy up the place. It is a dark, dingy room, furnished only with backless wooden benches and a few ancient kitchen chairs. On the average night more than half the audience has to stand. Some of the floor boards are loose, and the front panel has been knocked out of the old upright piano.

People remember that informal, pre-Preservation Hall period in their own ways. Richard B. Allen tells of Borenstein selling paintings while the musicians played for tips. He also recalls Borenstein's having bands play in his apartment on Mardi Gras day, and his making tape recordings of a band with trumpeter Willie Pajaud at a party. Borenstein apparently made quite a few tapes, but they were for his own pleasure only, and have not been issued as records. The jazz sessions grew out of even more informal sessions with itinerant folk-blues and gospel singers. Speedy Gonzales, a sometime piano player who worked for Borenstein for many years, both in his frame shop and in his apartment, and who continued to sweep up at Preservation Hall until his death in 1990, remembered the very first of these:

One night some guy from out of town came by and he had a guitar. He was trying to sing a little bit on the street so Larry got him to come inside. People started to take notice. He was in here singing, no accompaniment, just by himself. So Larry decides to pass the hat and "see what I

Typically New Orleans in feeling were the jazz parties on the patio by the Hall's rear wing. Participants at this one included (from left) Sammy Penn (drums), probably Kid Thomas Valentine (trumpet), Emanuel Sayles (banjo), Louis Nelson (trombone), George Lewis (clarinet), Noon Johnson (bazooka) and Slow Drag Pavageau (bass). Seated at the center are Mr and Mrs Larry Borenstein, and at the right, with glass, Mrs Aline Willis, one of the key early helpers at the Hall.

can get for him." So he passed the hat and a few quarters came in, and he gave it to him as a little token. And then from then on, different fellows would come in.

They were just freelancing, they'd come in and get in on the group so it wound up one time they had about a seven or eight piece band, just guys that decided to come in and play. And I think Kid Thomas was about the first group that was formed that played here at night like that. So from that, one day I came back and they were sort of organizing and different musicians were coming in to make known that they wanted to play or that they offered their services. That first guy was just singing some old folk songs that he knew. He just hung around and there was a few nickels for him and he had been sharecropping so he didn't get much money anyway. Every night or so he picked up four or five bucks. That was quite a bit.

Allan Jaffe later noticed that, mentally, people had a tendency to begin the history of the Hall – or of jazz, for that matter – with the day they discovered it. Whether or not this applied to drummer Leonard Ferguson, he certainly participated in one of the earliest sessions:

We couldn't call it Preservation Hall because there wasn't any such place, but it was an art gallery that Larry Borenstein had. It was the spring of '55 or just after, and I happened to come walking along there one night and I heard music coming out the door which was kind of unusual, and I looked in and there was Punch Miller, trumpet, and Raymond Burke, clarinet, and this little fella Erwin Helfer, a student at Tulane, playing piano, and some spectators. And Raymond said, "Leonard, can't you run home and get a snare drum and a cymbal or somethin' to help us out?" So I went home and I got a snare drum and I think two cymbals, and we played that way, and the crowd kept picking up and picking up, and the first thing you know, somebody passed the hat around and got money for the band, which the band hadn't been expecting – we were just having fun. And Larry Borenstein saw the money going into the hat, and the idea was born. People played, people kept coming in, and Larry was watching, watching.

Although Kid Thomas was not above the traditional practice of playing for tips at a party, he was no itinerant or sometime professional, but one of the few traditional black jazzmen who had managed, for decades, to keep a band working through thick and thin. Tom, as many of the musicians called him, claimed to have given Borenstein the idea of putting his jazz sessions on a regular basis:

Borenstein used to come over here to Marrero and he wanted me to come play at his place. He asked me, "Kid, how you'd like to come play at my place?" Well, I thought it was some kind of dance hall. But it wasn't no dance hall! I used to come over on Sundays when I wouldn't be doin' nothin'. Somebody else would play, all that.

[Borenstein would later tell people:] "This man and me, we're the ones got this thing goin' on." That's true! All we did was hand you a job. All them people you see there workin' at that Preservation Hall? Me and Punch [Miller], we started that. I was the first one started out that place and I gave the original idea to the man in the first place.

Cornetist Charlie DeVore's memories of those times are very specific – including the jail incident. His dating of the first jazz to have been played regularly at 726 St Peter Street was probably reliable:

I first arrived in New Orleans in June of '54. I didn't really get to know anybody until early '55. I was lucky to have been an observer in those years. And as far as I know, the whole thing started because Punch Miller came back from being on the road with the Royal American Shows. That would have been late '55. Punch came back to New Orleans for the winter of '55-'56. He was with the Royal American Shows until the season ended, the end of September, when all the State Fairs concluded around the country. So Punch probably got into town around October or November. They were trying to get a job for him playing somewhere. The thought was that Larry would let Punch get together a little band and play in the art studio and pass the hat. That was the first music there that I was aware of. But if Speedy says there were folk musicians there earlier, it could be true.

And then Larry, because of his business, wasn't able to get over to Algiers to Specks' Moulin Rouge as often as he wanted, so he started inviting Kid Thomas to come over to play. It seems to me he invited Thomas over on Friday nights. And I know the thing with Punch started up every Thursday night. So he had the two nights, Thursday and Friday. Thomas always recognized that Punch was there first.   Punch wanted to play six nights a week. Seven nights! They all did! Thomas always had a certain amount of proprietary feeling about the Hall. But Punch started there in the latter part of '55 – November of '55 kind of sticks in my brain – and Thomas came in some time in '56.

In those days Larry had all sorts of partitions. Everything was hanging; it wasn't opened up like it is now. There was a piano in the back against the wall by the carriageway, and Punch would stand back there. A partition divided that part of the Hall from the other part where it leads into the rest room facilities, if you want to call it that. Thursday nights, Punch would play, and Erwin Helfer, a good friend of Bill Russell's from Chicago, would play piano. Sam Charters [an ethnomusicologist who put out an important series of recordings of the traditional players in this period] came around quite frequently and played banjo or cornet. I was just starting to learn how to play and would kind of doodle in the back.

Thomas was up front, not too unlike the way it is now. The front doors all swung out and that's how the people came in. The paintings would be hung on these various partitions – one across the front and one right down the middle. Thomas played there because his band was too big to get into that little cubicle in the back.

About January of '57 we were having a little session with Punch, and Eddie Morris was playing trombone, and Thomas was there. It was a nice jam session, and I was there too, and we all got thrown in jail. They had a law on the books that prohibited blacks and whites from appearing together for entertainment purposes. Bill Russell saved all the instruments. We were playing and not paying much

An informal session on the patio behind "Mr Larry's Art Store" in 1960, when fine players were plentiful but jobs scarce, included (from left) trombonist Jim Robinson, bassist Slow Drag Pavageau, trumpeter Charlie Love, trumpet student Charlie DeVore, clarinetist George Lewis and clarinetist Paul Barnes.

attention, and all of a sudden Larry came bursting in and said, "Quick! Put your horns away!" And Bill said, "Quick! Put your horns away!" And I said, "Gee, whizz, I'm surely playing bad these days." Before I knew it there was a couple of big guys in blue suits and we gave all the instruments to Bill for safekeeping. And the guy pointed at Bill and said, "What about you?" And Bill looked at us and said, "I never played a note in my life!"

Doggie Berg had brought his drum sticks and been playing on an old skull he'd found propped up in a corner. And Joel Salter played banjo. They were a couple of guys from out of town who had stumbled onto what they thought was a great jam session. So that made six of us that got arrested. (Apparently, Joe Lyde had also been playing "chord" piano, but, lacking an instrument of his own, was able to disappear easily into the crowd.) We got thrown in the clink. Larry bailed us out, and then we had to go up in front of a judge named Babylon. We were charged with disturbing the peace for playing loud music, but Judge Babylon started right in about us baggy pants Northerners coming down and telling people in New Orleans what to do. Thomas and Punch and Eddie Morris are standing there, and they're really quite frightened because they know how the law works in the South.

This was when all the civil rights turmoil was starting with Martin Luther King and the early Montgomery boycott, and a guy like Babylon was really going to put it to us. He says, "I know this Kid Thomas, I've seen Thomas over there in Algiers for years and you just ask Thomas how he'd like it to be: like it is now or the way it was in the good old days? You'd want the good old days, right, Thomas?" And Thomas is nodding – Thomas is a very practical man. Poor Eddie Morris couldn't say anything at all. They asked him and he just stuttered. Boy, I felt so sorry for poor Eddie.

Babylon went on about we don't put cream in our coffee down here in New Orleans, and you can stuff it down our throats but we're not going to swallow it. And I said, "Well, your Honor, I'm looking at this affidavit and it says that we're being charged with disturbing the peace by playing loud music. Now, what has this got to do with putting cream in your coffee?" Oh, he got angry! A couple of the bailiffs moved closer and they had their hands on their clubs. He really launched on a tirade.

But, son of a gun, we got off. I think Larry had used his influence. And I guess the judge was concerned that maybe it could turn into some real civil rights litigation. But his lecture lasted 30 minutes or so.

After that, Larry knocked off having sessions with mixed bands. And from that point on, the sessions were never planned with any degree of regularity, just from time to time, and it would be all black bands. That may have been when Thomas started playing with his regular band. Before, he had been coming over and sitting in. After that Punch would have a whole black band to play with, and so would Thomas. Those two musicians were really the ones that are responsible for the beginning of that "kitty hall" approach, from '55 to '57.

Not long after Charlie returned to Minnesota, Borenstein resumed the illegal mixed sessions in his "kitty hall" – i.e., a place that relied on voluntary donations.

*   *   *

In February 1957, two bright, pretty girls arrived in New Orleans. Pat Davis and Nancy Collins were just out of college and had been having a carefree fling through America's "storybook" cities. They would stay until that summer, and were lucky enough to find an apartment on Pirate's Alley, the atmospheric, block-long byway in the French Quarter where artists and writers — including William Faulkner — had lived. On Mardi Gras day Larry Borenstein always had an open house. Pat and Nancy were among a

Entrepreneur E. Lorenz Borenstein in a characteristic pose; opinions on him ranged from deep respect to unqualified revulsion. One thing was certain: he played a key role in the creation of Preservation Hall and thus in the worldwide revitalization of New Orleans jazz.

group invited to view the parades from his balcony. Nancy needed a job, and Borenstein gave her one. Although she started by sorting frame pieces, she soon graduated to selling paintings to "mullets," which the American Heritage Dictionary describes as "edible fishes . . . found worldwide in tropical and temperate coastal waters":

> He didn't make a pass at me because I think it was too clear that I would not be receptive to it. But I know for sure that he did make passes at bright women, and it was quite widely known that he had various women of all sizes and colors and shapes and religions. That was just part of how he was. A man of large appetite? Yes.
>
> I had finished college and had a year of graduate school at Cornell, and Larry loved to show me off. He said, "She almost has her graduate degree," and there I am in my blue jeans on the floor sorting frames. He used to relish the fact that the people he hired were bright and well educated.
>
> Larry was a funny guy to look at. He was quite overweight and had a rather paunchy stomach, and I rarely saw him in anything except torn T-shirts. His stomach

hung way over his belt, and he loved to drink beer. He always had a day or two's growth of beard. When you met him you were impressed with the twinkle in his eye, but you kind of wondered who he was. He was certainly not pretentious, and you never thought he would have any money at all. He always carried a roll of bills in his pants, and occasionally when he would reach in, they would scatter, and we would pick them up and give them back. He certainly didn't have any airs, and even later, when he had become one of the biggest landowners in the French Quarter, he wasn't into status symbols and didn't seem to need the creature comforts most of us would have enjoyed with that kind of money.

But Larry knew an incredible amount about the things he knew about. He would always gather people to go home and have dinner. We would sit on the floor. The food was a joke. But he loved good music [people would spot him in a tux at classical performances], and the atmosphere would be stimulating, and the conversations would range among a wide variety of topics.

Borenstein liked having Nancy and Pat pass the hat for the musicians in the evenings because they looked young and wholesome and clean-cut, in contrast to the dark, smoky atmosphere. They weren't supposed to take no for an answer, but to shame the visitors into giving by saying something like, "Didn't you really enjoy the saxophone? Aren't they terrific?" Pat remembered that Larry was interested in the jazzmen both as artists and as people, and in sponsoring projects that would benefit everyone:

He hit on the idea that if he had the musicians come in they would lure more trade off the street and more people would see the paintings and therefore buy more paintings. I doubt that he would have done it just as benevolence if there hadn't been some commericial payoff, because it was time-consuming to arrange it. But he was genuinely interested in the artists. I remember going out with him to hear DeDe and Billie Pierce at a nightclub, and we went across the river once, and he would tell me how poorly they lived and how poor they were, and he was real interested in giving them a vehicle to earn some money while also benefiting him. But the emphasis was really on that this was something that they needed, and he talked a lot about the fact that they were so talented and yet they'd hit such hard times.

He was real kind to these musicians who were out starving in the boonies, and he brought them in and gave them an opportunity. He gave them all the money we got

A true living legend, bassist Papa John Joseph was born in 1877 and arrived in New Orleans in 1906. He played with cornetist Buddy Bolden, widely thought to have led the world's first jazz band, and worked with his own group in the Storyville district until 1917. Having retired to become a barber, he made a comeback at Preservation Hall and played his last note there in 1965. The pianist is probably John Robichaux, an historical figure in his own right.

in our hat, and the payoff for him was getting people into the art gallery to buy the paintings. That seemed a fair exchange to me.

People would walk by after visiting Pat O'Brien's, the well-known nightclub next door, where a trio including the venerable bassist Papa John Joseph often entertained. Hearing the music in the gallery, they would come in through the French doors open to the street. Borenstein would talk to them about the paintings and the artists. They would sit on the floor, stay a while, pay and leave. They were not encouraged to plunk down for two hours, and the musicians would often repeat the same songs after a short time. Nancy summed up a scene that would expand in size but be repeated in essence for many years thereafter:

The musicians were just the greatest. What I liked about them was that they had energy and they had enthusiasm, and they just looked like they were having a wonderful time, and they just radiated the spirit of jazz in New Orleans. So people who were in their presence kind of reflected this, and when they left it was like they were happier, they gained something from the experience of being there with the music. They'd walk in kind of beat and tired, and they would hear it, and they would leave with a lift to their step, or a smile, and they would take some of that energy with them.

Larry would be chain-smoking, in the back of the room. He didn't seem very involved. He stood a lot with his arms crossed, they kind of rested on his fat stomach, and he'd be leaning against the wall or column. But he was very astute, and he took in everything. He didn't miss anything. If anyone got rowdy or out of hand, he would go up and tap them on the shoulder or something and suggest they leave. So he was in total control.

* * *

To others, Borenstein's expanding trading and real-estate interests seemed to reveal a thirst for power and a style of doing business in which humanitarian scruples played no part. In a city which in a half-century of economic stagnation had grown tight, gossip-prone and inward-looking, he flaunted his disrespect for traditional ways of doing things. An adversary of the establishment, he not only associated with bohemians, radicals, gypsies, uppity locals and outside agitators, but happily dealt with shady-looking businessmen rumored to have Mafia ties. With his refined visual sense, Borenstein had a keen esthetic concern for the Quarter's distinctive, humane environs and did much to save them from decay and destruction; yet he had terrible relations with the Vieux Carré Commission, an ultra-respectable body charged with much the same mission. Rightly or wrongly, Borenstein developed some lifelong animosities. But even one of his enemies conceded:

Even if I didn't like him, I like to see a little man come in and break up the structure. This is a rigid town. This is a closed town. As early as the 50s, that whole real estate crowd who were responsible for the World's Fair fiasco would have liked to see the whole French Quarter torn down and replaced by skyscrapers. Larry broke the pattern by coming into the Quarter and buying a three-story building with no cash up front, and I admired him for that.

The wellsprings of New Orleans jazz continued to be the neighborhood brass bands even as the French Quarter was gradually taken over by the tourist trade. Pausing on a stoop in the early 60s near an unidentified lady are (from left) saxophonist Emanuel Paul, trumpeter Peter Bocage, trombonist Albert Warner and trombonist Chicken Henry – all of whom also played at Preservation Hall.

One of Larry's friends, the successful actor Severn Darden, put it this way:

Larry was extremely complex. His business and his life were at the same time totally separate and totally together. It's very difficult to explain. Larry really wanted to make a lot of money, which he did. He was always a week or two late paying an artist, the money gathering interest while they waited in Mexico for 35 dollars or something. He drove a very hard bargain. The real estate he bought was truly magnificent, and in many cases he didn't do anything but kind of keep it from falling down – keeping it for a later generation to fix up, which is happening now.

His house behind the Cathedral is really a study in strangeness. It's a beautiful house, a valuable piece of property. I went over to visit Larry. Larry wasn't there. It was boiling hot. In the room I was in, there were two chairs and a kingsized bed with no bedclothes on it, and a lightbulb hanging from the ceiling. Windows all closed, stuffy as anything. I'm sitting close to Sascha, Larry's daughter, having a conversation, and it struck me that this would be a great scene in a movie. Paint was falling off of everything.

During the middle of the civil rights thing we were in New Orleans with the Free Southern Theater, the first black-and-white theater group to tour the South since the

In an early Preservation Hall junket, musicians and helpers set out on Trans Texas Airways in January 1965; they were heading for Little Rock's Arkansas Art Center to play for the opening of the John D. Reid Collection of American Jazz (from left): George Lewis, possibly the writer Al Rose, DeDe Pierce, Cie Frazier, Billie Pierce, Jim Robinson, Charlie Hamilton, Raymond Burke, Kid Thomas Valentine, Sandra Jaffe, William Russell, Richard B. Allen, Paul Crawford, Slow Drag Pavageau, and Larry Borenstein and his wife Pat. Recalling the journey, Allen later stated that the "flight attendant was attractive but a Methodist."

1870s. Larry didn't want to be associated with the civil rights movement, and yet he gave us a lot of free space in his building if we wouldn't tell anyone. He was all for it, but he didn't want it to hurt business.

He always wanted me to open a theater in one of his buildings. I knew it would have been an interesting, difficult, but not impossible task to get along with Larry. I knew that if there was any possibility of his making any money out of it, especially if it was real bad and people went to see it, he would want to make a lot of money on it. If it was good, and people went to see it, he would want to make less money. And he would have even have lost money on it, probably gracefully.

Borenstein's peculiar blend of hard realism and generous idealism – some have called it paternalism – would be reflected, in altered ways, by Allan Jaffe and thus flow subtly into the behind-the-scenes atmosphere at Preservation Hall. Although Bill Russell did not believe in the profit motive, he attested that Borenstein always kept any agreement and was "one hundred percent honest and reliable." Nonetheless, Borenstein's ways of conducting business frequently led to stormy or suspicious relationships. This happened with several of the

French Quarter artists, despite the fact that he created mutually advantageous opportunities for a number of them. Some would work in the evenings at the gallery, doing quick portraits of the customers and musicians, which Speedy Gonzales would then frame – a system which later became popular around Jackson Square. Unlike many gallery owners, Borenstein would also provide artists with much-needed current income by commissioning or buying work outright. A master salesman, he would pay far below the price at which he might later sell; but this also meant he was often stuck with unsold pieces. Strong and unafraid of a tussle – at times he seemed to savor clashes with creative types – Borenstein ignited the deep-seated fears many artists have of being dominated or exploited. While some of them were doubtless irresponsible in their own right, it is not hard to imagine their feelings in cases such as one Nancy Collins remembered:

> As a reward one time, because I had done something for Larry, he said to me, I'm going to let Xavier de Callatay do a portrait of you. And I thought that was terrific because I'd never had one done. And I remember dressing up in a black dress and posing quite a number of times. While it wasn't flattering, it was certainly me. And Larry didn't like it, and he tore it up. The artist just had a heart attack.

Later Larry would sometimes behave similarly in Preservation Hall. Allan Jaffe observed:

> Larry's philosophy was that it is the music that's important and not the people. The people are just incidental to the music. He was not only that way with musicians, he was that way in life. What he was doing was important – he relished *doing* things. Making a deal. It didn't have to be his own. I saw Larry sitting and buying a million dollar piece of real estate, and somebody calls him up with some penny-ante complicated thing, and Larry would walk away from the other to go help somebody on a more complicated thing that he found interesting.
>
> On a good day Larry would have more creative ideas than I must have in a year. He was unreal – his mind just worked constantly.

Jaffe, who also enjoyed making deals, loved both the music and the musicians; but, when forced to choose, he put their interests first. Acknowledging this difference, Borenstein later told Jaffe, "If I had been running the Hall, it would have been just the same, except that I wouldn't have anybody working for me."

Borenstein forged an important alliance with the artist Noel Rockmore, who later became quite successful. Several of Rockmore's richly pigmented, darkly emotional paintings of the musicians could still, 30 years later, be fathomed in the dim light of the Hall. By one account, Borenstein's and Rockmore's was a love–hate relationship between father and son figures. Given Rockmore's tantrum-prone personality, the alliance was full of violent ups and downs. In 1968 Borenstein, also a sometime writer and editor, published a book entitled *Preservation Hall Portraits*. It featured many of Rockmore's paintings of the musicians, with essays by Borenstein, Bill Russell and Rockmore himself. In one passage, the painter gave a description of the chemistry between artist and entrepreneur:

Larry Borenstein's commission on the Preservation Hall series of musicians was a jolt to most of the work habits I've had, because they generally had to be done in one sitting. I think this had a very good effect, at least for a while, on my work. I think that when an artist is forced to deal with a new set of circumstances, he either sinks or swims, and I think that in swimming rather vigorously I learned, literally, new techniques.

I think it also helped me to put down spontaneously a very strong impression of each musician as he sat in the studio. I believe I could have gotten bogged down from the actual idea of the series of paintings had I used a slower technique. I feel strongly that all intrinsic or genuine developments in an artist are essentially against the grain – if the creator only repeats what he had done he naturally will go only so far.

The studio above Preservation Hall had a great deal of mood and atmosphere that was conducive to the series.

* * *

If Borenstein could be challenging, rude or arrogant, he could also be caring and compassionate. One of the areas in which he proved himself ahead of his time was the appreciation of naive or folk art, especially by black painters such as Bruce Brice, whose work later became quite valued. This seemed related to his interest in rough, primitive, vernacular

Over the years, as the Hall proper became increasingly crowded, many a visitor would view the musicians at this angle – from the carriageway. Here, trombonist Jim Robinson stands to play one of his forthright, skeletal solos.

jazz, the blues and gospel. His cultivation of Sister Gertrude Morgan demonstrated how he would sometimes devote much time and trouble to projects from which he expected little tangible reward. "She was ecstatic," remembered Larry's daughter, Sascha. "She had daily conversations with the Lord. My father was not a religious person, but he wanted her to paint because he thought she was important. I don't think he thought he was going to make a lot of money off it." Sue Coil, a New York editor and longterm friend of Borenstein and the Hall, also had fond memories of Gertrude:

Sister Gertrude Morgan was an old, old black lady. Nobody's quite sure how old – she really didn't know when she was born. She was sort of a one-woman religion. One day she started to paint. She painted on cardboard with poster paints from the dimestore. She did wonderful primitive paintings in which she always appeared dressed in white, from head to foot. And that was the way she dressed. Larry got very interested in her paintings and started carrying them in his gallery. They were all religious in nature and sort of mystical.

Gertrude was also a marvelous singer (see photograph on p.37). She made up her own songs. One of my favorites had the line in it, "Jesus is my airplane, and flies me through the sky." Larry rewarded her for her singing. She played tambourine, and she stamped her feet, and set up counter-rhythms, and then sang. She was utterly marvelous. He recorded her also.

Gertrude had a little chapel of her own in the house where she lived. When the landlord was about to evict her because the property was going to be sold, Borenstein bought the property and let her live there rent-free for many years until she died. This was typical of him, said Allan Jaffe, who learned a great deal from Borenstein in the course of their business relationship, and who later did similar things for musicians which he, too, steadily refused to discuss. It was also typical of Borenstein that he himself did not put up the money for Gertrude's house – it came from Jaffe's and Borenstein's real-estate partnership. Borenstein paid for Gertrude's funeral; but when local writer-photographer Mona MacMurray was about to mention this in a magazine article, he made her take it out.

Borenstein fancied himself as a patron of the arts. He always insisted that he never wanted to make money from New Orleans jazz or from other idealistic projects such as his early Preservation Hall book. He enjoyed creating environments which would foster esthetic enjoyment and intellectual discussion. On the other hand, he was too hard-headed not to use such gatherings to help him make business deals. For many years after he had turned over the operation of Preservation Hall to Allan and Sandra Jaffe, he used it as a place to make business contacts, impressing people with the fact that he was somehow the founder and boss even though by then he was merely sub-letting to Jaffe, and would usually refer those asking directly about Hall business to him.

Borenstein cared deeply about his friends and acquaintances. He saw no reason why anyone should suffer for lack of money, and quietly took care of several people's hospital bills. One of those was Speedy Gonzales, who recalled: "He'd give you a job, or he'd create a job for you. There might not be a job there, but he'd find something for you." Severn Darden remembered:

He was the central point of information of everyone on almost every level in the Quarter. From the time he got there, he knew where anyone was. You'd ask for somebody

Borenstein, whose 1950s art gallery evolved into a dingy, world-famous jazz room, was a masterfully offbeat entre-preneur in things as diverse as rare stamps and real estate.

you hadn't seen in 15 years and he'd say, oh, someone saw him on the beach in Hawaii. He would always ask me where people were, who I'd seen, how were they, how were they doing, what were they doing, were they happy? He was always very concerned with the people that had in any way been part of his life. Really concerned. He also liked being that center of information – keeping his people together, as it were.

Borenstein would spend hours, almost every day, helping people, counseling them in their business affairs and their lives. "We miss him terribly," said one of these, Jo Ann Clevenger, a successful restaurant owner. "He was wise in a humane way, not only in a business way. He was detached and analytic in the sense of asking, 'Will this bring you what you want?' He was moody and reflective. He thought things through, weighed them: 'If I cut myself short on this, how much am I hurting myself compared to the

Louis Nelson was one of the most enduring – and endearing – of Preservation Hallers, and his career at "Mr Larry's Art Store" spanned five decades, from the 50s to the 90s. An independent spirit, he often played under other sponsorship as well, particularly in Europe and Japan.

amount of good it can do over here?' He was hostile to bureaucracy."

Borenstein had strong feelings for the black people, and when leasing his properties to store owners forbade them to sell or display confederate flags or mammy dolls. Larry would never allow his children to sing *Dixie*, or anyone in the Hall to play it. His fondness for women was well known, but his attitude towards them was not narrow or chauvinistic. Said one who visited him with her children in January of 1981, two nights before he died:

He was a real mix, like any complicated person who gets a lot done. He was a hard-seeming person in a lot of ways. Larry was a person I didn't trust in some ways, and in other ways I felt such a friendship for him of just many years developing that there was a great caring there, and there was respect for a lot of things about him. There were

areas where I had to be responsible for myself in dealing with Larry. He had a deep spiritual side, and he hadn't found a religion that could quite make sense on enough points that he couldn't intellectually chip away at. But I don't think he was through looking. Larry and I had a lot of talks about religion, because I had started to study the religion of my family tradition as an adult with some college courses. None of this was heavy-weight material for Larry's kind of mind and doubts. But Larry gave me the opportunity to define myself. We would sit and discuss religion, and discuss what you could come to terms with as believing and accepting into your life. He was very interested in it. Larry lived a lot through other people, and I think sometimes that was misinterpreted as a lot of control, and I think sometimes it was an attempt at a lot of control. So he had his light side and his dark side. And I think he had a lot that was lighter than most people realize. The people who do things can be so marked because they do deal with reality, not just the perfection of dreams.

Four decades later it is hard to appreciate how extraordinarily difficult it was to get anything started or done, especially where black traditional jazz was concerned, in the parochial French Quarter of the 1950s. Many came, undertook some recordings or other documentation, tried to help in this way or that – but without any lasting effect from the musicians' point of view. If the live, authentic product was not to vanish entirely, a person of unusual toughness and resiliency was needed. Borenstein was that person. Even after Jaffe had taken over management of the Hall, Sascha Borenstein remembered:

My father would watch over everybody like a hawk. He wouldn't let anybody bring food into the Hall, even if it was some friends. And if any drunks came, he would bully them away. He had a real strong personality, and he was always interested to know exactly what was going on. I don't think he worked there; I think he was there every night just because he liked to be there. Nobody can be as strong in dealing with people as my father was. He was very powerful, and he could get what he wanted. If there was somebody playing loud music from a bar on Bourbon Street, all my father would have to do was go down there and yell at them and say, "Turn off this music! Now I own this building, and that building, and two buildings down the street. Turn it off right now!" And they would turn it off. Nobody else could command that kind of authority. He often was rude but it was all right. He knew which people it was okay to be rude to. He didn't have any ideas about "the customer's always right" that some businesses have.

Of the many things he did in his life, Borenstein was proudest of having set the foundations of Preservation Hall. The best final tribute to him was perhaps this passage from a letter written in 1961 by one of the more stormy and cantankerous musicians who ever worked at the Hall, banjoist "Creole George" Guesnon:

Dear Friend Larry I received your letter, and as usual it contained words of logic, and reason, that could only come from within the heart and mind of one with a deep-rooted sense of values. A rare quality indeed my friend! (in this world of today) and one that it took me quite a while to find out that you possessed.

Kid Thomas Valentine

Kid Thomas's Boogie

David R. Young

The following account was written in 1978.

Louis Malle's popular movie *Pretty Baby* opened with the sound of a sultry trumpet setting the mood for the entire film. The tune was *The Honey Swat Blues*, and Kid Thomas Valentine underscored the scene, an aerial panorama of New Orleans's red-light Storyville district at night, by blowing some unembroidered, sensual blues. People in New Orleans will tell you that 86-year-old Kid Thomas has never blown a phony note in his life.

As I approach Preservation Hall, I hear Kid Thomas's trumpet cut through the street noise like a blade. These aren't individual melodic notes so much as fiery clusters of notes, staccato bursts of jazz. Kid Thomas only hints at the melody, with humor and mischief.

"He's unique – probably the only trumpeter alive who was not influenced by Louis Armstrong," William Russell says. "Kid Thomas is playing with as much fire today as ever, with the same ratty tone, and I've been listening to him for over 30 years now."

The next number, *Kid Thomas Boogie*, brings the house down. It always does. Emanuel Sayles puts down an extraordinary boogie woogie on the banjo, but it's Thomas himself who really gets the joint jumping. He blasts a cluster of notes here, a cluster there, each time surprising the audience with the brashness of his trumpet, the rhythmic drive of his playing. When not blowing the trumpet, he's either banging a tambourine against his hip or whapping a slapstick to drive the band along.

Kid Thomas has always played a rough brand of jazz. He's led his own small groups since shortly after World War I, and from 1936 until the late 50s his was the house band at the Moulin Rouge, a dance hall across the river in Algiers frequented by working-class folks, mostly Cajuns. Recently, he took his Preservation Hall Jazz Band on an extensive tour of South America.

He takes his break in a small kitchen out back, where the soft light comes from a gas lamp in the courtyard of the hall. Skinny and nearly lost in an over-sized suit, wearing a bright green tie and black and white shoes, Kid Thomas stands in a loose fighter's crouch, punching the air with one hand to punctuate his rapid-fire talk and holding a po-boy sandwich in the other. He laughs often and is as animated as a teenager.

"Sometimes people ask me what I've got that's so special," he says. "You know what I tell them? I tell them I got what people like. That's right. People don't have fun any more. Don't dance. Dances, pictures – Clint Eastwood – that's the stuff, man. And the fights. I always go to the fights. And picnics at the lake, you know what I'm talking about. I played for all the picnics in the old days. Played on the trains and boats. Used to be, people had a ball. I still try to give them a good time. Here the people just sit around and stare at you. People don't understand this music at first. It takes awhile to get the idea. But once you get the idea, you want to stay all night."

The Enduring Louis Nelson
"Focus your mind, then play from the heart"
John McQuaid

The following is taken from an article which appeared in the New Orleans newspaper "The Times Picayune" in 1987

Stirring the sunlit musty air of Preservation Hall as he moved, 84-year-old trombonist Louis Nelson eased down on a cushion on a high-backed wooden chair and prepared to play, just as he's played for the past seven decades. He was the last man to arrive, and he took his time. He frowned a little. His thick gray eyebrows hung heavy over his eyes. He put the black vinyl case on his lap and unzipped it. Inside was his trombone, a Yamaha given to him by a Japanese jazz band at the world's fair here three years ago. Nelson took the two pieces out and gingerly fitted them together, flexing the instrument with his long arms and hoisting it up on his shoulder. The seven-piece band riffed through a series of tunes. Nelson sat on his chair and played. With his cheeks puffed and a little sweat on his forehead, he looked solemn. The sound was long and mellow, first uplifting, then mournful. "Concentration is part of a crucial equation a jazz musician uses each time he plays," Nelson said. "The second part is heart. You focus your mind on the horn, then play from your heart. And that's all you need. Playing the horn just came to me. I don't copy. When I pick up that horn, my mind is on how I'm going to play that particular number. I try to keep the correct time, to give each note the correct volume and the right value. If it's a whole note, I hold it. I don't chop it up or cut it off. I don't play 'pah pah pah,' I go 'mmmmmm mmmmmm.' It's smooth. It's in your mind, and it comes right out."

Louis Nelson was born in New Orleans on September 17, 1902. He was part of the black upper-class – his father was a doctor and his mother a teacher and musician from Springfield, Massachusetts, who had graduated from the Boston Conservatory of Music. Shortly after Nelson's birth they moved to Napoleonville, Louisiana, where his father traveled between towns making house calls.

"I heard a fellow playing – he used to play with a band out of Napoleonville," Nelson said in his gravelly, slightly Cajun-inflected baritone. "Don't ask me the name because I've forgotten. I heard him playing trombone before he was leaving to go to Lake Charles, and I said, one day I'm going to play trombone like that man. He had a smooth tone, and he gave the notes the full value. That's why I followed in his footsteps." Nelson trained under a teacher named Claiborne Williams, who taught him technique, breathing, and that intuition was superior to purely technical skill. "My teacher taught me how to take a breath. He said, 'Don't worry about the reading or anything. Let me just tell you about the main things you got to know and you'll get to reading after.'"

By the time he was 18, Nelson was playing with the Joe Gabriel Band out of Thibodaux, touring around Cajun country playing in large, airy dance halls for a dollar a night. It was only the beginning. He soon moved on to more prominent groups, eventually joining Sidney Desvigne's ten-piece swing band and playing their arrangements at tony locales such as the New Orleans Country Club and Southern Yacht Club. Monday and Tuesday, though, they would play for black audiences at the Pythian Temple in the Roof Garden and at the Bulls Aid and Pleasure Club. When

Desvigne moved to California and his band broke up, it was the start of tougher times for Nelson. In the early 1940s he joined up with trumpeter Kid Thomas Valentine in a jazz ensemble, but they could only get about one gig a week, playing in spots such as Speck's Moulin Rouge in Marrero and the Fireman's Hall in Westwego. They were dance halls that catered to Whites, where patrons would come in, dance a foxtrot or a waltz, and have a few. Nelson was forced to take day jobs driving trucks, first for the post office and then for a fish merchant. He was raising two children on his own and for a while gave up playing altogether. Times changed when the old jazz musicians, long out of the public eye, started jamming together regularly in the French Quarter in the late 1950s. By 1961, when Preservation Hall opened, they had a permanent place and a built-in audience of jazz aficionados from New Orleans and around the world. Nelson is one of the last of the old musicians who play traditional New Orleans jazz, a small group centered mainly around the gigs at Preservation Hall. But he has always been an independent, branching out on his own, arranging his own band and his own tours in addition to the responsibilities at the Hall.

Nelson has been married three times and has great-great-grandchildren he can't count. He's playing on his fifth trombone, and says he will keep playing until he dies. He is focused on the present, not the past. He never goes back to the old dance halls. What's the point? "Why should I miss 'em? I don't work there anymore. I'm doing good here. I'm finished with 'em. And when you're finished, you're finished. I just want to be myself. I don't have no big head. I just want to go there and play and sit down. I do what I got to do."

Chapter Four

SMITTEN WITH KALEIDOSCOPIC VARIEGATION

"Don't wake me, Barbara, I'm afraid I'm dreaming."
—clarinetist Emile Barnes

In August 1960 a new figure popped up in the goldfish-bowl world of the French Quarter. "Smitten," as he later said, with the "kaleidoscopic variegation" of New Orleans jazz, 22-year-old Grayson "Ken" Mills was determined to use the $9,000 he had recently inherited from a great aunt to record the music. While hanging around Jack's Record Cellar, a focal point for jazz buffs in San Francisco, Mills had begun corresponding with banjoist "Creole George" Guesnon. George had sent him a tape of a session which included himself, trumpeter Kid Thomas and clarinetists Israel Gorman, Steve Angrum and Polo Barnes. Mills intended to use this first tape to launch his new Icon label.

When he reached New Orleans, Mills went first to Guesnon's house, where he met Barnes and Gorman, among others. He soon found his way, as well, to Bill Russell's record store and to Larry Borenstein's art gallery. Borenstein told Mills he'd

The rollicking energy of the former art gallery was captured in this early 60s photograph (from left): McNeal Breaux (clapping), Wilbert Tillman (sousaphone), Andy Anderson (trumpet), Andrew Morgan (clarinet) and Alex Bigard (drums).

already heard of him – that he'd read something Mills had written in the avant-garde magazine *The Realist*. The two hit it off well, Mills later remembered. Borenstein let him use the patio behind 726 St Peter to record one session with Kid Thomas and another with trumpeter Punch Miller; these albums were issued that November. Possessed of a raw-earth instinct for divining poetic messages in the music – but lacking the historical perspective and musicianly discrimination of a Bill Russell – the young Californian would never lose his naive intoxication, his jazz-revivalist's sense of a crusade against cheapening mediocrity, or his bent for extravagant prose: "I was extremely overwhelmed when I heard a real New Orleans clarinet. Because it was weird. Totally different from records. That air down there! The heat and the moisture was different, right? It never really got grabbed, that tone. Polo Barnes would play inordinately excellent and intricate ideas and always squeak somewhere."

Mills returned to California, produced some records, and wrote a description of his visit to New Orleans and his recording sessions at Associated Artists which appeared in the autumn of that same year, 1960, in an obscure English jazz magazine called *Eureka*. Interviewed 25 years later, his memory diverged from other people's concerning the original location and uses of the gallery, and of the sessions which had been running there for five or six years previously:

I said, "Larry, can I hold sessions here and restore these guys' vigor? And try to recreate what once happened naturally by providing work and organizing as many bands as I can and as many sounds as I can so that I can record them? We can't record like this – they can't even put a song together. They're rusty, corroded." So he said, "Sure, you can hold 'em here." Then he came up with an idea, says, "I'm gonna clear out that room next door, that little art supply shop, you can hold them in there, you can use that for your work space." So I did. And that was my office, the front hall part of 726 [?732]. We're talking about late April, early May of '61.

I held one with [Ernie] Cagnolatti, and [Jim] Robinson. Kid Howard was just coming back from illness, Sheik [Colar] was nursing him, and Sheik had him play second cornet. And we had Emile Barnes and [trombonist] Harrison Verrett and Slow Drag Pavageau. That was my first one.

Ken Mills (right) ran Preservation Hall, with Barbara Reid, during its first summer -- 1961. With him are (from left) Louis Nelson (trombone), Punch Miller (trumpet), Emanuel Sayles (banjo), Alex Bigard (drums), Kid Thomas (trumpet), George Guesnon (banjo), Slow Drag Pavageau (bass) George Lewis (clarinet) and Israel Gorman (clarinet).

Then I had one with Polo [Barnes] and Punch [Miller] and Jim [Robinson]. I'm listening to this to see if it's worth recording. The kitty is dealing with the money. They're doing their rehearsing, and they're getting themselves back in shape again. And it's working very well. We're getting some pretty good crowds. We had a really nice Sunday with both Israel [Gorman] and George [Lewis] playing. Crowds were overflowing in the street. Israel and George went out on the sidewalk and played.

This is how it starts. I'm eating dinner at Bourbon House, and Larry comes in and he says, "I gotta talk." I said, "Okay." It's real early May, maybe the last day of April. He says, "I can't help but think there's some money in this, that there's work for these musicians, and it could be put on a logical sustaining basis. I don't know how it can be done, or if it can be done, but it can be done. You want to try it? I don't know how you're gonna do it. I'm leaving on a business trip for pre-Columbian artifacts in Mexico, so do you want to find some way to do it?" I said okay. I got hold of [Louis] Cottrell, the President of the Musicians' Union Local, and he comes down and we sat in Larry's office with our feet up on chairs, and I outlined what I thought would be a good thing to Cottrell. They were cool. What they weren't cool about was having a phonograph record coming into town that had been issued somewhere [else] and been recorded [here] outside of union aegis.

The biggest thing was the insurance policy and the burial policy for the widow. That seemed to be the big lure for the union – that the guy would be buried for sure and the widow would have something to live on – that's why the union was so important to them.

My first session, I paid the guys $35 a man, double for [Kid] Thomas. About the same for Punch. I didn't want to cheat 'em; I didn't want to pay them more than I could afford, either. For live performances, $24 for one-night stints, $18.50 for every night, was the rule then. However, Cottrell says, "If you can do it – it's very difficult to do – but if you can get a non-profit license, we have a rate for that." It was $13.50, double for leader.

By this time Mills had met Barbara Glancey Reid, who quickly became his partner in getting the Hall started. A friend of Bill Russell's from Chicago days, she had moved to the French Quarter in 1952 and been quickly absorbed into its bohemian arts and intellectual scene. She enjoyed longtime friendships with many of the local musicians, had offered important help to those recording them, and had assisted, as well, with Borenstein's kitty-jazz sessions. Reid was a sometime writer, interested in local topics such as voodoo and witchcraft; she had once planned to write a book with Russell on their mutual friend, the great gospel singer Mahalia Jackson. A gadfly who

Having originally come to New Orleans to record what had become an esoteric music, Ken Mills issued committed, true-grit discs before, during and after his short stint at the helm of Preservation Hall. With their bold covers and far-out liner notes, his original Icon pressings, such as those of Emile Barnes (left) and Punch Miller (right), became collector's items.

liked public relations, Barbara Reid would later run a strong but unsuccessful campaign for city council as a champion of the poor and the Blacks. One friend called her "the Auntie Mame of the French Quarter." Her active interest in old-style jazz predated her close friendship with Russell: in Chicago, she and her first husband, Bill Reid, had known such figures as reedman Sidney Bechet, pianist Jimmy Yancey and trumpeter Lee Collins. This background, along with her publicist's talents and network of local connections, proved valuable complements to Mills's intense focus on the music *per se*.

Barbara Reid had recently married pharmacist Bill Edmiston. Since the summer of 1960 they had been living with their infant daughter, Kelley, on the third floor of Borenstein's building at 732 St Peter, next door to the soon-to-be Preservation Hall. Barbara Reid did have her moody and difficult side. But Edmiston retained fond memories of her from that period when the Hall was formally coming together:

Barbara was great. Her judgment was wrong a lot, but her motivation was right. She was an honest person, the most honest person I've ever met. . . . She was a little bit driven, a type A personality. She'd give everything away. She gave those musicians their start. She'd give them anything. They didn't take advantage of her either. They knew she was working on something she liked doing. She was a mixer. She liked meeting people, and she liked them, and she liked their music, knew many of them very well personally, and I don't think they ever questioned that she was in it for anything but good. She always said she merged the two musicians' unions, black and white, and I guess she did.

In many ways we went our own ways. I had my job and she had her hobbies. And she was a great dreamer. She would dream up things and a lot of 'em wouldn't pan out, but I'd pay for them because I believed in her. We'd been following jazz musicians and she knew them all. She opened doors for me. Anything we would ask them, they would trust and they would do it . . . They knew that if the money in the kitty didn't come up, I'd write them a check, and I did. I know that I wrote one or two checks where they very sympathetically never cashed them. They knew what was going on, that we were doing that just to hang onto them. And they wanted to hang onto a good thing that they knew was growing.

That May, 1961, Larry Borenstein asked Barbara Reid to assist Ken Mills. Mills needed her immediately:

I said to Barbara, "Look, I know music, and I know musicians, but God, I don't know nothing about this other stuff." She said, "What do you need?" I said, "A non-profit license, because no way in hell can we pay the entertainment tax, buy the entertainment license. You talking about fierce big-time expense, $90 to $115 every night of our lives. A music that hadn't been presented live on a continuous basis since the Happy Landing [a local dance hall] in '57, and here we are conceiving of holding nightly sessions and relying on a kitty basket.

The idea evolved between Barbara and me. She knew a lawyer, Tony Vesich. He went to the State Legislature and got us a non-profit corporation license. Larry's out of town. He had said, "Find a way to do it. I'm providing the space. Do it." So we're doing it, the best way we can. He already knows Cottrell's suggestion. He leaves town knowing that's a possibility.

Borenstein had returned from Mexico and was leaving for California to get married by a Buddhist priest. As Bill Russell later told it, more than altruism may have been involved in Borenstein's turning over 726 St Peter to Mills: "Larry decided while he was gone it couldn't be an art gallery – nobody there to sell

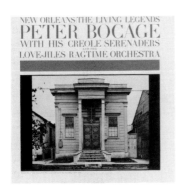

Many of the players soon to be featured at Preservation Hall appeared in a landmark series of recordings made by Herbert Friedwald for Riverside Records in early 1961.

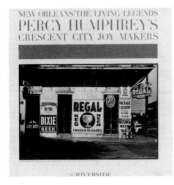

the stuff, he didn't want to turn the art business over to somebody else – so he decided to make a music hall out of it and turned it over to Mills."

Mills and Reid were not operating alone. Allan Jaffe, who also arrived in town that spring, stressed that there were a number of other people who worked hard and selflessly on the project. There was, for example, Mrs Aline Willis, one of Larry Borenstein's secretaries, who truly loved the music and came regularly to the Hall to do all the correspondence. In 1986 Jaffe said, "People ask me today, how did the Hall start? I say a lot of people in the neighborhood got together and got the Hall started."

In Borenstein's absence, Mills and Reid made rapid progress. The Charity Hospital License and a Mayoralty Permit were both finally issued on July 17, a few weeks after the Hall actually opened. The state charter of the non-profit corporation was formally filed and issued in Baton Rouge, the capital, on July 31. Some documents called the group the Traditional Jazz Association; others, the New Orleans Society for the Preservation of Traditional Jazz. The minutes of an August board meeting listed Ken Grayson Mills as President; Barbara Reid Edmiston, 1st Vice President; William Russell, 2nd Vice President, Sylvia Shannon [Larry Borenstein's secretary], Secretary; and William Edmiston, Treasurer.

A copy of the charter was eventually framed and hung on the wall behind the musicians, between the former gallery's two sets of French doors. Near the charter were other documents, along with hand-lettered signs proclaiming "EVERY CENT OF THE KITTY GOES TO THE MUSICIANS," "AUTHENTIC NEW ORLEANS JAZZ," and "PRESERVATION HALL / PRODUCED AND MAINTAINED BY GRAYSON MILLS / PSYCHOLOGICALLY SUS-TAINED BY BARBARA REID." The display was subject to frequent alteration; for example, the phrase "and maintained" was later blocked out. The signs were destined to be almost as controversial as they were memorable. Some helpers objected to the one about the entire kitty going to the musicians, because a portion always went for operating costs.

Before "Preservation Hall" had been settled on, the place was briefly known by other names, including "Slow Drag's Hangout" and "Authenticity Hall." An early visitor remembers one evening when Reid tore

Barbara Reid in a typical French Quarter street scene in the era when she was involved, along with Ken Mills, in operating Preservation Hall. A caring friend of many of the musicians, Reid later lost a bid for a city council seat as a champion of the downtrodden.

a brown paper bag into a flat sheet of paper, lettered in black crayon, "Perseverance Hall," then fastened the sign between the two doors with three scraps of masking tape. In years to come, many persons, including Reid, would credit her for coming up with the final name. Mills, however, later insisted:

> Here's the real way the name came about. "Authenticity," "Perseverance" – these were some of the names we were comin' up with. We were throwin' names around, me and Barbara. So I wrote down three things. One of them was "Preservation." "I want that!" she says. The name was never hers, and it wasn't mine. It was the product of an idea-logue.

In any event, it was a name that stuck. As time went along, "Preservation Hall" acquired brand-name value. While other aspects of the successful formula would occasionally be imitated, the name itself was the only part the management protected zealously and legally. (Nonetheless, by the late 1980s, a tourist trap half a block away on the corner of

Bourbon and St Peter had for several years been trying to siphon off some of the business by shamelessly displaying a big sign saying "Dedicated to the Preservation of Jazz.")

A well-wisher who drove a cleaning truck brought in carpet samples. A friend of Russell's named Ralph Collins picked up the groups of folding church seats which were still to be found in the Hall proper and carriageway 28 years later. Originally, these stood on the carpet sections in an arc around the front of the band. The main entrance consisted of the open French doors nearest Pat O'Brien's restaurant and the river, but people were also admitted through the carriageway on the opposite side, as they are today. For vocals there were two speakers, one in the carriageway and one in the Hall itself. (The amplification was soon removed and never replaced – another major difference from the Bourbon Street joints.)

* * *

The official opening was the night of June 10, 1961. Mills remembered the band consisting of trumpeter Kid Sheik Colar, clarinetist George Lewis, trombonist Eddie Summers, banjoist Harrison Verrett, bassist Slow Drag Pavageau and drummer Alex Bigard. Helping pass the hat were Barbara Reid, Sandra Jaffe, Marge Kidorsky (Mills's fiancée) and an off-duty Playboy Club bunny named Pat Gordon. A local television station, WYES, filmed the band playing such tunes as *I Thought I Heard my Mother Pray* and *I Can't Escape from You*, and interviewed Kid Sheik, Ken Mills and Barbara Reid. One of Barbara's statements on camera, when broadcast later, seemed to strike everyone as impressive: "We tried to restore the musicians' old pride in themselves."

Mills remembered, "Barbara had this marvelous hawking style that was totally fresh and innovative and in keeping with what we were trying to achieve in there. And yet it was still, 'Come on in here, have a look.' She stood in the doorway, smoking a cigarette, hawkin'." Reid's flair for publicity was much in evidence. Spreading the word about the Hall, she told everyone she knew and had a flyer printed up in 15 different typefaces. Versions varied slightly over the first few weeks (see illustration).

Reid appeared on at least two radio talk programs, and her friendship with local reporter Bill Stuckey led to his writing a long, favorable piece for an important local paper, the *New Orleans States-Item*. Writer James Asman, who happened to be in town at about the same time, did a major story about Preservation Hall for Britain's *Jazz Monthly*. However, the first of many articles to be printed in England and Europe over the years was probably the one appearing in the *Manchester Guardian* on July 9. Written by Roger Dunkley, it included this colorful passage:

The enthusiasm and performance of these aging musicians was quite amazing. With an average age of about 65 they played from 7:30 to 1:00 each night. The audience, in shorts and T-shirts, was composed mainly of residents of New Orleans. It included young couples with small children, who contrasted strongly with the patrons of the near-by commercial outfits. Throughout the evening crewcut young men in button-down shirts and dark Ivy League suits peered nervously through the open doorway and then led their partners off. Perhaps the lack of air conditioning dismayed them; more likely it was the display of completely uninhibited playing. To add to their suspicions, no one was asking for their money.

Of the performers I heard, Kid Thomas on trumpet was outstanding, still blowing surprisingly strongly at an estimated 73, and leaping up and down onto his chair, donning a huge floppy woman's bonnet, to play Happy Birthday to George Lewis, using a Coke bottle as a mute. At 61, Lewis is a thin, delicately-made Negro whose slender hands still produce a purer, more enjoyable note from his clarinet than most other living players.

But perhaps the most influential piece was a widely disseminated, unsigned Associated Press dispatch quoting Mills and the band members at some length. Although Barbara Reid's signs from that period said the Hall was open Wednesdays through Sundays, and Jaffe later stressed how empty the French Quarter streets were in those days, the article maintained that "Six nights a week, some 600 to 1,000 persons pack the hall – standing, sitting on the floor, overflowing into the steamy New Orleans night – applauding and listening intently to the oldtime jazz."

In light of the strong coverage which would

The flamboyant, down-home style of promoting the Hall around New Orleans in its early months was later supplanted by a policy of no advertising at all -- but plenty of unsought national publicity.

THE
NEW ORLEANS
SOCIETY FOR THE PRESERVATION OF TRADITIONAL JAZZ

PRESENTS

The Continuation of
New Orleans' Own Original *Rhythm*
IN ALL ITS INITIAL
☞ GLORIOUS SPLENDOR ☜

TUES
EACH ~~WEDNESDAY~~ THRU SUNDAY EVENING
8 P. M. TILL MIDNIGHT

A DIFFERENT BAND EACH NIGHT
Provided by a Purely Non-Profit Co-Operative
EVERY MEMBER OF THE FAMILY WELCOME

WE HAVE · NO DRINKS · NO GIRLS · NO GIMMICKS
JUST REAL MUSIC!

PRESERVATION
HALL
726 ST. PETER ST.
NEW ORLEANS 16. LOUISIANA

NO ADMISSION CHARGE—STRICTLY KITTY CONTRIBUTIONS

MENDOLA BROS., Inc., PRINTERS, 1305 Decatur St., New Orleans 16; Dial 523-1946

continue to be afforded Preservation Hall over the next quarter century, a media blitz like this might not seem so special. But against a previous silence reverberating back for decades – the musicians hungry and demoralized, the local jazz establishment virtually decreeing the old music dead – such sudden attention was an inspiring turnaround. Mills's diary included some comments overheard from the musicians:

Trombonist Albert Warner 7/8/61: "I just learned how to do it. I haven't been playing anything like this in a long time."

Clarinetist Emile Barnes 7/30/61: "Don't wake me, Barbara, I'm afraid I'm dreaming. This bunch puts me in mind of Milneburg years ago when me and this bunch was playing there."

Banjoist and vocalist Emanuel Sayles 7/26/61: From the bandstand, after a tune is finished, Sayles spontaneously cries, "Regeneration at Preservation Hall! Bring 'em back alive!" (Laughter and applause).

Enter Larry Borenstein. Bill Russell's memory of what happened after both honeymoons – of the Borensteins and of Preservation Hall under Mills and Reid – was probably the most objective:

> Everybody's ideas were entirely altruistic – nobody to cash in on anything. On the other hand it had been Larry's idea and Larry's business in a way. So they took it over, and when he got back he was burned up to find the thing had been incorporated as a business, and he didn't believe in signs all over the place about kitty contributions. It wasn't that Mills and Barbara were trying to cut Larry out of it entirely, but they just had this other thing going here.

That the conflict grew out of a clash of volatile personalities, as well as from clearcut issues, could be divined from the suddenly altered tone of Mills' later account:

> Larry disliked the non-profit structure of the operation. He wanted it put on a free enterprise, normal business basis post haste. It would have taken tremendous stores of capital. He had no control or influence on the decision making and operation and found himself increasingly out of synch with the mentalities in control. We're dealing with a martinet here who went bonkers whenever he was seriously crossed on anything in which he invested emotional and egotistic feeling. Many of his suggestions were adopted, such as the Coke machine. He held the belief that the musicians should pick their own personnel, but I had noticed what the buddy system produced: you would either get black Dixieland or something worse.
> Barbara and I still got along famously. Bill Edmiston said he marveled at it – never saw two people get along so well under pressure conditions. . . . In short, and in fact, Borenstein ripped our ass and saw to it that our phenomenal achievement was dismissed like the shadows of birds passed. He could, and did, re-create us as myths of his own making. And nobody who knew better – those eyewitnesses who were in the know – ever struggled to set the record straight because they didn't want to harm the music.

Some said the root of the problem was that Mills was primarily interested in his recording project, rather than in the business of running the Hall. Apparently, hundreds of people were flowing in and out of the doors without paying anything; the average contribution, by one count, was 13 cents a head. Reid, by these lights, was only marginally better than Mills

Rare bits of jazz-buff memorabilia, membership cards were issued for the short-lived society formed in July 1961 to operate the Hall as a non-profit enterprise.

at minding the store, even though her heart was in the right place. Merchant to the marrow, Borenstein repeatedly tried to get them to tighten things up, but they never would.

Mills replied that they were struggling to learn how to run a business despite the "help" of someone who had it in for them. Mills' accounts showed that in the three months from June 16 through September 12 the nightly take ranged from below $60 to over $1,000; it averaged $119, against average expenses of $104, leaving a profit of $15 a night. "We weren't flying by the seat of our pants," he remembered, "nor were we chaotic, torn by rancor, or loosely-knit. . . . Books were kept; bills were paid; we opened every night as scheduled; we owed nobody anything. . . . The public flow was handled professionally and cheerfully; maintenance was constant. . . . We didn't fail, as a project or as a business. . . . Nobody will ever know what we would have achieved there had we been left to what they considered our incorrigible designs."

One irony was that, according to Allan Jaffe, Borenstein had originally gone to some lengths to talk Mills into running the Hall on a full-time basis. Again, it is important to realize how difficult and thankless such an undertaking was in the New Orleans of that time. Many observers believed that Mills had no intention of remaining after he made his recordings. At a later point Borenstein asked jazz historian Al Rose to run the Hall; he refused. Another time, Allan Jaffe tried to talk Borenstein himself into running it – without success.

Twice the police shut them down for disturbing the peace, causing losses; Barbara Reid traced this to an anonymous caller who hated Borenstein and who stopped his calls after she explained the situation. In the process they were forced to hire a security guard. Reid obtained a formal letter from the mayor congratulating the New Orleans Society for the Preservation of Traditional Jazz for its efforts; Borenstein had it framed and hung on the wall. After this there was no further trouble from the police.

Part of the internecine discord stemmed from the fact that Ken Mills was operating the Hall as a kind of lab to test the musical chemistry between varying combinations he was planning to record. Recalled cornetist Charlie DeVore:

Veterans of many a down-and-out dive made their comeback at the Hall (from left): Emile Barnes (clarinet), DeDe Pierce (cornet), Papa John Joseph (bass), Billie Pierce (piano), and an unknown player (ukelele).

Ken would sit in front of the band and he'd have all the combinations that he thought would work. There were some musicians that could play quite well, and others that had been in retirement and perhaps never were really that talented. Like a no-name, no-blame trumpet player – I can't even remember the trumpet players he'd be using – but there was a wonderful trumpeter, Kid Howard, who wanted to play desperately, sitting out in the carriageway, kind of wistfully looking in.

I remember this vividly: Ken would sit there and watch the band, and he'd start issuing them orders, like, "Okay, play *Bucket's Got a Hole in It*." He wouldn't smile, he'd just kind of watch them, and then he'd order them to do this and that. Larry saw what was happening, and it was really an unhappy scene.

Among the balloons of intrigue and misinformation wafted over Preservation Hall in this period was the idea that the Ford Foundation, which had earlier provided the seed money for Tulane's Jazz Archive, was also – or should be – involved in the Hall. In the fine old tradition of New Orleans grudges, the city's jazz community is to this day riven with tensions dating back to the formation of the Hall. Part of the problem was that the Hall, like the Quarter itself, and much of the Central Business District, gradually lost its neighborhood homeyness as it came to be run more professionally.

Despite the stormy relations, appearances were maintained, and the experience of most visitors continued to be strongly positive. One happy recollection was that of a Philadelphia artist and longtime jazz lover named Marty Kaelin:

I followed the sound of a most archaic jazz, finding myself again at 726 St Peter. The music was that of the Love–Jiles Ragtime Band. Deciding to be more aggressive I stepped inside and [was] instantly told to leave by a young man I would come to know as Grayson [Ken] Mills. The following night there was a small gathering of college age youth seated on the floor. I joined them listening to Punch Miller, [pianist] Eddie Morris, [trombonist] Louis Gallaud. I had met Punch several days earlier along the street with George Lewis. I knew of Punch, even heard him playing with a Calipso band in a tent show in the late days of World War II.

Ken Mills and Barbara Reid, recognizing my interest being deeper than curiosity, quickly accepted me into the fold and it was at 726 I spent the evening hours for the remainder of my stay. The musicians as might be expected were the roster of Mills's Icon Records.

By day the soon-to-be Preservation Hall was a gathering place for musicians. Punch could be found there at any hour sitting alone the long hot summer days. I spent many hours talking – mostly hearing of carnivals, circus and minstrel shows. . . . Punch would sing the most obscure [songs] at merest mention and be reminded of a dozen more. We often went to Buster's [Buster Holmes' restaurant] to eat, but he kept up his stories.

Grayson Mills impressed me as an intense man, somewhat condescending, whose one ambition at the time was to capture the city's past music, to put on tape all those musicians overlooked or even thought long gone. All who care and love New Orleans music should be grateful.

Tulane University archivist Richard B. Allen wrote a friend that September: "This is heady stuff, raw, rough around the edges. But when your ear becomes acclimated to this, the usual commercial stuff sounds just too slick to suit you."

Borenstein could be patient with tenants, but not if he was fighting with them about something else. He forced the Edmistons to vacate their apartment next door on a short notice. His dislike of the signs took on the dimensions of a holy war, symbolizing everything he objected to in the way Reid and Mills were running the Hall. His original altruism was soon replaced by an insistence that Mills sublet the Hall from him for $400 a month. Mills did so.

That the youthful Mills may have brought some of Borenstein's anger on himself is suggested by the fact that at one point he started selling paintings of musicians in the Hall – by artists who were not part of Borenstein's stable – in direct competition with Borenstein's gallery next door. The predictably enraged Borenstein made Mills tell the artists to remove their pictures. Adding fuel to the fire were comments by various helpers concerning the level of taste shown by this or that other helper in announcing the bands or in trying to induce people to drop more money into the kitty jars. At some of the Society's board meetings, tension had risen to the point where runners were dashing in and out carrying the latest tidbits of intrigue. To a detached observer, the whole affair was assuming the dimensions of comic opera.

The denouement was not far off. True to his original design, Mills kept pressing ahead with his recording plans:

Borenstein and I had often discussed the uncomfortable feeling that a lot of brilliance was going into the ether and he had even suggested such things as running mikes down the columns and disguising them, and recording nightly, and then working out a method where it could be legalized later. I agreed with him. One night the [Kid] Thomas band was playing with George Lewis, and I broached the subject with Thomas of recording the performance and giving him the tape for his safekeeping so that later on we could hold a legitimate union session to cover the material.

Louis Nelson was leaning against the wall. He had me repeat the prospect, then nodded his head and said he thought it was okay. Lewis thought it was a good idea. As long as Thomas got the tapes, everything was cool. Thomas said, "Is that okay with you?" And they said, "Yeah." Except Sammy Penn, the drummer, wasn't told about it. After the first set he mixed in the foyer and talked with people. He really enjoyed jabbering – he was an articulate and colorful, excellent talker, with a very warm disposition. Then after the next set Sammy went to take a piss in back and happened to notice [Bill Russell's friend] Ralph Collins sitting there with a set of earphones on and my Ampex tape recorder. When Sammy came out, he spoke to Thomas about it and was quite animated.

Thomas went and talked to Larry. At that point Larry

An impromptu multi-media presentation in the Mills–Reid summer of 1961 featured (from left) ?Mother Margarit Parker, Louis Nelson (trombone), Kid Thomas (trumpet), Sammy Penn (drums), Emanuel Sayles (banjo) and George Lewis (clarinet); the artist is Xavier de Callatay and the spectator in the foreground is probably Ken Mills.

snuck around the back and pops in and there's Ralph sittin' there with the recorder. So Larry said, "This is it. This substantiates what I've known to be the case all along with you, that you talk the good line, but there's corruption in your heart." And Thomas? What's Thomas going to do? Rush up and say, Mr Larry, this has all been worked out? Larry's been waiting for this. He really starts kicking ass, and now I'm holding things up with my thumbs. . . . I saw how I had impacted them with the imbroglio of my creativity in approaches that they could use to my nefarious nature.

I went to [local musicians' union president] Cottrell the next day and explained what we had goin'. I said, "Louis, what if we held them under union aegis and stored them in escrow in the safe at Local 496?" "You can do it but you gotta phone ahead and one of us will come down and sit there." All right, we held one session like that with Punch Miller and [trombonist] Albert Warner and George Lewis, everything out front, Bill Russell sitting right in the middle of the audience turning the machine on and off, and the tapes go back with [union official] Sidney Montague to the union safe. That should have been the end of that.

But Larry kept on. He tried to get the board to impeach me, presented what he thought was a solid case to get rid of Mills, but they wouldn't do it. That was somewhere around August 14. So his next maneuver was, he wouldn't accept us as tenants. I wanted to get out of there, move it somewhere else, because I didn't want anything further to do with him. But Barbara had looked into it and said the best thing for us to do is stay put. And she said you can't leave us, we need you for various reasons. Especially they needed me because I was financing it all. So I decided to stay.

Whoops, that doesn't work either. Larry finally hit the format. He comes in and says the way our [sub]lease is written is very loose. He doubles it to $800 a month, wants the first and last month – some way or other wants almost two grand up front. So I look at it and I said that's it, I couldn't meet that. He says I don't blame you, I wouldn't take that risk either.

The rest was kinda fast and easy. At the board meeting I tried to get Barbara and Bill [Edmiston] to understand that this guy really had me in a corner, and I either had to be helped financially, or we had to move, or it was over. But she could see her dreams and all the love that she had put into this project . . . they were saying you've got to stay and you've got to put up two grand and you've got to do what you've always been doing. I said I can't do that. I don't have the funds or the means.

There was never any rancor among the board. The way it came down was, Barbara and Bill handed their proxies to Bill Russell, they gave their vote to him, and then they walked out. I couldn't understand why if it's succeeding we can't take it to another location, why she wouldn't support that. But now I'm alone here and I'm inclined to put an end to this. We voted and Bill [Russell] voted and that was the end of the Society. We dissolved it.

Borenstein and I sat down and carefully worked out the situation. He paid the legal fees and the dissolution of the Society, dissolution of the fictitious names, whereupon Jaffe bought it and published the name Preservation Hall. I held my last concert about the eleventh of September, counted the money, paid the musicians. And then as easily as turning the key on the lock, walking into a going business, Jaffe started fresh, opened the doors, booked a band and held a kitty. It was never rancor, disruption or anything else. The only thing is, Barbara and I weren't there. We were gone.

Barbara Reid, of course, was crushed. While she would find plenty of other fish to fry, her longstanding friendship with Larry Borenstein was permanently affected, and she would carry anger and sadness about Preservation Hall for many years. Yet, said

Blasting away on a hot summer night at the Hall in 1961, when the music room still opened directly onto St Peter Street, were (from left) Jim Robinson (trombone), Wilbert Tilman (sousaphone), Andy Anderson (trumpet), Alfred Williams (drums), John Casimir (clarinet) and Emanuel Sayles (banjo).

Clive Wilson, a trumpeter and leader who later played at the Hall occasionally, "No matter how bitter Barbara was, she would always say, 'The musicians are working, it's all right.'" Her bitterness eventually left her, and in retrospect she even told a friend she was glad things had gone as they had: "Grayson and I were no business people, and we probably wouldn't have done as good a job as Jaffe did, managing the Hall." When Barbara passed away in 1983, Jaffe opened the Hall one afternoon so that family and friends could gather there in her memory.

In a letter dated August 18, 1961, Richard B. Allen described the situation:

Larry Borenstein has rented part of his St Peter Street art empire to Grayson Mills, the kid from California, and Mills is now having sessions six nights a week with a different band each night. Some of the sessions have been very good, especially John Casimir's and Kid Thomas's. Of course, some nights it is pretty bad because Mills has a tendency to mess around with the bands' personnel. I hope this thing can be sustained on a "clean" basis in spite of all the internecine strife. It has developed into a bunch of backbiting, gossipmongering, petty rivalries which so often characterize the peripheral people of the jazz world. At least those of us that are really involved in it can be nasty on a larger scale. I hope they don't waste too much of Russell's and my time. Certainly, it is a worthwhile project to put a little money in the musicians' pockets, but not at this cost.

Less than a month later, on September 11, Allen wrote this memo for the files of the Jazz Archive at Tulane University:

A week or two weeks ago the Society for the Preservation of Traditional Jazz was dissolved. The work of the non-profit society will be continued, starting Wednesday, September 13, 1961, by Allan Jaffe and his wife, Sandy, on a profit (or loss) basis. I will be their assistant. The sessions will be continued at the same location, and the name "Preservation Hall," which is distasteful to several people, will not be used. It will be called simply "726 St Peter Street." Larry Borenstein will continue as landlord at the same rent.

In the interim, Grayson Mills is continuing to run the place, assisted by Ralph Collins and Allan Jaffe. During his stay, Mills has recorded several more bands under union contracts at 1110 Royal Street. These included Israel Gorman's band and Kid Sheik's band.

Since the dissolution of the society, she [Barbara Reid] has come back only once. Ralph Collins allowed her to watch the kitty that night. I don't remember who got her to stay away after that, but I remember it was not Grayson Mills.

Out of all this bickering, back-biting, and gossip-mongering, the person who has the highest tolerance seems to be Allan Jaffe. He seems to bear no malice towards anyone involved. As for myself, I think that I have been involved in jazz a little too long.

To others, the uproar of those few months in 1961 seemed like a tempest in a teapot. Still, these were the beginnings of something that would ripple out more widely than anyone then imagined.

And the musicians? Their offhand remarks sometimes contained more wisdom than the well-meant perambulations of their boosters. Recalling the incident of the hidden recorder that caused so much contention, Kid Thomas just cackled gaily. "It was comical, man. Comical!" Of Ken Mills, Kid Sheik said simply, "He loved the music more than the money."

A World You Couldn't Expect
Visiting Kid Howard's Mom

Henry Blackburn

Kid Howard used to live just three blocks from the Hall. He wanted me to come by and see his mom, who had had a stroke. I had never been in a black New Orleans home, and I don't think I had ever been in one of those classic long, narrow, lovely "shotgun" houses where you come into the front room and then they've got the dining room, and then the bedroom, and the kitchen, and the patio, and you have to walk through those to get to any particular room. The feeling of coolness and stillness when you come out of the overpowering heat! I don't know what it is about the design of those houses. Of course, they keep all the shades drawn, and you come into it and at first you think you're in a funeral parlor, but then you find out that it's really very pleasant, and you can just sort of retreat.

It's a world you couldn't expect would exist because of the subdued lighting and the coolness, and a little lady, in a very clean white cotton gown, a little bit of nothing on a pillow with a funny thing over her head, a hair net; one side of her face drooping, one hand useless at her side. Nothing you can do but sit on the bed and smile and talk to him about how he cares for her, explore what treatment she's getting and reassure him that they're in good medical hands. But the peace in those homes and the pride that they have in their homes and their families and in their loved ones. The cleanliness is striking.

Kid Howard always wore a very crisp white cotton shirt. When he'd come in off the street, he'd put on a clean cotton shirt, with his bright shiny black pants. It's just a tradition of properness and cleanliness and godliness. It was very striking to me. In all my earlier years of living in the South, I never had the pleasures of that company or friendship.

Play with Pride
Chatting with Narvin Kimball

"My father was a musician. He was a stickler. He taught me, if you are going to play, put yourself in a position where you play with pride, and with dignity." Although Narvin Kimball's father, Henry Kimball, died in 1932, he is still widely remembered in New Orleans jazz circles. The noted guitarist Bud Scott, who worked with the elder Kimball as early as 1904, later called him "the greatest bass player I ever heard in my life."

And Narvin did learn to play with pride and dignity. Carefully turned out, sitting very straight and nearing 80, this banjoist, singer, songwriter and bassist presented himself to his public with an air of sweet righteousness. Unlike the more instinctual jazzmen, whose appearances, while equally professional, were a public thermometer of their current emotions, Narvin said, "When I play, I come to work. And when I finish work, I'm ready to leave. I'm one of the first ones there, and I'm one of the first

ones to leave. The sole intention is: this is a night's work, and it has to be together. And I'm gonna do my best, because I don't know by whom I'll be heard. My philosophy of playing is to do it with the same enthusiasm that I played the very first time I played in my life. Every night is beautiful to me when I'm playing music." Kimball developed a whole philosophy about sound waves in the air, vibrations of the banjo head and the drum head, harmony spreading out like the branches of a tree. A singer or musician should "go softly up to the mike," approaching it "the way you'd wake a baby."

A sharp dresser, he told how, in Texas, he was proudly shown a painting of himself by a man who had bought it for $1,200; why, wondered Kimball, did he himself get nothing out of it? "And there are gold plates being sold with my picture on them," he said resentfully. A thoughtful, gentlemanly, careful man, he received letters from all over the world, including one from a man pretending to be a fellow banjo player, who, in reality, was conducting an academic survey. Behind Kimball's winning public smile was a thicket of old scars.

One of the vital polarities in New Orleans jazz is the constant tension between the steady background beat, set up by the rhythm men, and the more "playful" players working against and around that beat. It is this tension which, like the dialogue in a good stage play, drives the musical story ahead. Clarinetist Willie Humphrey was a great risk-taker, a gentle jiber, a master of the bent tone and the off-beat phrase. He and Kimball played together, on and off, for more than 60 years. As early as 1926, they were working a Mississippi River steamboat in the highly regarded Fate Marable band. Below, Kimball gives a sense of the inner creative tension, that looseness against tightness, which provided such a lilt to their touring Preservation Hall ensemble:

"Well, a person like Willie is unpredictable. You never know what he's gonna do. When Willie's playing with me, he'll look over at me, and I know what he means. He wants me to punch. *Punch!* He wants me to be right there behind him, see? And I'll get behind him, and I'll be playing the rhythm just a little bit heavier. When I said he's unpredictable, some of the things that he's making are incredible. And it so happens that since we have been playing together as we have, we understand each other very well. I know what he wants, and I try to give it to him. And sometimes you'll look over there, and the meaning is that he's pleased. So, it's a beautiful relationship that exists between the two of us while he's playing. Or sometimes he'll look at me and he'll frown – he's not pleased because he isn't

hearing what he wants to hear. Then again, he'll tell me, 'Pull your chair over. I want to hear the banjo. I want to hear your parts.' But sometimes when I move over, I'm moving over too far, and I'll be shadowing the pianist that's behind – he wants to be seen – so I'll have to move back."

Kimball's lovely voice projected beautifully. It was long a highlight of performances in the Hall and on the road. Long ago he and his sisters sang in a "kitchen trio" while washing the dishes. Later he sang in high school and college choruses. After World War II he performed in a vocal quartet called the Four Tones, which included fellow jazzmen Fred Minor, Alvin Alcorn and Louis Barbarin (all of whom later appeared at Preservation Hall). But it was only from the 70s onward that Kimball sang on a professional basis.

Although highly regarded for his left-handed banjo technique ever since the mid-1920s, Kimball did not touch that instrument for 25 years. Instead, from about 1935 until about 1960 he played string bass with swing-oriented groups like Sidney Desvigne's orchestra. Such practicality was characteristic of those Preservation Hall players who possessed the skills needed to switch.

Typical, as well, was the fact that Narvin also worked a day job from the lean 30s onward. Pride of profession marked his career at the Post Office: "In 35 years I was late maybe three times, and not a single day off without pay." Wearing both hats often meant that he had to "sleep fast," getting home from clubs at two in the morning and rousing himself at four to start pounding the pavements with a mail sack. Only after retiring in 1973 was he able to accept band tours longer than his annual two-week vacation. Whatever Narvin Kimball did, he did with pride and dignity.

Chapter Five

EACH ONE IS RIGHT

"As long as this music is serving a purpose, as long as it's functional, as long as the integrity of it remains, it will remain a vital music."
—Allan Jaffe

Fresh perspectives were needed after the Mills–Borenstein turmoil; and if these had not arrived in the persons of Allan and Sandra Jaffe, Preservation Hall would not be what it is today.

Jaffe's personality gave him a different outlook and approach from those of the earlier Hall managers. He fused several apparent opposites. By nature he was a loner, tough and independent, private with his thoughts and emotions. People often felt distanced by his hard-to-decipher blue eyes and unexplained silences. Paradoxically, he was actually a very friendly man, maintaining a wide network of warm associations. And Jaffe was extraordinarily generous: he did more for more people than many of them knew, or than he would have thought of admitting. He laughed a lot and enjoyed a lot. Many remember him best in connection with wonderful meals at Galatoires, or giant feasts for the whole band and myriad hangers-on, most often paid for by him, out in Milwaukee or

Surging through the French Quarter, a crowd of "second-liners" engulfs the famous Eureka Brass Band in a parade shown on network TV in the 60s -- among the earliest of such segments which would give the Hall and players valuable publicity for many years.

The warm yet inscrutable smile of musician-manager Allan Jaffe, shown here wrapped in his helicon, summed up the Hall's special atmosphere of welcome, mystery and subtle authority.

London or Seattle. He also endured some hard personal sufferings in silence. Operating as a team in the Hall's early years, the Jaffes exuded a strong extended-family feeling, an instinct for nurturing and protecting with longterm continuity.

A lover of the quirky and offbeat, of downhome plainness and practicality, Jaffe also enjoyed accumulating power, especially outside the usual old-boy channels – which helped make him a natural ally of Larry Borenstein. Unlike Borenstein, he never went out of his way to alienate the entrenched elements, but worked cooperatively with them as the case demanded. On the whole, though, his approach was to ignore local aristocrats and others used to operating in networks, and run his shop his own way. This made some say that Jaffe tended to cut people out, and had a holier-than-thou attitude. Such impressions were doubtless fed, in part, by his long pauses in speaking, which seemed to diminish over the years, as did his need to demonstrate being the one in control.

An indifferent dresser, he hated pretentiousness. Nonetheless, he was a strong supporter of received traditions – be it his sons' Bar Mitzvahs or a brass band funeral – which he felt evoked inner truth and humanity. According to trombonist Frank Demond, this ability to span apparent contradictions was the key to Jaffe's success: "Allan was one in a million. He had the warmth and sensitivity – and the toughness. It didn't have to be his way. In a way it had to be exactly his way, but in another way he let go completely."

Jaffe's complex character and interests were shaped, in part, by the circumstances of his youth. Born in 1935, he grew up in the small town of Pottsville, Pennsylvania. His father's father had played a horn similar to the modern euphonium in a Russian Imperial Army band. The father, Harry Jaffe, taught stringed instruments at the Settlement Music School in Philadelphia, but soon opted for business instead. He moved 85 miles northwest to Pottsville, where he opened a wallpaper and paint store. Yet he continued to play music as an avocation. As a boy, Allan Jaffe would listen to his father and two paperhangers play polkas and popular tunes at home. All three members of the trio played mandolin, violin and banjo by ear; they would pass the instruments around, taking turns.

After brief flings at piano and cornet in elementary school, the young Jaffe settled on the tuba in junior high school. By the eighth grade he had progressed rapidly enough to earn a place in the city band. This ensemble followed a long Pottsville tradition of serious-drinking, capable brass band musicians, dating back to pre-Revolutionary times. As a high school sophomore Jaffe played in the public high school band, then won a tuba scholarship to the Valley Forge Military Academy, where he spent his junior and senior years. Here the well-trained English director rehearsed his 50-piece, all-scholarship ensemble every day of the week. The group played for US Presidents Eisenhower and Truman, an interesting precedent in that, as a member of the Preservation Hall bands, Jaffe would later perform for every US President from Kennedy through Reagan.

At the University of Pennsylvania, Jaffe joined a

concert band, but found it disappointing, and stopped playing regularly. Working his way through school by waiting on tables in sorority houses, he took several humanities courses but majored in economics in the undergraduate division of the Wharton School of Business, from which he received his BS degree in 1957. In his senior year he became involved in the new field of computerized market research in a project at Gimbels Department Store, then stayed on as an employee for two additional years.

Some related Jaffe's later success in managing Preservation Hall to his business-school training. He was dubious about this. "You do learn the rules of the game – how to talk to the people who go to the business schools and end up being the ones in control," he said. "Learning to program the computer also helped in that you had to ask the right questions." On the other hand, "The better the schools got – the more scientific methods were applied – the more you stopped using common sense." He had already gained a healthy respect for common sense by hanging around his father's shop:

It's a tedious job. You just sit and listen. Listen and understand. I used to tell my father how bored I was sitting in his store, waiting for customers. He said, "That's easy. There's so much work that has to be done here." I said, "What has to be done?" He said, "If you don't know what has to be done, you don't belong here." I started to understand what he was talking about. The glamorous thing was waiting on customers. But what had to be done was keeping the dust off stuff, and having the books in order.

Such feet-on-the-ground training was later reinforced by watching the humble way Bill Russell went about supporting New Orleans music:

If you want to help, the first thing to do is look for a broom. That's literally what Bill Russell did, and that's what I learned from Bill Russell. The place where musicians needed help wasn't in playing their horn. It was running to the store for them, and paying a bill for them, getting medicine. Those were the areas where they needed help.
Look around. What has to be done? "Oh, I'll sell records." And that's what Bill does. He sits there and talks to people, and it's wonderful. Now, when people come to work at the Hall, it's basically that. You sit there for five

Jaffe with the Olympia Brass Band on Bourbon Street; he played regularly with them in New Orleans, and with the leading Preservation Hall bands on tour.

minutes and you decide somebody wants a glass of water, or they're out of ice cubes.

Under Jaffe, Preservation Hall became, at least in principle, a kind of jazz store in which management opened and closed the place, took care of the housekeeping chores, and essentially strove to stay out of the way and let the musicians do their thing, which is not necessarily easy:

Managerial skills? Probably my strong point is not doing anything. If Willie comes in and complains to me about Sing, and Sing comes in and complains to me about Willie, and Percy complains about something, I can listen to it and not have to make a decision about what to do about it. I have to work at that, too. That type of tolerance doesn't come easily. I can remember one musician who used to come into the Hall, hustling for tips. It used to kill me. I used to want to throw him out. He'd do little things I thought were degrading to him. Sitting and restraining myself, being calm about it, was what eventually made it work.

I mean it was his place. The Hall is the musicians' place. If I had told him what to do, it would no longer be his place. If it was no longer his place, then it was no longer

Willie's place and it was no longer Percy's place. The Hall, I think, to the musicians, really is their place, more than it's my place. And I think that's important. If one musician is doing something that is making it bad for the other musicians – it doesn't happen that much, but if it does – the musicians themselves will eventually stop it. Or you can control them in a less Machiavellian way than stopping it. There are songs that we don't play because every time we play the song, there's an argument. Rather than settle the argument, we just don't play the song.

What is a better hallmark of a New Orleans musician than to say, "I'm better than the rest of the guys"? Every one of us in reality is similar in saying that "I'm better than the rest of them. I play it right and they play it wrong." The secret is, each one is right. And everybody is really enjoying the music at their own level. That's the way the jazz lovers enjoyed it? Well, fine. That's the way the other people liked it? Fine. I don't want to tell somebody how to sit and enjoy it. I know how I enjoy it, and I don't want to tell someone else to enjoy it the same way I do.

*   *   *

There were other respects, too, in which Jaffe's approach and background were different from those of the typical jazz enthusiast. His interest in the music had developed more along social lines than in the manner of an exacting connoisseur combing through rare record bins:

> While I was in prep school I would get to concerts and I heard Armstrong play and Benny Goodman and we used to be able to get into jazz clubs. I heard Bunk Johnson records at college. My roommate's cousin had a very popular Dixieland band at the time out of Princeton and we used to go hear them. I used to run parties at a fraternity house and I used to hire bands. Each school sort of had their own Dixieland band, and there were other people who knew about King Oliver, Louis Armstrong and Bunk Johnson.

Unlike most fraternity boys, however, Jaffe had an innate habit of looking, in every field, beyond the easy allurements of show-stopping technical flash, to the less obvious values of diamonds in the rough. Said Curt Jerde, curator of the Jazz Archive at Tulane in the 80s, "Allan has a way of dismissing academic arguments about the music as fatuous, and saying, 'Keep it simple.'" In this, if not in other ways, Jaffe

```
      IF   IT   IS   MUSIC
             Contact
      PRESERVATION HALL
               for
  ALLEN JAFFE  -.-   Bass Man
              with
  Dejan's Olympia Brass Band
  522-2841            523-8939
```

would become a natural protégé of the Hall's grandfathers, Russell and Borenstein, those seeming opposites who attracted, and after whom he named his first son: Russell Lorenz Jaffe. (He made saxophonist Harold Dejan, leader of the rough-hewn Olympia Brass Band in which Allan played tuba for many years, the godfather of his second son, Benjamin.) Although the embittered Ken Mills would remain understandably cool to his successors, he nonetheless confirmed that

Jaffe had an instinctual, inarticulated understanding of the music. It's unusual for a raw rube out of Philly to naturally go for something so strange as that music was. Because that music was so tactual and indifferent by regular musical standards that you almost had to understand the language of that music to like it. It had to speak to you, and it did speak to Jaffe.

Precisely because it spoke to him in this rough vernacular way, rather than in a fine-arts way, some of his choices of performers, over the years, would sometimes seem less than perfect to the ears of many who cared deeply about the music.

Factors of greater concern to a manager than to a critic – reliability, commitment, loyalty, longevity of service, overall advancement of the enterprise – weighed heavily for Jaffe. The musicians tended to credit his strong leadership for his and their success, and to point out that he had an unusual ability to withhold anger in certain crucial situations, even though at other times, as Willie Humphrey said, "You might see him say some rough things to some people. He's pretty smart. He knows how to treat people. He's got a whole lot of friends, and they try to help him."

Jaffe's rough-grained side helped make him more like the musicians than the music-lovers. It showed up, for example, in his dislike for the kind of recording session in which producers fuss over things at length, asking the players to repeat the same song several times, then later fine-tuning the mixdown as they work toward some standard of perfection. Strongly preferring the slice-of-life approach, his instinct was closer to that of most New Orleans musicians, who have tended to see recordings not as holy writ but as one more job. Jaffe venerated the idea that New Orleans jazz is functional music – even though (or perhaps because) there were those who claimed Preservation Hall concerts had removed it from its native functionalism. Typical of his statements to interviewers was this one, made during a nationwide telecast of the Percy Humphrey band:

> As long as this music is serving a purpose, as long as it's functional, as long as the integrity of it remains, it will remain a vital music. It will remain as important a part of American music as it always has been.

* * *

The business student's extracurricular musical interests had drawn the young Jaffe into a familiarity with Philadelphia's concert stages:

> I used to be in all the operas and a lot of ballets, carrying swords and stuff. The Met would come there, the Philadelphia Opera, all the good ballet companies would come through. They had a group of people that, if they called you, you would come or send someone reliable. I did that for about three years. So walking backstage was no longer something new to me. I knew what a prima donna was like, and I knew what a stagehand was like. I wore black makeup one time to carry Tibaldi in Aida. Four of us had to carry her on a chair after a ballet with Margot Fonteyn, and everybody came back to a party that night we were having at the fraternity house where we had a Dixieland band that I had hired. It might have been Tony Spargo; he had this funny kazoo.

Jaffe also helped arrange a couple of jazz concerts at the students' union. He was thus becoming familiar with booking procedures and the concert stage, and aware of the growing national college market for jazz. One later result was that his first thought on hearing, for example, the wonderful duo of Billie and DeDe Pierce in New Orleans was not, like most connoisseurs, that these people ought to be recorded or interviewed in their own "natural" environs, but that they ought to be out there on the college concert circuit. Arriving in the French Quarter in early 1961, Jaffe would soon meet other out-of-towners interested in the music. But while their interest "was in writing and documenting, I have no interest in writing and documenting. What I was trained for, and what I enjoy, is management and promotion." Unlike

The roll call of creative spirits who had occupied portions of the old Creole mansion at various times included photographer Dan Leyrer, whose studio remained unaltered on the second floor of the rear section. Here, Leyrer made a photograph for an album that became an all-time best-seller. Pictured under the Hall's trademark sign are (from left): Slow Drag Pavageau, Jim Robinson, Emanuel Sayles, Willie Humphrey, Cie Frazier, Percy Humphrey and Sweet Emma Barrett.

Borenstein and the others, Jaffe would correctly predict that, if there was to be a real payoff for the Preservation Hall musicians, it would be in touring:

> People in New Orleans didn't realize how much interest there was in the music around the country. In the 50s practically every college campus had a Dixieland band, and for anyone who really listened and became serious about it, it was only a few steps, maybe through Turk Murphy and Bob Scobey and Lu Watters, back to the New Orleans roots.

The social environment of Pottsville had also foreshadowed that of New Orleans in some interesting ways:

> Pottsville had a very established black population. The first black to shed blood in the Civil War was from Pottsville. The first defenders who came to Lincoln when he called for volunteers were from Pottsville.
> There was the right side of the tracks and the wrong side of the tracks. I sort of was right on the tracks. I was the only one among my friends who lived right downtown on the main street. We lived above the store. There were two polka bands, one across the street from us and one on the corner. They were much louder than the bands in New Orleans. They would start every Friday night and go all the

In pictures as well as words, the media quickly discovered that the rugged performers made good copy. Leading the simulated parade here, during the 60s, was the venerable Louis Nelson, also featured in a color spread in "Gentleman's Quarterly." From left: Cie Frazier, Slow Drag Pavageau, an unknown trumpeter, Nelson and an unknown photographer

way through the weekend. I was used to that loud music.

During the 40s, through the war and afterwards, Pottsville was a wide-open town. It had one whole street that was like the strip. Behind us was a famous brothel that advertised in the yellow pages. I mean this was a street like out of Catfish Row, with balconies, and the girls in silk dresses out on the balconies and out on the street. Indian Town Gap was a military reservation near Harrisburg, and Pottsville was the closest wide open city, so a lot of soldiers would come through. And coal miners.

Jimmy and Tommy Dorsey are from a couple miles away, and Les Brown. The Dorsey brothers played in all those places when they were small. Pearl Bailey used to entertain there. Pottsville had a dance hall where all the big bands played. Black bands came through and played. King Oliver played there. One of the musicians who came and played had to have been Jelly Roll Morton. But I didn't hear the Oliver and Morton records in any real sense until I came to New Orleans. Most of what I heard were polka bands. Those were for the Poles and other people who worked in the mines. There were all these ethnic groups but they stayed as these groups. They had their own churches, they had their own days, and everybody supported everybody's days, and everybody got along. There was Lithuanian Day and Czechoslovakian Day, and Russian Orthodox and Greek Orthodox. And my father being in the paint business and the art business, all the priests and such would always be coming into the store to buy stuff to decorate the churches. On a Sunday we'd go to three or four different picnics. And the Welsh! God, we had a lot of Welsh in there. I used to sing in the Welsh choirs. The Molly McGuires were a group of Irish that protested working conditions in the mines and they hung many of them. That was the beginning of unions. They were all from the Pottsville area.

It was the county seat, a small town of 20 or 25 thousand. The blacks were maybe ten percent or less, but it was an established, older black population. They lived pretty much all over town. The president of the senior class ahead of me was black. The captain of the football team was black. One year the head of the national honor society was black.

I was going to hear Louis Armstrong play for dances up at Lakewood while I was still in Valley Forge, and the more I heard about the music, the more I realized that I liked the idea of it being a functional music that served a purpose in people's lives. I thought that a city must be interesting that had that kind of functional base for its music. That's one thing that began to attract me about going to New Orleans. The people who I was in the Valley Forge band with, we were all there working, all on scholarships, and we kept very much apart from the rest of the people at the school. The other kids were there for all the typical reasons why people go to military academies, including we had a lot of children of people in the military, and kids considering the military as a career. There were a lot of very wealthy kids too. It was a boarding school on the main line which is the old society section of Philadelphia.

I think that the idea of the groups staying together and still mingling is what this country is starting to revert back to. It's being able to get along and still keeping to your own traditions.

While working for Gimbels in Philadelphia, Allan Jaffe began dating Sandra Smolen. Born in 1938, she had studied English and journalism at Harcum Junior College and the University of Pennsylvania, and was now working as a secretary. Jaffe had been nurturing a plan to travel around the US and get jobs in different cities as soon as his research project was finished. In 1960, when he had completed his required basic training in the army, they decided to get married:

I said, "What do you think about quitting your job and we'll move somewhere and start over again?" She said, "Great." So we did. We quit our jobs and got married the next day and left town within a week.

New Orleans was where we went first because of my interest in music, and Sandy's. Sandy was particularly an Armstrong fan. I transferred my savings account to New Orleans so I'd have some cash when I got there. But first we toured all over Mexico for three months. It was truly "foreign." In some ways it's the same as New Orleans, which was the most foreign place we could go where they still spoke English.

Intending to remain in New Orleans for two years or less, the Jaffes arrived in late March or early April of 1961. They found temporary residence in the French Quarter. Allan quickly landed a job in a door factory near the airport, but quit after about three days. Through a friend of Sandra's, he then found a position at D. H. Holmes, the well-known large department store which bordered the Quarter along Canal Street. He hoped that this job would allow him enough time to pursue musical interests. But the Jaffes were in town several weeks before they could connect with the jazz scene:

Hanging around the Jackson Square area a lot, we got to talk with a lot of artists. We told them we were moving to New Orleans and asked them if they knew anything about New Orleans jazz and where we could hear it. They would inevitably ask if we had met Larry Borenstein yet. We'd say, "No," and they'd laugh. "You'll meet him. Ha, ha, ha, wait till you meet him." Like: "Well, you're in for it."

Then one night we were driving down St Peter Street, right there where the Hall is now, and I saw two guys with instruments in brass band uniforms, with their hats on, like in a picture on a record album I had. It was [trumpeter] Kid Sheik and [trombonist] Chicken Henry. I quickly stopped and parked. They had gone into Bill Russell's shop. We waited for them to come out. They told us they were going to play a job over at the Friends of the Cabildo, the museum on Jackson Square. We went over and found out it was open to the public. Dick Allen was giving a lecture, and the brass band played a couple of numbers and walked out.

We followed them and said, "Where are you going?" They said, "We're going down to Larry's." We followed them, and they went to Larry's gallery at 732, next to where the Hall is now. We got to talk to the band and met Dick Allen. They played one number and left. We hung around and talked to Larry, and he invited us to a big jam session he was having that Sunday.

That Sunday was the first time we got to hear a real New Orleans band play. I remember I put a dollar in the

Rarely recorded, trombone great Earl Humphrey was featured late in his career on an LP made at Preservation Hall in 1966 (from left): Cie Frazier (drums), Humphrey, DeDe Pierce (trumpet), Orange Kellin (clarinet), Lars Edegran (piano), Leonard Brackett (producer for Center Records), Twat Butler (bass); Bill Russell acts as recording engineer.

kitty for the two of us. Several different bands played in the course of the day, at least two front lines, at least two or three on each instrument, sometimes at the same time, sometimes they took turns. George Guesnon was there, Israel Gorman and Emile Barnes, Louis Nelson. It was against the wall in the back of the Hall.

Larry was having these sessions, sometimes two in a weekend, sometimes he could go for a couple of months without having any. They were not even planned. Some musicians would come and say, Larry, we'd like to come over and play next Sunday. Or someone else would arrange it. Ken Mills came back to town, and we talked to Larry about doing things on a regular basis. In June that started. Ken was arranging the bands and also was going to make up any shortage between what was taken in at the door and the union scale. Sandy was passing the kitty, and I was responsible to see that the band had drinks, and to keep drunks out and stuff like that. Then came all the political problems.

Ken wanted out. Larry asked Sandy and myself to [sublease] the building and to run the Hall. Which we did. We took over in September of '61.

The worldwide appeal of the old-style jazzmen came partly from a nostalgic perception that they had come from a romantic subculture in "days beyond recall." Blind trumpeter DeDe Pierce was featured on the cover of England's famous "Sunday Times Magazine" on June 26, 1966.

THE SUNDAY TIMES *magazine*
OLD MAN RIVER

Practical matters came first. Ken Mills could not bring himself to open his books on such things as which musicians he'd been hiring to the man Borenstein had picked to replace him. Drummer-bandleader Barry Martyn remembered Jaffe stopping by Bill Russell's shop one day:

He said to Bill and me, "I've got to set up a roster of bands for at least next week. Do you have any idea of who'd fit with who?" I deferred to Bill, naturally. Between the two or three of us sitting there, we did manage to come up with a roster of good bands. And I guess Allan then went out and hired them, and that gave him a week's breathing space to get the other things together. That's how I remember it starting. Then I went away to England and back next year, when Preservation Hall was fully operational because of Allan's business acumen. They threw him the ball and he ran with it.

Bill Russell helped around the edges, sweeping, offering his quixotic good cheer, being available for background chats, and working hard at interviews of musicians in connection with his job as curator of Tulane University's Jazz Archive. In September of 1962 he closed his record shop across the street and went to Missouri to take care of his ailing parents. Returning after they had passed away, in November 1964, he lived in Larry's building next door and would open up the Hall each night around eight o'clock.

Richard B. Allen was working days at the Jazz Archive, of which he would soon become curator. He had recommended Jaffe to Borenstein because he thought the Hall needed a businessman in charge. Allen's taste and dedication were valuable to the Jaffes in the first months. "Dick Allen used to come in and work the nights I was away at my Army Reserve meeting," Jaffe recalled. "He gave us an awful lot of help in contacting the musicians and seeing that the schedules were kept, and paying the musicians." But then, amid a general splintering of personalities and policies within the jazz community – and on a lawyer's advice – Allen withdrew from the Hall. In a 1967 memo he offered a taste of the kind of challenges facing anyone hoping to build bridges between the musicians' clannish old subculture and the modern commercial world:

During the days when the Jaffes took over Preservation Hall from Ken Mills there was a policy of hiring as many different bands and musicians as possible. Within a short time, perhaps two or three months, all the non-trumpet playing bandleaders began to hire [trumpeter] Kid Clayton. One week Clayton was scheduled for every night except one. At this time I was responsible for the signing of contracts, and helped set policy even though I would not become a partner. Jaffe had made me this offer, but I refused. I managed to get one bandleader to hire Ernie Cagnolatti, his regular trumpet man, instead of Kid Clayton. There was quite a bit of resistance on the leader's part and some bitterness. At this time Kid Clayton was having lip trouble, not being able to play one chorus without fluffing badly. He sang frequently to cover up. Why did the leaders hire him?

The policy of using a wider variety of bands and musicians, and of sticking to more conventional groupings, was spelled out in typed, mimeographed schedules distributed to the fans and musicians. "Boy, that's great," exclaimed devotee and cornetist Charlie DeVore in Minneapolis. "They really seem like sharp people, and they are essentially outsiders. They'll go into it with an objectivity that perhaps the others don't have down there. And they have all the right combinations. I tell you the first mailers I got from Allan Jaffe were just wonderful. Many of the bands were the same groupings used on the Riverside sessions in January of 1961." For example, the lineups for the last two weeks of September 1961 were as follows:

Punch Miller's Bunch . . . . .Tues., 19th
Peter Bocage & His Creole Serenaders. . . . Wed., 20th
Punch Miller's Bunch . . . . Thurs., 21st
Jim Robinson's Cosmopolites . . . . Fri., 22nd
Kid Thomas Algiers Stompers Sat.,23rd
Kid Clayton & His Happy Pals . . . . Sun., 24th
Peter Bocage & His Creole Serenaders. . . . Tues.,26th
John Casimir's Young Tuxedo Band Wed.,27th
Kid Howard's La Vida Band. . . . . Thurs., 28th
Percy Humphrey's Crecent City Joymakers. . Fri.,29th
Jim Robinson's Cosmopolites. . . . . .Sat., 30th
Kid Thomas' Algiers Stompers. . . . . .Sun., Oct 1st

Jaffe knew that, if the Hall was to survive on a permanent basis, it would have to become financially self-sustaining. For that to happen, overhead costs would have to be reduced. One of his first changes, therefore, was to use quartets instead of seven-piece ensembles three nights a week. Such so-called "short bands" were an old New Orleans tradition. Luckily, some fine quartets were available under leaders such as George Lewis and Willie Humphrey. Lewis happened to have been on tour in Europe when the Jaffes took over. But he was soon back, working two or three nights a week in the Hall in varied groupings, as did a few other popular musicians. A schedule from December 1962 shows how the rotation pattern had lengthened:

Kid Thomas & His Algiers Stompers . . . . Sat., 1st
George Lewis Quartet & Jim Robinson. . . . . Sun., 2nd
Punch Miller's Bunch . . . . Mon., 3rd
Sweet Emma & Her Jazz Band . . . . Tues., 4th
The George Lewis Quartet . . . . .Wed., 5th
Jim Robinson's New Orleans Band . . . . . . Thurs., 6th
Punch Miller's Bunch with George Lewis . . . Fri., 7th

Pianist Charlie Hamilton, born in 1904, played with the legendary Evan Thomas's Black Eagle band, circa 1927, but soon gravitated towards larger dance bands. Returning to basic jazz when it regained popularity in the 60s and 70s, he became a regular at the Hall and on tour.

Percy Humphrey's Crecent City Joymakers. . Sat., 8th
The George Lewis Quartet . . . . .Sun., 9th
Willie Humphrey's Hot Four . . . . Mon., 10th
Billie & DeDe Pierce with Louis Nelson. . .Tues., 11th
Peter Bocage & His Creole Serenaders . . . .Wed., 12th
Sweet Emma & Her Jazz Band . . . . Thurs., 13th
Kid Thomas & His Algiers Stompers . . . . . . Fri., 14th
The All-Stars with Jim Robinson, Kid
Howard, George Lewis, Joe Watkins,
Alcide Slow Drag Pavageau & Dolly
Adams . . . . Sat., 15th
Billie & DeDe Pierce . . . . Sun., 16th

Other ensembles appearing during this period, but not shown on the above schedules, included Creole George Guesnon's New Orleans Stompers, Paul Barbarin's Jazz Band, Bill Matthews' pick-up groups, and the Burke–Crawford–Ferguson Band, a white group that played occasional Sunday afternoon concerts. Add to these Kid Sheik's Storyville Ramblers, which included a number of the best men, but which, in late 1961, was out playing an extended gig at Cleveland's Tudor Arms Hotel, a job arranged earlier by Mills and Borenstein. There were regular meetings of the bandleaders to discuss affairs of common interest, such as hiring practices and union matters.

Soon after taking over, Jaffe closed the French doors on the river side through which most visitors had been entering the Hall directly. This was done partly to reduce the amount of sound escaping into still-residential St Peter Street, and partly to make crowd-handling more efficient. Henceforth Sandra Jaffe, or a friend named Ione Anderson, collected donations in a big wicker basket under the wrought-iron entrance to the carriageway adjoining the Hall proper – a system which would remain unchanged for more than a quarter century. For a while, Jaffe put up a sign there saying "Entrance," with an arrow. And for a month or two in the fall of 1961 he changed the name from "Preservation Hall" to "726 St Peter." At that point banjoist and singer Manny Sayles wrote a song about 726 St Peter; he later wrote another one about Preservation Hall.

*   *   *

Besides the schedules, the Jaffes continued to send out occasional mimeographed sheets, but in a more formal, dignified tone than had prevailed earlier – as in this example:

Mountains of memorabilia, letters, collectibles and instruments gradually accumulated in what became a private historical archive in the rear wing of Preservation Hall.

You Are Invited
To a
Birthday Party
In Honor Of
PAPA JOHN JOSEPH
Who Will Celebrate His 90th Birthday
Sunday Afternoon November 29th
at
Preservation Hall
2:00 p.m. to 5:00 p.m.

At 2 o'clock the Eureka Brass Band will
lead a parade through the French Quarter
to be followed by a party in the
Preservation Hall patio

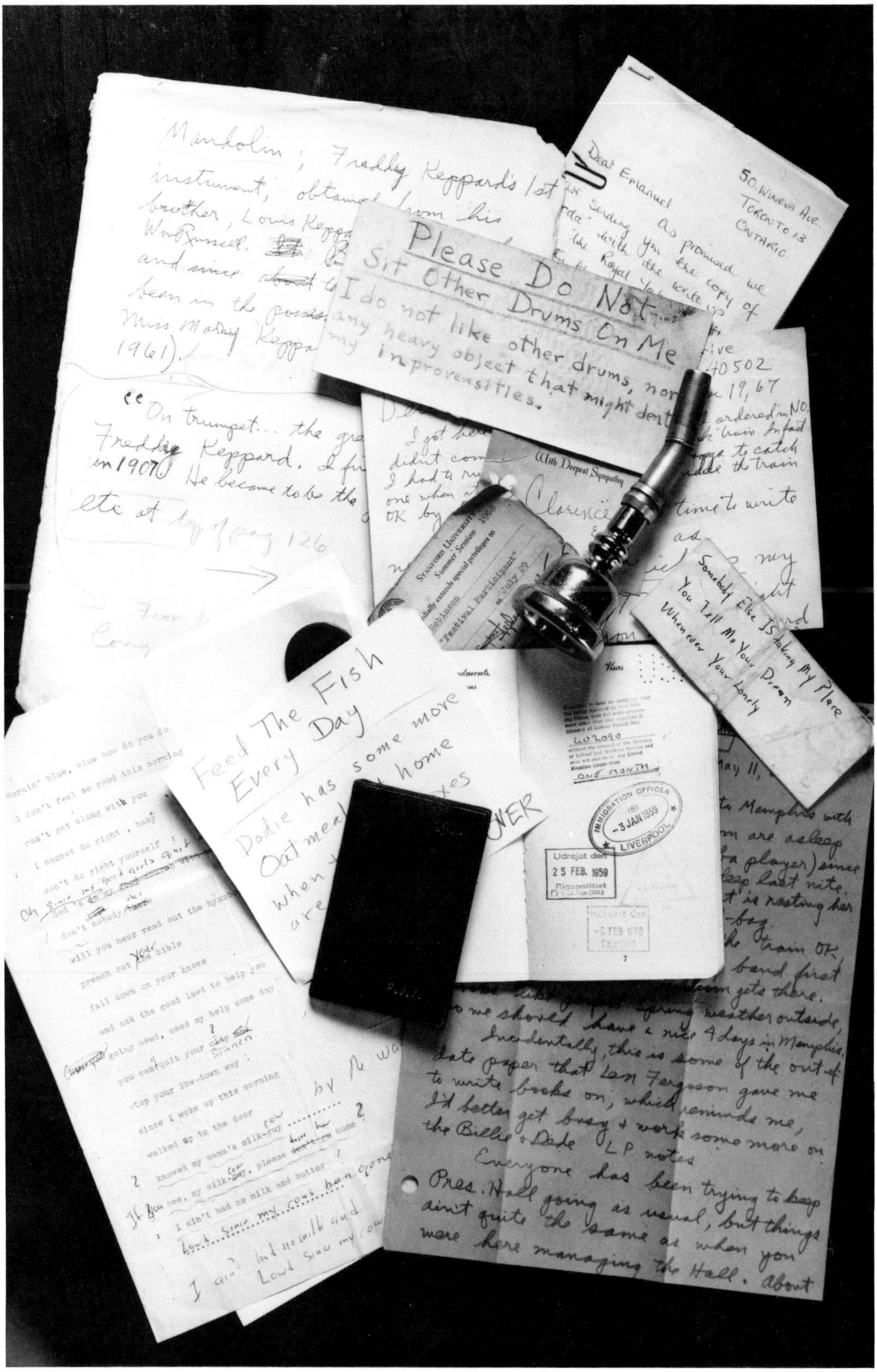
Please Do Not
Sit Other Drums On Me
I do not like other drums, nor any heavy object that might dent my improvensitiles.
Feed The Fish
Every Day
Dodie has some more
Oatmeal
Somebody Else IS taking My Place
You Tell Me Your Dream
Whenever Your Lonely
Dear Emanuel
50 Wineva Ave.
Toronto 13
Ontario
With Deepest Sympathy
Stanford University
Summer Session
Festival Participant
Immigration Officer
Liverpool
-3 JAN 1959
Udrejst den
25 FEB. 1959
Rigspolitiet
Mornin' blue, blue how do you do
I don't feel so good this morning
preach out your bible
fall down on your knees
and ask the good lawd to help you
stop your low-down way
since I woke up this morning
walked up to the door
Incidentally, this is some of the out of date paper that Len Ferguson gave me to write books on, which reminds me,
I'd better get busy + work some more on the Billie + Dede LP notes
Everyone has been trying to keep Pres. Hall going as usual, but things ain't quite the same as when you were here managing the Hall. About
"On trumpet... the
Freddy Keppard.
Mandolin; Freddy Keppard's 1st instrument,

Another flyer read:

JAZZ AT PRESERVATION HALL

Preservation Hall, located at 726 St Peter Street in New Orleans' French Quarter, celebrated its first anniversary June 10, 1962. The Hall presents Traditional New Orleans Jazz concerts every night, 8:30 – 12:30, featuring the legendary men of New Orleans who helped create the music we now call Jazz. Supported only by contributions, all the bands at Preservation Hall are paid union scale.

These musicians were not working in the city regularly for many years. The Hall was established to provide these much romanticized musicians with a place to play and be heard.

When Preservation Hall was started only four bands were playing there. Now the Hall presents more than 15 bands, a different band scheduled every evening. There are no drinks or food served. The people come in and sometimes find a seat on one of the few chairs or benches. Most people stand or sit on the floor. An estimated 1,500 –4,000 people come to the Hall weekly to hear these men play.

Managed by Allan and Sandra Jaffe, the Hall presents many famous New Orleans Jazzmen who have retained the spirit, inventiveness, drive and musicianship which is a mark of their music.

Preservation Hall also sponsors parades and concerts featuring the internationally famous Eureka Brass Band. It was also difficult to hear the Eureka, but now on a Sunday afternoon you can see and hear them winding their way through the French Quarter. There are also periodic special Sunday afternoon concerts and on some Sunday mornings New Orleans Gospel and Street Singers appear at Preservation Hall.

The earlier policy of no paid advertising was continued; Barbara Reid's activist style of media relations was dropped. Nevertheless, Preservation Hall still made good copy, and press interest continued to grow. In the waning months of 1961 the local papers carried at least four newsy items about the unique enterprise. And Don Marquis, a New Orleans jazz historian, wrote a Sunday supplement feature for Cleveland's main newspaper, the *Plain Dealer*, built around the Sheik band's appearance in that city. An earlier issue of the same paper had carried some lighter perspectives on the band.

National attention increased steadily. The Canadian jazz magazine *Coda* carried a long piece in

Mingling with members of the highly respected Eureka Band, circa 1965, was music critic John S. Wilson. His columns in the "New York Times" and elsewhere gave the Preservation Hall bands favorable coverage over three decades.

December 1961 about the general resurgence of jazz activity in New Orleans, beginning with the landmark series of Riverside recordings made by Herbert Friedwald eleven months earlier. The article described Preservation Hall carefully and intelligently, the only cautionary note being on a matter that would not cease to concern seasoned listeners:

> New Orleans jazz and the musicians who play it have always performed, primarily, to a dancing audience and this is the one drawback to Preservation Hall. There is the possibility of the music suffering when played to a listening audience, a large number of whom belong to the floating tourist trade that believe that jazz must be fast, noisy and flashy and that the performers are "clowns." The music is functional at dances and is natural. Fortunately, in almost all cases, the music has remained that way at Preservation Hall.

The *Coda* story also gave considerable space to the opening of the New Orleans Jazz Museum on Dumaine Street on November 12, 1961, with a parade by the Eureka Brass Band, and to extensive filming of the New Orleans jazz scene by NBC for "David Brinkley's Journal," an event which gave the Hall its first important national TV exposure.

The Jaffes in one of their countless press interviews: they always tried to keep the spotlight on the musicians, rather than on themselves. But many reporters were tempted to take the easier way, filing simplistic accounts of the youthful northerners who had "saved" the old-time players by "starting" the Hall.

In 1962 the half-dozen hometown stories on the Hall were outnumbered by news features in such faraway places as Duluth, Chicago and New Haven. Britain's *Manchester Guardian* carried a feature on the Eureka band, the Museum and Preservation Hall; the *Christian Science Monitor* ran a three-column spread on the Hall with a photo of Percy Humphrey. In an article in the *New York Times Magazine*, Pulitzer prizewinner Hodding Carter referred to "One of the truly great centers of American Jazz, Preservation Hall."

In 1963 local and regional items about the Hall continued to appear at about the same rate as before. But there was a swelling tide of interest in the national print media. *Town & Country*, *Cosmopolitan* and the *Christian Science Monitor* (again) all commented favorably on Preservation Hall. Even more significant were the reports in *Time*, *Downbeat*, *High Fidelity* and the widely distributed features service of the *Associated Press*. John S. Wilson's long, knowledgeable piece in the September issue of *High Fidelity* foreshadowed coming decades of his enthusiastic columns as the jazz reporter for the *New York Times*. On January 25, *Time* led off its show business section with an article half devoted to the brass band funeral of the powerful clarinetist John Casimir, and half to Preservation Hall. But in a weird clash of tone, *Time*'s warm, positive copy was undermined by whoever gave it its jingly, hostile subheads: (Widow's Wail; Lips That Fail; Rick-a-tick-tick for the Lately Sick).

In his long, sprightly *Associated Press* piece, Sid Moody walked a fine line between admitting that the music is often not what it was and celebrating the fact that "the old men (and a few women, too) can still play with a drive, swing, and, when the spirit is upon them, with a joyful exuberance all too rare." Much of this story was given over to a sensitive discussion of a new series on Atlantic Records entitled "Jazz at Preservation Hall"; the bottom line, which few buffs would contest, was that the Riversides of January 1961 were a lot better.

Charles Suhor's *Downbeat* article of January 17, 1963, was as wisely dimensional as anything written on the Hall, before or since. While not wholly accurate about events in the Mills era, it caught something of that elusive mix of ingredients which would continue to flavor the enterprise:

> Within a given month, as many as 50 of the reactivated jazzmen might be heard, from relatively well-known musicians like clarinetist George Lewis and trombonist Jim Robinson to figures virtually unknown outside of purist circles. . . . Jaffe began acting as an agent for the hall's bands on bookings and tours, bringing in money to keep the hall operating during the slack tourist season. (The Baton Rouge, La. Symphony Orchestra and Houston, Texas, Contemporary Arts Society were among those contracting for groups from the hall.) He also initiated record sales in the hall's patio [carriageway], but, true to the policy of nonhustling, the records are simply made available to visitors.
>
> The widespread recognition of the hall has not changed its essentially informal, productive atmosphere. A wider audience is being reached – including the social register, the college crowd, and an amalgam of personalities from Lucy Bird Johnson to Norman Thomas – but the admixture of rapport and respectfulness that always had characterized the hall's audiences remains. The musicians still play with a vigorous, unself-conscious abandon, reflecting their primary concern with musical expression and their lack of ensnarlment in commercial considerations.
>
> Jaffe is highly sensitive to the combination of human and musical elements that have determined the hall's

success. . . . However, it would be a mistake to view the current revival as a purist's paradise in which an idyllic past has been recaptured.

There is the palpable fact that many of the hall's musicians were not, and are not, important jazzmen. *Down Beat* reviewer Gilbert Erskine has pointed out the fallacy of the widespread romantic notion that any New Orleans musician owning a horn and playing street parades in the early 1900s must necessarily have been an important link in the chain of jazz history. . . . Moreover, even the best jazzmen show the effects of the failing lip, the wandering facility, and the shortened breath. It is a tribute to the strength of their conception that their art has a high degree of realization even though their technical problems are often severe. On a good night at the hall – and there are many – a group will communicate the essential jazz spirit despite the individual technical weaknesses of its members, indicating that the whole is indeed greater than the sum of its parts.

*   *   *

Despite such publicity, Preservation Hall remained financially precarious during the early 60s. Allan Jaffe continued to work at D. H. Holmes for the first two years; Sandra, too, had a job. They lived in the quarters adjoining the patio to the rear of the Hall proper. Many nights, Bill Russell, the Jaffes and helpers such as Gail Sams and Dodie Smith would sit on the benches in front of the band to make it look as if someone were there listening. If the kitty fell short of union scale, Jaffe made up the difference out of his own pocket. "Allan and Sandy worked hard," remembered Jaffe's mother, Fannie Jaffe, 25 years later. "I knew they were losing money. But when they went home at night they were happy." In the 80s Allan Jaffe reminisced, "I used to stand out on the street and not see people all night long. It was just a very different city. Now, we sometimes get more people in the first set than we used to have in a whole week." He had gone into the venture prepared to lose $1,500 if it came to it. Privately, Larry Borenstein had told Richard B. Allen (but not Jaffe) that he was prepared to bail Jaffe out if that proved necessary. It didn't. But it took almost two years of operating in the red before the enterprise became profitable.

Borenstein and Jaffe saw eye-to-eye in many ways, but differed about some, in which cases Jaffe

Jaffe sharing a happy moment with Harold Dejan (right) in the late 80s: Jaffe was a regular member of Dejan's scruffy-looking, commercially successful Olympia band, and the Olympia was hired one night a week at the Hall.

made his own decisions. Bill Russell later explained:

> Larry never had any financial interest in Preservation Hall. People thought Jaffe ran the place as a front for him which wasn't true at all. Larry used to come in there and he'd complain about things. Quite often Jaffe would take his advice, but Larry never did try to run the place. Jaffe turned down his ideas as often as not. Like putting up bleachers in back of the hall where the standing room is: Larry wanted to do that. As you notice, Allan didn't do it.
>
> At certain times Borenstein objected to certain people playing there, but for good reason I can guarantee you. And Jaffe out of friendship for Larry wouldn't hire them. Not that he was afraid of Larry. Larry gave Jaffe a lot of advice. He never had anything to do with the day-to-day running of it.

Borenstein had never believed it was possible to make money presenting jazz. "If I had, I would have done it myself," he said. Whereas Jaffe held staunchly to his belief that they should be selling only music, Borenstein kept urging him to "maximize" things: to try to use the music to sell other products. Indeed, Borenstein himself continued to use the Hall not only for his own esthetic enjoyment, but to sell paintings of the musicians, some of which were priced above $1,000. He was there almost every night, giving the impression he was at least partly in charge, and nabbing prospective clients for his other varied enterprises.

Borenstein, among others, remained pessimistic on the prospects for concert touring. Jaffe kept after it, however, and in the end was proved right. While attendance at the Hall itself grew gradually in the 60s, and swelled dramatically in the 70s, it would be the economics of touring that gave Preservation Hall its real financial backbone and brought quite a number of the wizened performers middle-class living standards on a regular basis for the first time in their long, hard lives. From the later 60s onward, stable and profitable relationships with booking agencies led to regularized national and international schedules, featuring three separate Preservation Hall bands in demanding tours which included some of the most famous concert halls in the world.

Unlike Ken Mills, who had liked to experiment with different musical combinations, and Borenstein, who was constantly thinking up new business angles, Jaffe was the kind of shopkeeper who never changed anything once it was working. A second grade teacher had confided to Jaffe's mother that, whereas some children were book-wise, this one was street-wise. Gifted at divining and channeling the flow of human affairs, Jaffe nurtured a remarkable synergy between the creaky little room on St Peter and commercial realities like TV appearances and the high-paying tours. Through that nurturing, Preservation Hall gradually acquired brand-name identity as a stable, beloved bit of Americana.

* * *

One key to the Hall's long-term prosperity was that Jaffe had, from the outset, sought to align his motives with those of the musicians themselves, rather than with the jazz aficionados' on the one hand, or the booking agents' on the other. This helped keep things at ground level, and to support that one-to-one directness, that sense of participation among performers and average listeners, which was the sort of social gumbo that had originally nurtured the music. Jaffe's instinct for this perhaps had to do with his growing up "right on the tracks," as he said, in two worlds but of neither – which is indeed how artists of many sorts live, and which can make them hard for other people to understand. He was tougher than nails in some ways, softer than butter in others. His relationships often had an ambiguous quality. He seemed always to want to flow from the heart but often not to be able to allow himself to. This made

Redoubtable bassist Chester Zardis, who had played with many of the all-time great New Orleans jazzmen since before World War I, came to the Hall soon after it opened and was still going strong until a few weeks before his death in 1990, three months after his 90th birthday.

some people feel uneasy in his presence. He was painfully sensitive to the whole process of giving and receiving favors and to his position as a protector of the musicians, his close family and the Hall's extended family – much of what his life was about. Late in his own life, Jaffe's father recounted how, as a young boy, Allan would often come home missing a sweater or another possession because he had given it to someone more in need of it.

Jaffe credited the musicians for their own success. In earlier decades, he pointed out, everyone knew that to be a New Orleans jazz musician was a poor way to make a living, despite amenities such as local status and plenty of partying. But among the surviving veterans, attitudes began to change – once they saw that the Hall was not the sort of uncaring, fly-by-

night operation they had long been accustomed to. While many of their buddies had died in the 40s and 50s from heavy drinking and related difficulties, those robust and lucky enough to have survived felt they were being offered one last chance. Given the possibility of decent jobs and respectful treatment, a number of the jazzmen stopped drinking altogether, or cut way back. It was a mark of their confidence in Jaffe's firm, dedicated efforts that 60- and 70-year-olds who had already tried going out on the road many times, only to be stranded or disappointed, were now willing to try it yet again – albeit for very little money at first.

In the mid-80s, Willie Humphrey said he had figured the Hall might last ten years at most. Why, then, had things turned out so much better? "Jaffe's management," he replied, "has been perfect." By 1985 bassist Chester Zardis, as old as the century, had seen plenty of jazz entrepreneurs come and go. Asked what he thought of Jaffe, Zardis replied, "He's the best man around here yet. Everybody likes to work for Allan." One hastens to add that Willie and Chester are among the two dozen or so key players who have benefited most from Preservation Hall. While their views are not universal, neither are they atypical.

Human nature being what it is, over the years one musician would be bad-mouthing Jaffe, while another scurried around during the day bringing him home-made pecan pies, while yet another accused that one of trying to play Stepin Fetchit instead of learning how to play or sing right. Several would point out that this boss was shrewd enough to keep alive the geese that were laying the golden eggs. Jaffe's college friends kept telling him he was crazy to waste his life on such an unpromising venture. Those closer to him saw how deeply, and intangibly, it was feeding him.

Each one is right.

Trumpeter-bandleader Percy Humphrey, a bedrock realist, put it this way in recounting the comeback of the irrascible pianist and singer, Sweet Emma Barrett:

> I used to go get people out of retirement – I knew they could play – and talk 'em into playin' again. Sweet Emma was one of 'em. She had retired, quit – disgusted. And I

went and got her. I say, "Come on, work with me."

"Agggh."

"Come on, try it, I need you."

Jaffe made Sweet Emma my boss, because she was a good drawing card, and she worked hard. Disagreeable, but a good mixer. She knew how to talk to people, and I kept her in front.

She would say, "How can I get in touch with you? Because I'm workin' every day." She didn't have anything else to do but sit at her phone. And insult the people. And don't you know a whole lot of people liked it? And she got along with them.

Even Jaffe, she done told him some rough stuff. [Percy does a squeaky-voiced imitation:] "I say I goin' talk to people that way." She didn't bite her tongue 'bout nothin' or nobody. And he [Jaffe] and his wife and some of the rest of the group practically nursed her back to health, or to life, 'cause she was almost dead. She was livin' there [in the rear quarters of Preservation Hall with the Jaffes].

[Percy imitates her voice with indistinguishable sounds like a crow:] "I won't give a . . . I won't even . . ." She wasn't happy 'til she got out. But after she got out, got well enough to maneuver working around a little bit, the boss put her back to work at the Hall. That's the kind of attitude that keeps this Dixieland stuff going: people that you work for, and they know you, they know what you can do, what you are capable of doin', and they continue giving you a chance. Allan Jaffe really gave her a new life.

The Jaffes in front of Preservation Hall in the mid-60s: Sandra took a less active role after their children were born, but returned to run the Hall in the late 80s.

Billie Pierce

Happy Inside
by Terry Rustin

Over three decades, the leading Preservation Hall band played nearly 100 concerts at Stanford University in California. The following article appeared in the student newspaper, the "Stanford Daily," in 1969:

Billie Pierce is not only one of the greatest living Dixieland piano bangers, she's also a fantastic gumbo cook. The same pudgy hands that smack out seven notes each beat on *Tiger Rag* worked all day Friday, cooking up a washtubful of real New Orleans gumbo over a Coleman stove for her "army" of music makers. "I couldn't be no cook, though, sugar," she disclaimed. "Too much work . . . 'sides, I already got a piano." But neither she nor her husband of over 40 years, hornman DeDe Pierce, are afraid of work. "I like to keep busy, ya know, honey?" says Billie. And DeDe told how he'd been a brickmason from his early teens until he lost his sight some ten years ago. "I'd work all day for my father – he was a builder, ya know – and playin' the bands at night. No, he didn't

like me trumpet playing. 'Waste of time.' Then I married a piano player. Hoowhee! He said, 'We ain't never gonna get no work done 'round here now.' He was right, too. You play 'til three, four in the morning, you ain't much good on the job next day."

DeDe is getting older, and it shows in the deep lines in his face. But his smile is still quick and happy, although he's often uncomfortable. Wednesday, he had a tooth extracted, and had to play the usual two concerts that evening with a swollen jaw. "Don't got but one trumpet player in the band," he laughed. Then, a bit pensively, "Got to have 'em all out, one of these days. Don't know how I'm goin' to play then, with dentures. I played pressure all my life, on my teeth, you know . . . but some fellas does it, I don't know how. Just have to learn, I guess."

Billie takes real fine care of DeDe, helping him into the shade, bringing him "somethin' cool." DeDe and I sat there while Billie peeled and chopped and stirred a myriad of things into her gumbo. Someone called out for us to make sure Billie was doing everything right. "I got my good eye on her!" DeDe announced. But Billie let us know who was boss. "Baby, when I'm kitchen mechanic, you just stay out of here. And take that off my table. I like to keep my table in order."

Into the gumbo went veal, beef, chicken, sausage, shrimps, crab, oysters, and an endless array of spices and vegetables. "I never could learn to cook," DeDe admitted, and Billie was quick to confirm it: "He can't even boil himself an egg." "Yeah, I've sewed and knitted and kept the house, but I never could get a cookin' license." Then a broad smile filled his face, and DeDe let out a sly chuckle. "Hey, Billie, remember on that bus, when the Band was travelin' on that bus through the mountains, with that storm and rain and wind?" "Yeah, baby, I remember." "Everyone was asleep, and I said, 'OK, I'll drive now.' And they all woke up, everyone! Hoowhee! 'My turn now,' I said. Boy, that sure woke 'em up!"

Billie and DeDe Pierce are real people, honest, open, and full of love. Their own lives have been hard ones, so now they are especially pleased to be able to bring gladness and music to people all over the world. "We been to Europe, oh yeah. Went to Rome. That was a real treat for me. Seven countries in 21 days. Copenhagen, Stockholm, all those places – we was there. Snow and ice outside, but boy was it happy inside!"

The gumbo was finally ready at about 4:30. How long do you cook gumbo? "Til it's done, sugar. You just got to be able to tell." Ten gallons of gumbo and ten pounds of rice, wine, bread, and crackers. "I'm done," Billie announced, turned off the flame, sat down and lit a cigarette. "Couldn't find no filé, but Jim (Robinson) still won't eat it. He only likes okra gumbo." She was right, too. Jim wouldn't touch her marvelous creation. "I only eat okra gumbo," he declared, but that didn't stop anyone else. "Billie, you're a doll." "Thank you, honey," she smiled, and her chuckle let us know that she appreciated the compliment. "I think I'll keep her for a few more years yet," DeDe decided. "Too much trouble finding another piano player."

Or another gumbo cook.

Onstage during a concert tour of the Middle West, circa 1970, Billie Pierce shares a light moment with Allan Jaffe.

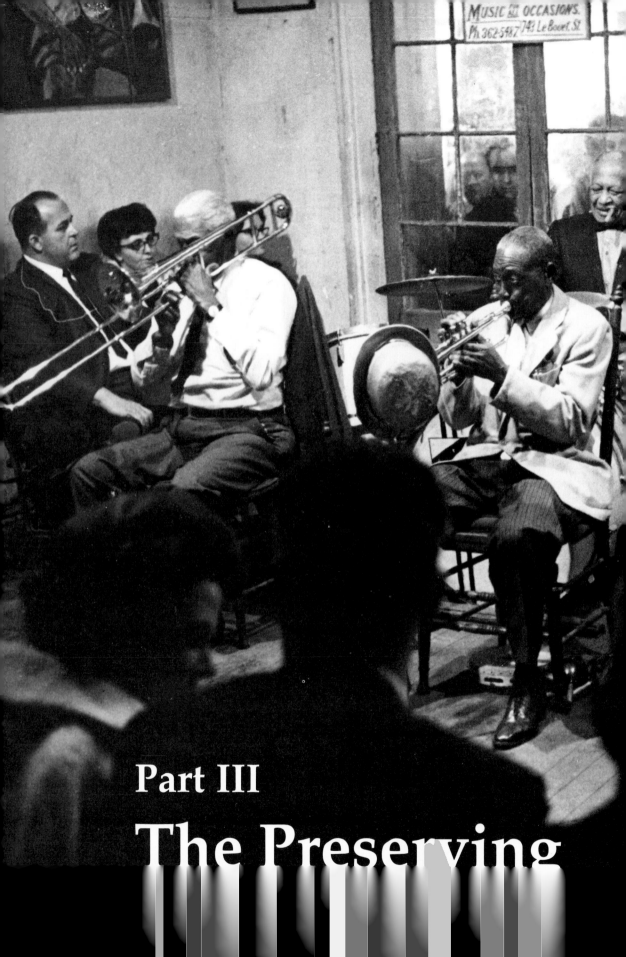

Part III
The Preserving

Chapter Six

HALLELUJAHS AND HUMBUGS

"Come on over! Come on over!"
—*Billie and DeDe Pierce*

Unparalleled in the history of jazz, the longterm success of Preservation Hall took place in a context of rising demand, shrinking supply and able management. Like other artistic products, authentic New Orleans jazz, as it became rarer, was assigned greater "market value." Demand was stimulated by exposure to wider audiences, increasing tourism to New Orleans and America's revaluing of her ethnic and cultural roots. By the 80s, however, management would be facing some challenges – the toughest being the gradual passing away of the irreplaceable older players on whom the Hall had built its reputation.

Part of the magic was the Hall *per·se*. Its "non-commercial" atmosphere proved increasingly attractive to visitors from a society being steadily engulfed by shopping centers and mass entertainment. The role of the Hall as a kind of subtle theater was not lost on Borenstein and Jaffe. Although many of the veterans themselves would have preferred to make their comeback in a more "spruced-up" setting, Jaffe wisely never forgot his first impression of 726 St Peter: to a northeastern college boy, it had evoked the romantic atmosphere in which jazz had been born. And for the next 25 years he

The zesty sense of life expressed by the older generations of New Orleans players was epitomized by Jim Robinson. While the formal simplicity of his style was widely copied, Robinson's emotional immediacy -- ranging from hoarse joy to whispering tenderness, and from sly teasing to outright anger -- sprang from a social and musical alluvium which few moderns could assimilate.

meticulously changed nothing whatsoever about the place. If people chose to believe nothing had changed in 75 or 200 years, that was fine with Jaffe. He wanted to let visitors feel they had happened onto something intriguing and wonderful. No signs revealed whether the Hall was even open. The mystique was heightened by other deliberate ambiguities.

If this was shrewd, it was not cynical. Both Borenstein and Jaffe loved the French Quarter's historic structures, wonderful food, quirky people and mysterious atmosphere. They disliked media hype and fancy improvements – and ran the Hall accordingly. It saddened Jaffe to see the wonderful old French Market truncated and sanitized to make room for a new tourist version; he gave the example of its famous meat market being replaced by a statue of the butchers. That was exactly the kind of theme-park improvement he would not permit at 726 St Peter. Too many well-meaning locals had always wanted to treat the city's traditional music as a relic and consign it to the past. The jazz played at the Hall, he believed, was contemporary music. Like the musicians, he was not so much interested in "preservation" as in ongoing life, activity, commerce. Indeed, the music became much less like what had been heard in earlier decades than many visitors assumed. And Jaffe's comment on why he finally bought the premises in 1984 was entirely in character. Despite a $600,000 price tag that he knew was excessive, "I bought it because I could afford it," he said, "and because I didn't want the landlord telling me when to close my business."

Although it lacked a dance floor, the Hall was a good place to hear the music. Partly because of its steadily growing reputation as the mecca of traditional jazz, audiences were extremely receptive. They listened and watched, instead of talking and clinking glasses and being forced to buy drinks. The acoustics were good – rather intimate. However, among the large crowds of later years it would be difficult to hear soft passages or soft bands, and particularly the unamplified piano, from anywhere except in the very front. The players did as they wished. Jaffe was wise enough to know that the older generations of New Orleans musicians needed no stage directing to appeal directly to people's hearts. Their natural warmth was entirely unforced – as if this were a private affair rather than a show. Jaffe often said that he thought of it as a nightly party. In these ways the Hall carried some of the feeling of the music's earlier, informal settings.

In other ways, of course, it did not. By the early 1970s, at least, the French Quarter audiences were comprised of tourists rather than locals. Most came only as onlookers for one set, 30 or 40 minutes, rather than participating all evening as had patrons of the old dance halls or steamer excursions. Race was not the barrier it had been before the civil rights revolution of the 60s. Nor was there the same kind of cut-throat, price-cutting competition for jobs. Wages were consistently higher than union scale. Another difference, after the early years, was that management, rather than the bandleaders, did most of the hiring of individual musicians. Regular players were guaranteed a night or two a week, virtually for as long as they made themselves available. If this sometimes made for feeble playing, it also enhanced the visual theater and acted as a kind of hedge against the inexorable losses due to sickness and death.

Spanning two worlds, Frank Parker grew up within the basic New Orleans jazz culture but spent much of his professional career working with such rhythm-and-blues artists as Fats Domino, Ray Charles and Johnny Otis. Returning to New Orleans and traditional jazz in 1970, he gradually became a mainstay at Preservation Hall, succeeding Cie Frazier as the regular drummer with the Percy Humphrey band.

A "drummers' drummer," Louis Barbarin was considered by some to be even better than his more famous brother, Paul. Having begun before World War I, he played with virtually all the historic New Orleans bands from the 20s to the 80s – notably those of Desvigne, Celestin and, in the last years of his life, Preservation Hall.

The more the world around it changed, the more charmingly anachronistic this funky place seemed. The louder were the speakers along brassy Bourbon Street, the more authentic and honest this unamplified music sounded. The slicker nostalgia advertising and video cassettes became, the more disarming were six or seven septuagenarians wearing baggy pants and unmatched shirts, carrying battered cases, shuffling or being helped in, both here and on some of the world's most prestigious concert stages. The stiffer the admission prices at Pete Fountain's or Al Hirt's joints, the happier patrons were to wait in long lines along the sidewalk, drop their dollar or two into the wicker basket, slip a dime into the Coke machine (until it was finally removed), stand or sit on the floor, and buy a record from hoary Bill Russell, authenticity personified as he perched near the dozing cat on a stool as rickety as the building itself.

Preservation Hall marked the unremarkable: in our era, the ordinary has become extraordinary. It testified, as well, to the resilience and adaptability of a music that had sunk to a nadir by 1960. If this product of an all but vanished subculture had once been functional in terms of taxi dances, crab boils and cornerstone layings, it had now proven functional in terms of the mass society.

* * *

Jaffe could be sharp and sarcastic when he felt the situation warranted. But he also gradually built up a worldwide network of warm associations which helped make the Preservation Hall carriageway and sidewalk a stimulating social crossroads not only for traditional jazz lovers, but for individualists in many fields, particularly the arts. He took a kind of covert delight in introducing people who, as he said, "should know" each other. This spontaneous sort of networking, while it might yield few immediate or direct benefits, fostered the Hall as a center of energy and synergy, of helping and being helped.

Over the years many people, from photographers to party-givers, from doorkeepers to doctors, gave of their time and interest to a degree and with a spirit that no straight commercial enterprise could ever match. Jaffe's natural talents as entrepreneur included sensing whom to trust and encourage within the widening ripples of this Preservation Hall "family." Some, especially musicians, were admitted free. Some could count on a rustic place to stay when they were in town. Musicians might be steered to needed jobs or invited to accompany the Olympia Band in a parade.

When Hurricane Camille blew saxophonist John Handy's house off its pillars, a group of volunteers, including an architect, spent two weekends setting it right. One day in the early 60s, an Englishman named Richard Knowles discovered Chinee Foster sitting in Congo Square, down at the heels, long out of work, and wishing he could get back to playing drums again as he had decades before under famous leaders like Buddy Petit and Papa Celestin. Knowles turned him over to the Jaffes, and they helped him to rehabilitate himself – Allan being tough with him, Sandra being kind and compassionate. Other networking functions, such as visits to indigent musicians and their families, overlapped long-established local customs, the Hall merely playing a catalytic role.

One "super fan," a striking middle-aged blonde named Stella Webb, attended so long and faithfully that a special gold chair, with a red velvet seat and a gold fringe, was finally set out for her. Remembering the lean, early years, when she had sometimes comprised the entire audience, Webb said, "I was there every night. I heard all of the old, old musicians there, and I have seen many of them die, and I've loved every one of them. There was not one of them that I didn't, and they knew it, too. Yes, I dearly loved them. And of course we told everyone we possibly could about it." One evening Webb called long distance and the band left the stand to go out into the carriageway and play into the telephone for her. The audience was no less mystified by this than other audiences have been by equally strange doings, such as some curmudgeonly bandsman suddenly shouting and waving away a non-existent tape recorder.

Dodie Smith Simmons, a black Orleanian, also discovered the Hall in the early 60s. She was then a student and a staff worker for CORE, one of the groups active in the civil rights struggle going on across the South. Before long the beautiful young lady was getting to know the jazzmen, and supplementing her meagre income by working at the gate. The Hall's commitment to the black vernacular music of New Orleans included support for the civil rights movement. Lawyers and other activists, fresh from the battle lines, frequently came to New Orleans to regroup and relax. They sometimes used parts of the Hall, and of Borenstein's other buildings, as havens where they could throw down their sleeping bags and confer without fear of being bugged.

Yet it was typical of the ironic crosscurrents of the era that some of Simmons' fired-up young friends accused her of being "Uncle Tom" because of her fondness for the older players and for a style of music identified with the "bad old days." She stood her ground. Having grown up hearing New Orleans jazz played at parades and picnics, she accepted it as something wonderful that was "just here, part of New Orleans." Like other friends of the Hall, Simmons saw the musicians, not through political or social filters, but as the vibrant human beings they were. After school, she often found herself heading for Billie and DeDe Pierce's humble dwelling:

The minute they saw you it was "Come on in!" They cooked like they were cooking for 20 people. They didn't

Dodie Smith Simmons was one of the dozen or more helpers-out who remained close to the Hall for four decades. Working at the front gate, visiting the sick, answering the phone, traveling worldwide to assist the musicians, devotees like Mrs Simmons lent a consistent, caring warmth to a business that was always more than a business.

have much money, but they always made you feel welcome. When people came from out of town and wanted to meet them, they'd say, "Come on over! Come on over!" They'd just make everybody feel like they'd love them forever. I used to go by Billie's house because she'd sing all the dirty songs – the ones she didn't sing at the Hall. But Kid Thomas was my all-time favorite. He was like a father to us girls. If he didn't like the guy we were going out with, he'd tell us, "That guy ain't no good. He don't mean you no good. Stay away from him." He'd come up and cook for us sometimes, red beans and rice. And he would talk to us and give us advice. Ten times out of ten, he was right.

*   *   *

Another of the Hall's roles as a "mecca" was to help New Orleans-style musicians from around the world tie into the basic lineage of jazz and brass band performance. Many had listened intensively to the music on recordings, but needed to imbibe those all-important subtleties which can only be acquired through direct exposure to the living roots.

Globe-trotting Preservation Hallers inspired countless trad jazzmen throughout the world, and particualrly in Europe. Here, Louis Nelson (right), who often appeared as a guest star with foreign bands, traded licks with Doggy Hund, leader of the Maryland Jazz Band of Cologne, Germany.

Knowledgeable helpers like Dodie Simmons began organizing after-hours jam sessions which gave the visitors a chance to play with some of the veterans. At the same time, such get-togethers sometimes helped rusty local men get their "chops" back and be heard again. As with the social networking, the custom long predates the Hall and continues quite independently. This impulse to "put something back in the pot" – passing along what was once passed to you – springs from deep within the subculture that produced jazz. Some of the most prominent of the older musicians, such as trombonist Louis Nelson and banjoist/guitarist Danny Barker, were long known for giving generously of their time and interest to the younger generation.

After the early 70s these gatherings, both public and private, happened most often in the spring, when many revival players and fans were in town for the French Quarter Festival and the New Orleans Jazz and Heritage Festival. But the 60s and early 70s were *the* years for musical cross-fertilization, because so many of the older players were still alive and vigorous. The following note by Richard B. Allen illustrates the Hall's catalytic role (Wilson, Edegran and Sancton were talented young white players; the others, except Jaffe, were black veterans):

Saturday afternoon, the 23rd of October, 1965, there was a jam session organized by Clive Wilson and Lars Edegran. Included in the band, which played at Preservation Hall, were Clive Wilson, tp; Lars Edegran, p; Tommy Sancton, cl; Eddie Summers and Jim Robinson, tb; Alex Bigard, dm; Allan Jaffe, helicon; Slow Drag Pavageau, b; and possibly a banjoist or guitarist. All of the musicians did not play together at one time. However, there were some trombone duets which Clive Wilson seemed to enjoy. There is a possibility of Jaffe's arranging for this band to appear in a movie, as the director overheard them by accident. According to Clive Wilson, Jaffe will probably change the personnel.

* * *

"You Europeans have funny ideas about jazz!" erupted the normally soft-spoken Dodie Simmons one night to an English jazz writer. She was collecting money at the gate. "Would it surprise you to learn that no black jazz musician in New Orleans has ever played jazz for fun? Black musicians in New Orleans play jazz for money. They always have, still do, and probably always will. Jazz has always been one way out of the ghetto. That's why so many black musicians have left New Orleans over the years. If the money looks better some place else, away they go."

Well aware of this fact of life, Jaffe directed his marketing efforts not to the jazz specialists, but to the general public – with the result that the idealistic buffs were sometimes puzzled by his decisions. In the sensitive matter of replacing an older musician who has passed away, for example, few realized how much consulting Jaffe did with the other band members, or the degree to which their counsel was affected by factors other than pure esthetics. As in many fields, one almost needs to have been there oneself to appreciate the difference between the producer's and the consumer's points of view.

While Dodie Simmons may have overstated the case (there had always been informal sessions, "rehearsals," unpaid rituals, etc.), she had a right to straighten out the starry-eyed Englishman. Among other things, her husband, John, happened to be an English trumpeter active in the booming resurgence of jazzy brass parade bands. John Simmons felt he might never have come to New Orleans in the 60s had it not been for Preservation Hall. Lars Edegran, a busy bandleader, felt much the same way:

> I think Preservation Hall has had a very big impact on all us young musicians who came here. I don't think a lot of us would have come here if it weren't for Preservation Hall. Without Preservation Hall a lot of those old guys wouldn't have been playing, at least not where you could find them. When I first came to New Orleans, it was really a focal point where we'd go every day. I basically learned to play from Preservation Hall – from listening to all those guys, and sitting in with them.

The place has been a nerve center, as well, for countless other musicians who came to town periodically, then carried their "lessons" back home. Among those who developed their own relationships with one or another veteran were cornetist John Paddon and his lady, singer Lulu White. They, in turn, welcomed many of the Orleanians to White's warm home in Boston, England. Paddon's playing showed how deeply he had imbibed the New Orleans feeling. He said:

> It is my firm belief that you cannot learn to play New Orleans music by listening to records. You just cannot get the idea of it. I never started to play anything like New Orleans music until I started to play with guys from New Orleans. They're expressing their beliefs, their way of life, and until you know what it is, you can't begin to express it or get the same feeling. The European guys try to twiddle their notes faster than the guy next door, or blow a bit louder, or play things a bit quicker: there's no cooperation.
>
> The first New Orleans guy I ever played with was Polo Barnes. The first tune we played, I was playing the lead after my fashion, and he was playing around me with his clarinet. Everything was fitting so wonderfully, and I thought, "Go ahead and just play." I went for a phrase, got nearly there, and I knew I couldn't get the top note. He put it in for me! And quite naturally. He knew damned well I wasn't going to finish it off, so he just came in and finished it off and made it one whole piece. From then on, I began to realize what these guys were doing.
>
> Alton Purnell [a well-known pianist and singer who was apparently born in Preservation Hall] put Lulu on the road to singing. He spent all one Sunday at our claptrap piano, telling Lulu how to sing. He said, "You're not an opera singer – forget the singing. You're telling a story to someone. Tell it to them; take an interest in it."

While much of the learning happened informally, a few of the veterans actually gave lessons. Clarinetist George Lewis was one; drummer Cie Frazier was another. English-born drummer Trevor Richards would never forget the ways Frazier put his teachings across:

The whole thing would revolve around certain numbers that Cie would play for you. He'd sing the numbers and play the drum part. In other words, he'd be introducing you into the correct way to accompany certain numbers as a drummer. Being a great musician and a good reader, he knew how the parts went. He'd sit down and say, "Now you play it." He'd play it and sing it, and he'd talk about playing the beat and certain little variations.

Cie Frazier's style was definitive, his lineage deep, his lilting sweetness a gentle cover for crisp rhythmic discipline. Rare among jazz percussionists of any era was his constant awareness of the band's overall sound and of the architecture of each tune. He was the quintessential Preservation Hall drummer.

And then in the evening when he was playing with Billie and DeDe Pierce, for example, in the Hall, he'd say, "Come and sit in," and he'd be sitting beside you, watching you, and as soon as you did something he didn't like, he'd reach around you and start to hold your hands with the sticks and say, "No, like this." He'd make it like a lesson with the Hall full of tourists watching and wondering what the hell's going on! It was really embarrassing if you did something wrong, and he'd step in and start telling you how to do it.

While many out-of-towners only pick up some of the surface features of New Orleans jazz, which they may or may not retain, the English clarinetist Sammy Rimington Sr was one of those who imbibed the teachings on a spiritual level:

George Lewis had said if you ever come to New Orleans, visit me and my daughter, Shirley. And I came the following year – April or May of 1961. I was 19. I'd never been to America in my whole life, and it was like a dream come true. The first place I went was Preservation Hall. It was the only place I was related to the music. I introduced myself to Allan Jaffe. Allan had a Lambretta scooter then, and he said, "I'll take you around the streets." He showed me Burgundy Street, St Philip Street, Bourbon Street, Dumaine – all the names from all the tunes on the records – but when you actually see the streets you relate to it completely differently. It's more magical, somehow.

It was difficult to play with the musicians then, because of segregation, but Allan said to me, "Kid Thomas is at a private party over across the river. If you want to go along, you're welcome." Later, I actually played with the Kid Thomas band for a wedding. It was just my two weeks' vacation, but, oh! It was incredible.

Preservation Hall looks exactly the same in 1985 as in 1961. It's pure acoustic music, no amplification, but let's face it, it's more touristic now. I went down there the other night. The place was packed. It was cozy, the people were happy, you could have a blow, a sit-in – fantastic! It'll always have that, I think. It's calm, magical. It's got some charisma.

I felt something from George Lewis that is inseparable. You can't lose it. It's there, forever, as long as I live: part of him.

When I think of all the guys I knew that are dead – they had a completely different philosophy on playing. It was an older style, a thing that's almost lost, a lost art. There are young guys inspired by it. You got to get to the roots.

*   *   *

The other side of the coin is that, while note-for-note copying of the style of a revered musician may be a useful learning aid, no true New Orleans musician ever ends up sounding like the clone of another. While they respect lineage, they always encourage the younger players to "be your own man." Trombonist Jim Robinson, for one, resented hearing his own parts imitated, at least by those who were

Like scores of other Preservation Hall sidemen, drummer Dave Oxley was rarely in the spotlight. Yet he projected a wonderful enthusiasm and laid down the beat with an assurance gained from decades of experience playing in road shows with such legendary figures as Bessie Smith, Ida Cox and Chris Kelly.

becoming professionals and hence competitors. Sensitive listening will usually detect a forced quality, something insincere, a lack of realization, in a musician who spends his life trying to be almost as good as another. Imbibing the "lessons of the master" means arriving at inner freedom and individuation. Trumpeter Percy Humphrey, who knew Louis Armstrong from a young age, was able to receive this lesson properly:

We used to play on the 30th of May, a day they used to call Grand Army Day in Chalmette, Louisiana, at a cemetery where the soldiers were buried. My grandfather used to bring members of his orchestra to entertain the public down there. Louis, and certain others, were in the Jones home [the waifs' home]. We would take the intermission, and they would come from another road, way across the back end of the cemetery, and we would hear 'em wailin',

Off-hour uses of the Hall as a catalyst for encouraging related musical activities included, particularly during the spring "Jazzfest," late-late private sessions for musicians from around the world. In this 1984 set, an Australian trumpeter led an impromptu jam session of Europeans, Asians and Americans (left to right): Luciano Invernizzi (trombone), Soren Houlind (drums), Geoff Bull (trumpet), ?Don Heap (bass), Thomas L'Étienne (clarinet), unknown (piano), Junichi Kawai (banjo) and Lillian Boutté.

comin' to us. I been knowing Louis and a whole lot of the jazz musicians ever since then. They were older than I was, and I wasn't doin' anything but beatin' on the tambourine. Louis and I always got along fine, and every time he would come to New Orleans, he come at our front room, and play something for my grandfather. I'd be right there listening, and when I get a chance I'd be talkin' with him.

[Later, playing occasional Mississippi River excursion trips in bands opposite Louis:] Every time that particular ship would come up, the promoter would hire me to play with whatever band he had. And on one of the occasions, Louis told me, "Don't try to imitate me or nobody else. Do your best to develop a style of your own. Play to satisfy yourself, and the people you playing for." He said, "Don't worry about what anybody else thinks. Only the people you workin' for, and the people you playin' to, and you happy with it. So let it stay that way. Do your best. Always do the best you possibly can."

See? And I thank him, and every time he would see me, he'd say [growling], "Yeah, heah, ehhhh! I hear you!" Say, "You doin' okay!" That's all he'd say. We'd shake hands, and any time he was anywheres close where I could see him and talk to him, I'd do so.

A certain sanctimonious mist tended at times to float around Preservation Hall. Perhaps inevitable, given its mecca-roles, and perhaps related to the quasi-religious fervor of some segments of the revival movement, the pink clouds were relatively harmless. But the place was really too dynamic to need them. It became many things to many people. For some visitors, it was a place to get your picture taken or have a record autographed. For others it presented a chance to engage in sentimental "Crow Jimism" – an inverse bias that assumes any musician who is old and black and from New Orleans must be good. For some foreign musicians it was a shrine at which to perform ancestor worship and receive some sort of implied certification.

Most local jazzmen, on the other hand, simply appreciated the Hall because it was a better place to work than Bourbon Street. Again, when at one point somebody asked Louis Armstrong what jazz was, he said simply, "It's what I do for a living."

Nor was Preservation Hall the be-all and end-all of traditional jazz. By the late 80s there was far more of it being heard, both at home and around the world, than when Larry Borenstein began holding his informal sessions. But while the Hall played an important role, especially in keeping the "pioneers" working, it would be a mistake to identify it too closely with that broad, rising current of activity. Neither did the music played at the Hall set any particular norm of quality or authenticity. Jaffe believed that there had never been any such thing as "pure" New Orleans jazz, except in the minds of individual listeners, each with his or her own idea of the correct way to play. The jazz heard back in the Storyville dance halls, or on Bourbon Street, or in the Hall, or at dozens of festivals around the US and Europe, had always evolved from year to year – even from day to day. Preservation Hall was established to sponsor a certain group of inspiring musicians. As they passed away, it tried to fill the ranks with compatible replacements. But it never claimed to be definitive.

* * *

Is it the climate? New Orleans does have its halcyon days, often in October. The music, too, has its sweet and gentle passages. And in one way or another the

players are constantly expressing a lot of love. Helping each other is a longstanding tradition. Manny Crusto, for instance, who was not only an accomplished brass and reed player but also an excellent instrument repairman, was known for having fixed many of his friends' horns for little or no money.

But: for much of the year New Orleans is alternately hot and sticky, cold and dank. Whether it's this, the emotional demands of the music, or whatever, the city and/or its music have always seemed to breed bad-mouthing, disagreements, even out-and-out fights. Known locally as "humbugs," these are as likely to erupt right on the bandstand as anywhere else. In the Preservation Hall back room, a dimunitive 75-year-old banjoist swung a jug of wine at an 85-year-old clarinetist twice his size. Backstage in a theater during a Preservation Hall band tour of the Soviet Union, two septuagenarians had forcibly to be pulled apart. Drummer-bandleader Barry Martyn, having taken many of the veteran

On a concert stage near San Francisco in the early 70s, one listener startled band and audience alike by leaping up to dance around Jim Robinson -- who clearly loved it. In an interview published in "The Jazz Record" in 1945, Robinson had spoken of the sort of exchange that is close to the heart of New Orleans jazz: "I enjoy playing for people that are happy. I like to see people happy. If everyone is in a frisky spirit, the spirit gets to me and I can make my trombone sing. If my music makes people happy, I will try to do more. It is a challenge to me. I always want people around me. It gives me a warm heart and that gets into my music. When I play sweet music, I try to give my feelings to the other fellow. That's always in my mind. Everyone in the world should know this. If we really love our music, we would be more happy and friendly. Just keep living and loving your music and keep no evil in your heart."

jazzmen on tour, confirmed that such humbugs are common:

They squabble all the time about nothing. There's nobody in the world like New Orleans musicians. The way they play – the way they put their personalities over – it's like shit or bust. The people always love them, because everything's up front, all out in front for the world to see, including all the squabbling and nonsense. King Oliver once told my trombone player, Clyde Burnhart, "Look, man. The biggest tip I'm ever gonna give you: don't ever hire more than two New Orleans musicians in a band at the same time. If you get a third one in there, they'll be fighting and squabbling and God knows what."

I saw one of them at Preservation Hall the other day cussing the audience out. Only in New Orleans would you find it. In New York, or in Chicago, when you hire a band, they never open their mouth; they just play what they got to do. That's what makes New Orleans music so great. To hell with techniques and all that: it's a human emotion. Everything's out front with them. They get contrary – goofy. So many crazy things happened in Europe. And in Preservation Hall, this one drummer got in an argument with the bass player, and so he turned all his drums to face the carriageway, so he wouldn't look at him. Went to all that trouble! Who cares, you know? Another drummer got mad one night with people looking in the window, and started cussing at the people, shaking his fist at them. People outside? What the hell, they ain't hurting nothing.

Nor is this form of Louisiana hot sauce confined to the musicians. Once, Allan Jaffe tried long and hard to heal a rift between Borenstein and someone important to the Hall. Borenstein finally told Jaffe to stop trying, because "I've already got too much of an investment in disliking her."

Jaffe himself did not remain immune to the city's old factional rivalries. For generations, a bevy of jazz institutions which clearly should have been working together more often engaged in covert warfare: the Jazz Club, the Jazz Archive, Preservation Hall, the Louisiana State Archives, the Jazz and Heritage Festival, the Jazz Museum, Louis Armstrong Park, the Tourist Commission and others. For the good of the musicians and the music, Jaffe and others worked to foster better relations and more viable solutions, but with only limited success. Indeed, Jaffe was street fighter enough never to allow his own scars quite to heal. He vented some of his permanent peeves to writer Tom Bethell in 1974:

Although born in New Orleans, Preston Jackson moved to Chicago at the age of 14. Probably for this reason his playing showed less of the rugged brass-band fundamentalism than that of the Crescent City's "tailgaters." From the 20s into the 40s he worked with leading northern bands including transplanted New Orleans greats such as Johnny Dodds and Jimmie Noone. Finally reverting to his roots, Jackson returned to New Orleans, where he appeared often at Preservation Hall in the 70s and early 80s.

I asked Allan Jaffe what the attitude of the New Orleans jazz "establishment" was when Preservation Hall opened up. "About the same as it is today," he replied with something resembling a grimace, implying that that attitude had not always been too friendly. "When Sweet Emma started playing at the Hall," he said, "someone in the New Orleans Jazz Club told her that it would ruin her reputation. And when David Brinkley was down here, doing his program on New Orleans jazz early in 1962, he went to the Jazz Club, and everyone told him that they were the ones who were saving jazz, and that no one else was interested in saving it. So Brinkley asked them, "What about Preservation Hall?" It had only been going for a few months then. Do you know what Dr Edmond Souchon, who was the most important man in the club then, told Brinkley? He told him that we were Communists."

In some ways, Jaffe feels, the Jazz Club hasn't changed much in the past decade. "Why," he asks, "when they moved the Jazz Museum from the Sonesta Hotel over to Conti Street recently, did they have an all-white band for the occasion? I mean, they had Kid Ory's trombone and some white kid blowing it. Then they had to get someone to cut a ribbon. So I said, "Why not use Booker T. Glass?" He is just about the oldest musician left in the city. But no, they had to get some official from City Hall."

The humbug background is worth keeping in mind when considering some of the challenges and complaints faced by Preservation Hall over the years. Success, of course, always invites criticism, and the Hall's unique formula also involved some special dilemmas. But minor resentments that would be easily shrugged off anywhere else were carefully stoked and tended for decades in the steamy hothouse of the French Quarter.

There were always mutterings around the general issue of control. Long accustomed to dealing with local club owners, steamboat magnates and such, the older musicians generally respected and appreciated the kind of strong-willed leadership that came naturally to Borenstein and Jaffe. Yet these same players greatly valued their own independence. They grew up scuffling for short-term jobs, making short-term commitments and maintaining certain prerogatives, such as collecting tips. Although inexperienced at first, Jaffe came to understand and honor their lifeways, partly through his participation as a musician himself in the brass bands.

On the other hand, he and Borenstein were doing something that had never been done before, and which was therefore bound to cause at least some friction. Although the two of them always remained close, they disagreed on a key issue: Borenstein felt that the Hall should sign longterm, exclusive contracts with the musicians, whereas Jaffe felt that such agreements would not only violate their traditions but prove unenforceable. Jaffe was in charge, and he did it his way: the musicians remained independent contractors, free to take any other job after completing a tour or a night's work. And they did.

But the situation was not quite that simple. Jaffe would not have been as successful as he was if his marketing instincts had not included a vital element of longterm strategy. The Preservation Hall concept hinged on a certain group of players, and it was important to be able to rely on at least the most prominent of them to some degree. Loyalty and consistency were particularly important for the tours, which were scheduled far in advance.

The kernel of Jaffe's genius as entrepreneur was his ability to mediate profitably between an old, individualistic, impacted, charming subculture and today's mass commercial society. His mediation included tender concern at some junctures, bluntness at others. One has to have felt Jaffe's anger to know its power. More often, he held it in reserve, using his forceful personality to establish the implicit controls that he felt were necessary. Although truly generous, and a man of few words, he could be rough on anyone he saw as a phony, or as seriously undermining the Hall. In the process a few niceties tended to fall through the cracks. This is true of any efficiently run business. But the Hall was so often perceived in idealistic, unbusinesslike terms that some onlookers and players were offended.

An early challenge came in the form of the rival "kitty halls" – nearby jazz rooms established by Ken Mills and others, more or less on the Preservation Hall model. On the whole, Jaffe and Borenstein appeared to view them benignly. They tried to maintain cordial relations; Larry, for example, was actually a good friend of Al Clark, who ran the most successful of them, Dixieland Hall. One of Jaffe's fundamental wishes was to help foster an ever-broadening base for traditional jazz in New Orleans, so that the music would re-seed and revitalize itself. The kitty halls were evidently part of such a base.

On the other hand, competition was competition – and that included not only rival halls, but key musicians suddenly disappearing to go off on tour under some other aegis. Jaffe appeared to have established no general policy in such cases, but to have handled each case pragmatically. There were complaints that he would penalize musicians for taking jobs that competed directly with the Hall by not hiring them for a period of time. Objective attempts to verify such allegations yielded only one or two confirmations. A savvy local musician obser-ved that one heard the same thing about every regular gig in town, and that Jaffe was a particular target of jealous whisperings because his jobs paid the best.

One competitor, Southland Hall, opened directly across St Peter Street with the stated purpose of driving Preservation Hall out of business. In this case Jaffe did specifically announce that any musician who worked at Southland would not work for him. But the upstart enterprise soon folded, and several of the musicians who had worked there, including clarinetist Raymond Burke, later returned as regulars to Preservation Hall.

Worthia G. "Show Boy" Thomas, as befits his name and personality, landed his first job playing for a baseball game in his home town of Napoleonville, Louisiana. From 1929 on he traveled widely with show groups such as the Rabbit Foot Minstrels, the Clyde Beatty circus band and the Jay McShann band from Kansas City. Remaining in New Orleans after 1960, he became known to Preservation Hall listeners as the trombonist who played the fewest notes and who vented the most dislike of flash photography.

Dixieland Hall was open almost twelve years – from January, 1962, until December, 1973. It was a period during which Jaffe himself apparently mellowed; his policies toward the competition likewise seemed to soften. The cases varied. Clarinetist Louis Cottrell, who also happened to have been local president of the black musicians' union, was one of the faction that remained exclusively at Dixieland Hall. However, such Preservation Hall mainstays as Kid Thomas, Emanuel Sayles, Albert Burbank, Sweet Emma Barrett and Jeanette Kimball all worked at both places.

Chris Botsford, a key Preservation Hall staffer who arrived in 1970, summed up the "control" issue in the late 1980s:

I remember Allan saying, "There's plenty of room for two places like Preservation Hall." He was clearly in support of the idea, particularly then, when the availability of musicians was greater. I never sensed any resentment on Allan's part against Dixieland Hall or the subsequent efforts of Heritage and Tradition Halls. What pleased

More facile than many of his contemporary New Orleans trombonists, Waldren "Frog" Joseph saw action with Joe Robichaux' big band in the 30s and later performed with popular French Quarter outfits such as those of Octave Crosby, Papa Celestin and Paul Barbarin. Besides his regular appearances at Dixieland and Preservation Halls, he was featured during the 70s and 80s with Clive Wilson's New Camellia Jazz Band at major hotels and other popular local venues.

Allan was to see musicians working. His objection, basically, was musicians not simply coming to him and saying, "I have this offer, would you mind if I . . . ?" Just showing him evidence of a little loyalty. And that's it. I don't think he would ever say, "No, you can't."

Larry was often more annoyed. Larry would get upset when they wouldn't pay absolute loyalty to the Hall. It was the way he did stuff – his bluntness – that bothered people.

Leaders like Barry Martyn, who have run independent tours that included Preservation Hall musicians, said that they would consult Jaffe in advance as a courtesy, and never encountered a problem. Unknown out-of-towners who phoned and happened to get Larry Borenstein sometimes received a different response. For many years, prominent Preservation Hall musicians such as Louis Nelson, Kid Thomas and Chester Zardis traveled abroad regularly as guest stars, without any confirmable penalties. In at least one case, that of Orange Kellin's New Orleans Joymakers, the situation worked in reverse: Kellin and Lars Edegran uncovered some good, forgotten local players and mobilized a fine band for a European tour. On returning, these musicians began playing regularly at the Hall.

Those who have been responsible for scheduling, such as Jane Botsford, Chris' wife and Jaffe's right-hand assistant, pointed out that it was hard to bring in a new player to replace someone who left for a while, then fire the new one as soon as the first one came back. "Just trying to be fair to everyone is terribly difficult," said Chris Botsford. "You're not just talking about someone doing a set job. It has to do with artistic things, and families, and what people expect to hear, and some tours paying more than others, and do you book a band a year in advance and have a whole different band show up?" An onlooker could see that tensions sometimes stemmed as well from poor communication, or from a conflict between deep-rooted southern folkways and modern assumptions about how work is organized.

All this was but a footnote in an overwhelmingly positive story. Considering the stringent controls of the very few other entrepreneurs who had ever managed to market New Orleans jazz successfully – the tough old Streckfus Brothers with their riverboats, for instance, or Louis Armstrong's coldly calculating agent Joe Glaser – Preservation Hall was the most caring, committed and effective link anyone could have forged between the anachronistic world of the old jazzmen and the mainline US culture. In the philosophy of pianist Sing Miller: "They goin' run this place like they want. I goin' live till I die."

* * *

Knowledgeable listeners frequently shook their heads over the endless strings of solos heard at Preservation Hall. They contrasted these often dull, overlong, ring-around-the-rosie routines with the more exciting and demanding ensemble jazz heard in earlier decades. Driving, cross-rhythmic, poly-phonic ensemble choruses are certainly at the core of this music; and Jaffe, Bill Russell and others at the Hall acknowledged the solo problem in no uncertain terms. But the guiding philosophy remained: no interference. There was truth in the oft-heard argument that the Preservation Hall system of playing for swarms of tourists who loved to applaud for the solos, and who usually stayed for one set only, accentuated the problem. But the tendency to overdo

Illustrating the frequent family connections of the traditional jazz musicians of New Orleans, Homer Eugene was, with his brother Wendell Eugene (also a trombonist), a nephew of Albert Burbank, Paul and Louis Barbarin and Danny Barker – all of whom (except for Paul) appeared at Preservation Hall at one point or another. In addition to his jazz appearances, Homer Eugene was often to be seen parading through the streets of the city with the Young Tuxedo Brass Band.

solos was not confined to, or fundamentally caused by, the Hall.

New Orleans jazz has always been functionally adaptive in terms of the environment and event involved. No rarified, hermetically sealed fine art, it is a participative, "y'all-come" folk phenomenon – whoever the folk might be. One reason this music survived so long, while other popular styles appeared and disappeared, was that it was able to mold itself to changing circumstances.

One basic circumstance, at least after the 1950s, was that it proved virtually impossible for any full-time, professional, seven-piece jazz band to survive permanently without a formula that would draw large numbers of customers to every performance. In the rare band that could steadily command $500 a night, five nights a week, a musician could hope to clear $15,000-$20,000 a year before taxes. (Benefiting from high fees on the road, some Preservation Hallers did better than that for years. Trombonist Jim Robinson, who for most of his life had never lived in a house with indoor plumbing, was said, at his death in 1976, to have had $100,000 tucked away.)

Many traditional jazzmen preferred to play for dancing. But that market died before swing went out and rock came in – before the Hall even opened. Trumpeter Punch Miller, the first jazz musician to play at Borenstein's gallery, had just returned from years on the road with tent and show bands. Nostalgia about the past could not alter the fact that yesterday's clambakes and rent parties had been supplanted by today's shopping malls and conventions. Audiences conditioned by decades of jazz festivals, community concerts, movies and TV shows were more passive, and more conditioned to the star or solo system.

Functionally, the ensemble style seemed related to dancing, the solo style to concert listening. But that equation was never hard and fast. The amount of soloing often had as much to do with individual preferences and abilities of the players as it did with functions and events. Certain instruments, such as the piano and the clarinet, seemed to invite the kind of technical virtuosity associated with solo work more than some others, like the trombone or bass. Musicians who worked long years in "short" bands of from one to four pieces – as did clarinetist George Lewis, or the piano-cornet duo of Billie and DeDe Pierce – learned to be inventive soloists out of necessity. Those who played supporting roles in brass bands and other large ensembles were less likely to develop solo skills. Also, the same band might play quite differently at differing functions; longtime fans clearly recalled this in comparing the ensemble sound of the 1950s George Lewis band at uptown society dances with their solo style in concert halls.

Scholars believe the earliest jazz bands used few, if any, solos. Judging from the early recordings, the musicians often even performed the same ensemble parts with little or no variation from one chorus to the next. When solos did begin to appear, they were often written out rather than improvised. Clarinetist Emile Barnes confirmed this in a Tulane interview. At least one great soloist, Sidney Bechet, may have constituted an early exception: this was suggested by Ernest Ansermet's 1919 review (see Chapter Two). The incomparable Louis Armstrong greatly expanded the role of the solo, leading the way toward swing in the late 1920s and early 1930s. Subsequently, many modernists abandoned ensemble work altogether. To some extent, influences from swing, Dixieland and bebop – all products of the North and West – fed back into the jazz played in New Orleans as early as the 30s, but especially from the 50s on.

In a 1960 interview, DeDe Pierce said that there was by then more solo playing than in the old days; how long the trumpet men stayed "up" depended on the strength of their lips, which had been stronger when they were younger. He added that certain musicians had always "featured" solos more than others. Willie Humphrey said similar things. A widely traveled, lifelong professional, who sometimes needled others with musicial one-upmanship, Humphrey thought that the reason some of the older bands played mostly ensemble was that many of the players just didn't know how to play solos.

A fair number of later-day traditional jazz enthusiasts honed their tastes on the kinds of loosely knit ensemble bands recorded in New Orleans in the 40s and 50s. While those records had their own special beauty, revivalists who made primitivism a virtue, and equated it with the constant-ensemble style, tended to forget that such Preservation Hallers as the three Humphreys, or Polo Barnes, or DeDe Pierce, or Jeanette Kimball, or Sweet Emma Barrett, or Narvin Kimball, or Manny Sayles, or George Guesnon, or George Lewis, or Albert Burbank, or Cie Frazier, were all skillful soloists decades earlier. Even Kid Thomas' dance-hall bands balanced ensembles and solos, as did the "classic" recording bands of the 1920s – with the notable exception of Sam Morgan's.

The general point is that ensemble play *and* solo play, tightly organized *and* loose arrangements, were all firmly rooted in the New Orleans jazz heritage. Solos were not bad or good in themselves. There was good and bad dance music, there was good and bad concert music and there were good and bad solos. The concert format did encourage solo playing, and some Preservation Hall soloists were better than others.

Still, some sort of intelligent esthetic has always guided the best bands. The mindless formula of a chorus or two of ensemble going in, followed by a long string of solos (without interludes or backing from the other horns, and often including even a bass solo) and a final chorus or two going out, did seem a

Jeanette Kimball's jazz background was unique. Growing up in Pass Christian, Mississippi, she was the only member of her family interested in music. As a child she "lived at the piano" and received three lessons a week from a graduate of the New England Conservatory. In 1926, at the age of 18, she was auditioned in her home by Papa Celestin – and quickly hired. Mrs Kimball stayed with Celestin's successful traveling bands until 1935, when she left to rear her children, play less demanding gigs and teach piano. In the early 50s she rejoined Celestin and remained with the band and its successor, the Papa French band, for 20 more years. Widely recorded and much in demand, Mrs Kimball gravitated from Dixieland Hall to Preservationm Hall in the 70s. There, her graceful style and ladylike presence remained a mainstay into the 1990s.

decadent modern trend. As for blaming this on Preservation Hall, one could point out that some who complained the loudest were revival-era musicians who played exactly the same way in different settings. Other protesters happily traveled from one jazz festival to the next, from California to Switzerland, listening to similar routines.

Because Preservation Hall was looked on as a mecca, it was sometimes expected to set standards in a way none of its founders or managers ever had any intention of trying to do. The aim of the Hall was to support the players, however they chose to play, for better or worse. Said Jaffe: "The main thing we always wanted to do was to present the music so people had a chance to listen to the music on the musicians' own terms."

Before Anything Else
Chester & Robbie

Once Preservation Hall became established in 1961, word spread quickly among the old-style musicians of New Orleans. Most of their names soon became known to the Hall through the grapevine. As time went along, a few others – such as drummer Chinee Foster and banjoist Father Al Lewis – were uncovered by jazz buffs and nudged out of retirement. Only one of the central figures at the Hall announced his availability by letter. Having moved to the nearby town of Cade some years earlier, he penned these auspicious lines to the Hall's manager:

Cade La
Aug 24 – 1963
Dear Mr. Allen Jeff

I am writing of my self I am a Dixie Land Bass Violin Player I have [been] born and raise in New Orleans I have

[been] away from New Orleans 10 Years I have seen all of my old timer Picture in the Paper that why I am writing tell George [Lewis] I am sending him a Letter I want to join his Band if he need a Dixie Bass man I am not doing anything
Yours truly
Chester Zardis
PO Box 15
Cade, La

It soon turned out that Zardis had had a fascinating career. He had played with many of the best-known early New Orleans bands, including those of Kid Rena, Buddy Petit, Chris Kelly, Jack Carey, Kid Clayton, Fats Pichon and Bunk Johnson. His musical memories stretched back to the days he and Louis Armstrong had spent in the Waif's Home as teenagers.

Chester would become, for more than a quarter century, a vigorous mainstay at Preservation Hall. In this period he earned worldwide acclaim as the last of the great old-time bass men, frequently appearing as a featured guest star on such far-flung shores as Australia, England and the European Continent. If one word could sum up the sound of this remarkable bass man, it would be *power*.

Another of Chester Zardis' contributions was his influence, both direct and indirect, on younger generations of traditional bass players. In this he exemplified the role of Preservation Hall as a catalyst in the worldwide resurgence of New Orleans jazz. Such "teaching" occurred not only inside the Hall, on the concert stages and on the records, but also in direct, one-to-one encounters, both personal and musical. This passing of the torch flowed naturally from the older musicians, since that was the way they themselves had received the lineage – even though, as Chester noted, "You don't find it no more like that. Today everybody lookin' out for themself."

Chester was proud of one of his finest students, Robbie Schlosser, whom he called "my scholar" or "my boy." Later a busy professional jazz bandleader in the San Francisco area, Schlosser cherished some warm memories of his tutelage:

The lessons Chester Zardis gave me were among my earliest, and his inspiration is always with me.

I met Chester about 1975. During the late 70s and early 80s, my wife Bunch and I visited New Orleans for a week or so at least once a year, and we'd stop in Preservation Hall nearly every day. Most of that time, Chester worked there twice a week. He would arrive at least an hour before the band began, and Bunch and I would get there early too, to chat with him and the other musicians as they showed up. On most occasions, we'd talk about music. Whenever bass playing came up, Chester would punctuate the conversation with an example demonstrating some technique. Then I'd try it, and he'd help me get it.

As I understand it, playing bass in a New Orleans style band is both deceptively simple and also absolutely crucial to the band's beat. When the band really cooks, everyone's decisions are smooth and together, and all the musicians strive toward a shared ideal. It's as though they're holding a relaxed conversation, coordinating their comments as they all retell a familiar story.

On a few occasions Chester asked me to stand by him in the band, so I could hear this "conversation" from the bass player's perspective. This was a great help. Often, as I heard him in the band, I would imagine how I would play if I were in his place and I heard what he heard.

Several times, Chester asked me to play a 30-minute set with the band. He'd sit on a stool beside me, or on the side of the room where I usually sat, and we'd talk about the music after each tune or after the set.

To see what Chester was doing was astonishing. And every time I hear him play, every time I hear him get the tone that he can on the bass, and put the accents in the notes just where he does, and the particular notes that he chooses to put in, to hear him do that, and to see the effect that it has on the rest of the band – it's absolutely fascinating, a wonderful thing.

One thing I've learned from the musicians who play at Preservation Hall is the attitude of the musician who considers his trade providing entertainment. And when Chester plays, he plays the bass to enhance the band's ability to entertain the people.

Let's call it providing a certain kind of texture. You'll play for whatever the soloist seems to be doing. Or is the band winding up? Is the band reaching a culmination, or is the band kind of hunkering down and really digging into what they're doing? You play the appropriate texture to help the band get where it's going. And Chester seems to play the bass that way. He doesn't simply plunk out: bang, bang, bang, bang – the right notes on the right beats. The notes don't mean a thing. The beats don't mean a thing. The meaning of the music that Chester plays comes from the context, comes from what the band is trying to do at the time.

Passing the lineage:Robbie Schlosser (left) and Chester Zardis were a perfect example of the sort of informal student–teacher relationship which marked Preservation Hall from its inception.

If the band wants to make a kind of quiet, subdued background, because someone else is working on a particular thing that wants to stand out, then Chester would behave as though he hears that it would be proper for the band to be a receding frame for this picture, to spotlight what that particular guy is doing right now. So he'll call very little attention to what his bass is doing, but instead he'll just keep the time, keep the time. And then when that business is over, if the band wants to explode into something, then Chester will play whatever notes would indicate that some change has taken place, or he'll put a syncopation or an accent in.

I jokingly say to people that I went to New Orleans once a year for half a dozen years to get my batteries recharged, and came back with some inspiration, but there's a lot of truth to that. When I'd be going, I'd be looking forward to it for weeks. And when I came back, I really cherished the memories.

A couple of times, Chester invited Bunch and me to come over to his house. He'd have some food for us, and we'd sit and we'd talk. Once in a while he'd get up and pick up his bass and say, "Hey, it was like this!" And he'd play a thing, and then he'd say: "Here, you try it." And so I'd try it, and he'd correct me, or he'd make another suggestion, or he'd show me: here's the way I like to play, hold your hand this way, the way you're playing doesn't get you where you want to go. He'd express it the way he was accustomed to expressing it. It was close to the way he was taught.

In between we'd sit down and drink a little beer, and eat a little crackers and cheese and ham, and then he'd say, "Now, try it again. No, it's not quite right. Tone's real important. Try it again.

No, now let me show you how." And then he'd do it again, and again, and again. And then I'd say, "Okay, let me try it now." That's all we did, all one afternoon, just this one little thing, in between the crackers and beer, just trading back and forth.

He told me that one time he was in a band on the back of a truck, and he played a certain introduction, and it really got a big response. A lot of people really liked it. And he said, "This is the way it goes. You put your fingers up here . . ." And he'd go ahead and do it, and I'd try to do it, and I'd miss a couple of notes. He felt it was a distinct melody, a distinct line, and I couldn't just fake a note that was close, so he had me repeat it and play the right notes, exactly the right notes.

He would always stress the tone, that whatever note you play is not as important as the tone that you play. The sense that he had was that it should sound pretty. It should sound really nice – full, big, robust tone.

He liked to keep his bass around, keep it leaning on the wall, or lying on the floor, and, when he would walk by, get up and play a little bit on his way to the other side of the room. Just to have it a handy thing so that, at a moment's notice, he could pick up the bass, and make it a part of the way he does things, part of the way he would be going around during the day. Just pick up the bass, and without any special preparations, without any special care or concern, be able to make the bass speak really pretty. And the technique of making the right notes was something that practice would give you; but the idea of having the pretty sound, the pretty tone, is something about which he would say: "That comes before anything else."

Chapter Seven

THOSE GREAT OLD GUYS FROM NEW ORLEANS

"Sounds like you need a tent."
—Stanford University official

Family fun in Minnesota: the air was cool, the welcome as warm as ever for this early visit of the Preservation Hallers to Minneapolis (from left to right and front to back): DeDe and Billie Pierce, Sandra Jaffe, Mr and Mrs Charlie DeVore (major local supporters), Willie Humphrey, Jim Robinson, unknown friend and Cie Frazier.

Almost as soon as Jaffe arrived in New Orleans in the spring of 1961, he foresaw that the real payoff for the musicians would be in touring. By the time he took the helm that September, a tour of sorts was already in progress: Kid Sheik's Storyville Ramblers had been booked for two weeks at the Empress Room of the Tudor Arms Hotel in Cleveland. They were followed by bands led by Kid Howard, Punch Miller and Noon Johnson. Kid Sheik's group returned for the Christmas holidays and stayed until shortly after New Year. None of these engagements was formally under the Hall's auspices, however. Despite strenuous efforts, it was not for another year and a half that the idea of widely traveling Preservation Hall bands really began to bear fruit.

Helping pave the way was a circle of jazz devotees in Minnesota's Twin Cities – a favor Jaffe never forgot. They included Dr Henry Blackburn and Charlie DeVore, both of whom had spent considerable time in New Orleans and were on their way to becoming fine part-time jazzmen. Cornetist DeVore had been stationed in New Orleans while in the Navy in the mid-50s, when the old dance halls were still going strong. He had participated in some of the

Onstage at historic Congo Square, Percy Humphrey was joined by some well-known sitters-in, actor Woody Allen (clarinet) and research MD Henry Blackburn (soprano sax). The occasion was the first New Orleans Jazz Festival in 1970. Allen was in town recording the sound track for his film "Sleeper" at Preservation Hall; Blackburn served as the Hall's unofficial medical consultant for four decades.

impromptu sessions at Borenstein's Associated Artists' Gallery. In the process he had become a good friend of many of the musicians, particularly Kid Thomas, whom he had vowed to help "almost as a blood oath." Dr Blackburn was a research physician at the University of Minnesota. In coming decades his work in epidemiology and the prevention of heart disease would win him international eminence. He would also act as a kind of unofficial medical consultant to many of the Preservation Hallers. Furthermore, for decades he would find himself in the happy position of being able to hire the bands regularly for national conventions, sometimes sitting in himself on saxophone.

Another Minneapolitan who has often performed at the Hall over the years was Butch Thompson, a gifted professional pianist and clarinetist. Thompson later led the house trio on Garrison Keillor's long-running "Prairie Home Companion" radio show, on which Willie Humphrey occasionally appeared as a featured guest. Other helpers in the Twin Cities included members of the Hall Brothers' jazz band, who in years to come sometimes played at train stations and airports to greet the veterans.

The Twin Cities situation was a good example of the kind of local support which long marked the far-flung travels of New Orleans musicians. From a purely commercial standpoint, the success of the Preservation Hallers among the general public would soon eclipse the need for such support. Yet that worldwide network of close friends would remain part of the "soul" of this quirky, humane operation.

In July, 1963, Jaffe and Borenstein journeyed from New Orleans to Chicago on the Illinois Central Railroad with a band consisting of Kid Thomas, George Lewis, Louis Nelson, Emanuel Paul, Joe James, Joe "Twat" Butler and Sammy Penn. Their first booking was on Saturday 20th, at the Red Arrow, a Chicago jazz spot where Lewis had often appeared with his group in the 1950s. But their prime engagement was two days later. On Monday, July 22, they were booked into the Guthrie Theater, an important concert hall in Minneapolis.

Success was by no means assured. Aside from the fact that Monday has never been the most auspicious night for anyone to play anywhere, none of these musicians, except Lewis, was experienced at playing to large concert audiences. None was a spring chicken, and pianist Joe James was in very poor health.

However, months of painstaking advance work had been done by Blackburn, DeVore and others. Money had been raised at local jazz events to pledge a minimum guarantee, reducing the Guthrie's risk. The Orleanians were put up in local homes. A series of jobs was lined up for the coming week. These included private parties, concerts at a shopping center and at the University, and an afternoon "jazz lawn party" at the Athens House restaurant (which thereafter became an annual event). Appropriately – and diplomatically – the group was billed as "Preservation Hall Band / leading New Orleans musicians / directed by Kid Thomas and featuring George Lewis."

The Guthrie concert proved a huge success. Thanks to plenty of publicity, the 1400-seat hall was virtually sold out. The performance was superb: Jaffe would forever regret that he had not recorded it. Startling everyone, the 67-year-old Thomas pulled out a full bag of humorous antics, such as playing in the balcony, and up and down the aisles, in a woman's

A smash hit in Japan, a Preservation Hall band featuring George Lewis (left) played 94 capacity concerts in 32 cities to some 320,000 listeners in 1963. Following massive media exposure, Lewis's clip-on tie was auctioned off at a benefit for $150. Rounding out the front line were Louis Nelson (right) and Punch Miller (center).

white bonnet – tricks for which he later became widely known. The acoustics were perfect, the atmosphere was warm and intimate, the response was ecstatic. The local newspapers covered the event in glowing terms, and the follow-up jobs also proved very popular.

On the heels of this first bona fide Preservation Hall tour came an even more spectacular one. In mid-August, 1963, Allan and Sandra Jaffe took a Preservation Hall band on a monumental three-month series of 94 concerts in 32 cities across Japan. Forty of these took place at Festival Hall in Osaka, the largest auditorium in the country with a seating capacity of some 3,000. Every concert was sold out, and it was estimated that in sum the band played to more than 320,000 people, not counting numerous radio and television shows.

Besides George Lewis, who acted as leader and introduced the band, the personel were Punch Miller, Louis Nelson, Joe Robichaux, Emanuel Sayles, Papa John Joseph and Joe Watkins. The response was truly overwhelming. The musicians were mobbed for autographs and attention wherever they went. After John Joseph celebrated his 89th birthday, each audience tried to outdo the last in presenting him

Though the band donned tuxedos for the concerts, Lewis tried a kimono in a teahouse (top). Having been warned the Japanese rarely showed emotion, the musicians were astonished by an outpouring that included stamping, jumping onto the stage, shouting requests, and clapping even for the spoken introductions to the tunes. Dazed by legions of autograph seekers were (bottom) Punch Miller (seated) amd Papa John Joseph.

with birthday cakes, which attained gigantic proportions.

Typically, there were also internecine humbugs. George Lewis accepted an offer to bring a band back the following year under his own name rather than the Hall's. The great clarinetist did so again for a third year – 1965 – in an atmosphere of worshipful veneration.

* * *

Thus the groundwork was being laid for touring on a regularized, professional basis. In February, 1964, a different Preservation Hall band, including both Nelson and Lewis, journeyed north by train. After playing dates along the way, they found lodgings at the University of Minnesota and worked a variety of local gigs. That October, yet another Preservation Hall group came to perform at the Tyrone Guthrie Theater and elsewhere. This time, Jaffe made sure the Guthrie concert was recorded; and a day or so later, he and Bill Russell stayed up all night editing the tape (the musicians' union having insisted this be done before they left town). Over the next quarter century the resulting LP would far outsell all other Preservation Hall recordings. The players were Percy Humphrey, Willie Humphrey, Jim Robinson, Sweet Emma Barrett, Emanuel Sayles, Alcide "Slow Drag" Pavageau and Cie Frazier.

Jaffe had spent many months fruitlessly knocking on the doors of New York booking agencies, trying to line up longer tours. In 1964 a breakthrough finally came: Cliff Menz, who ran a reliable, low-key agency out of Council Bluffs, Iowa, booked a five-piece band for an intensive three weeks that took them all the way from Texas up to North Dakota and over to Pennsylvania. The group consisted of DeDe Pierce, Willie Humphrey, Jim Robinson, Billie Pierce and Cie Frazier. Jaffe drove everyone, plus (later) two of the musicians' wives, across those many miles in a station wagon with a U-Haul trailer. Jaffe expanded the ensemble to six pieces by joining them himself on tuba. Audiences were enthusiastic, and Menz was soon booking the band for more college and community concerts. He collaborated with agents specializing in other areas to send them to the

Southeast, the Northeast and the Northwest. In 1970 Klaus Kolmar, of Kolmar-Luth Entertainment in New York, took over many of these bookings.

The most prestigious concert dates, however, were to come via Stephen Baffrey in California. Baffrey later explained:

I was working on fundraising at Stanford University in 1962 and 1963. One of my field responsibilities was the New Orleans area, and that's how I discovered Preservation Hall. I used to spend as much time as I could there, as a tourist. Then, a year or so later, I became the producer of the Stanford Summer Festival. I looked ahead to the day when we could present the Preservation Hall Jazz Band.

In 1967 I booked them for a specific period without having a performing space available. We were having a staff meeting, and one of our very stuffy lawyers listened to me say I had booked these people and didn't know where the hell I was going to play them. He said, "Sounds like you need a tent." He meant that in jest, but in fact it was the perfect solution. We had to go all the way to University President Wallace Sterling to get approval for the tent.

The steamy, informal tent shows were extremely successful. The tent had to be enlarged each year until 1969. At that point the Festival ended, Baffrey left and the tents disappeared. But the same band, later led by Percy Humphrey, would continue giving concerts elsewhere at Stanford for over 20 summers, making that university the site of more Preservation Hall performances than any other place in the world except the St Peter Street establishment itself. For a number of years, the band and their families stayed at fraternity houses and eating-club complexes, which were otherwise sparsely used during the university holidays. Many, many friends, old and new, came to visit. There were always several parties, and the well-known French Quarter restaurant owner Buster Holmes flew out to cook personally for the band (see Introduction).

Ranging well beyond Stanford itself, the pleasantly hot California summer tours remained special for musicians and staff alike. Sandra Jaffe had been diverted from her work at the Hall by the birth of her children, Russell (in 1969) and Benjamin (in 1971). Having lived in the rear wing of Preservation Hall, behind the patio, for nine years, she and Allan moved into their own house on nearby St Ann Street

An unforgettable face and demeanor were possessed by banjoist Father Al Lewis. As often grumpy as gay, he sang and played in an earthy style. Toting the world's most overstuffed flightbag across the continents, he also carried a high reputation among fellow jazzmen who had worked with him for many decades.

in the fall of 1970. The growing children accompanied both Jaffes on many of the California trips during the 70s and 80s. Sandra made intermission announcements, helped sell records and such; and over time the boys had a chance to observe the ins and outs of tour management.

Many of the musicians had children, grandchildren and other relatives living in the Los Angeles or San Francisco areas. California had, in fact, been a major destination for New Orleans jazzmen from the earliest days, when famous players like Kid Ory, King Oliver and Jelly Roll Morton appeared there. Transplanted Orleanians such as trumpeter Amos White, bassist McNeal Breaux, trumpeter Leo Dejan and pianist Alton Purnell would frequently turn up at concerts or invite the band for home cooking.

Working now as a freelance agent, as well as a media commentator, Steve Baffrey had begun to book the Billie and DeDe band ever more widely. His was just the kind of innovative, venturesome, warmly personal promotion this iconoclastic outfit needed:

> It started slowly, as a labor of love, but then it began to build fairly prominently into a business relationship. I suggested what a wonderful, successful, loving attraction we had discovered in the Preservation Hall Band, and convinced people to share our experience. That would be typical with the Ravinia Festival outside Chicago, and the Blossom Festival in Cleveland, and the Saratoga Festival in New York, and Lincoln Center. Mondavi Winery is a

A downpour at an open-air concert in Savannah, Georgia, in 1977 inspired impromptu rainwear and quick thinking by umbrella carriers including Hall staffer Alvin Lambert (behind clarinetist). The musicians (from left) are Frank Demond (trombone), Ernie Cagnolatti (trumpet), Louis Barbarin (drums), Manuel Crusto (clarinet), Narvin Kimball (banjo) and Sing Miller (piano).

perfect example of people who have really taken the band to heart over the years. A place like the Concord Pavillion is slightly different – it's not a big party as far as they're concerned. We deal with quite a few promotors who are strictly commercial and remain at arm's length.

Basically, you want to play every date for a nice, big, fat guarantee. But you can't always do that, and sometimes in order to entice some of the big places, where we've ultimately been very successful, we had to kind of sneak in on a percentage arrangement. I was taking the risk. I've had my share of both profits and losses over the years. There are enough solid guarantees so that, once I know I have a certain amount of money in hand, if I feel like taking a risk with some of the money in order to open up a new venue for the band, I can do it.

I have control of all the summer touring. The rest of the year is broken up among the other agencies by territories.

The Preservation Hall group's strong point is their absolute consistency. And the very endearing qualities that make up the band. The fact that it doesn't change is both a strength and a weakness. We have promotors who say, oh, I can't do that same thing two years in a row; and others who say, my goodness, don't ever change it, I want the same thing every year. A lot of clients say, it's those great old guys from New Orleans, and they don't check the roster to make sure it's Willie or Percy or whoever.

A minority of the audience are technical jazz fans. They are Preservation Hall fans. They like the ambience, and the style, and the bounce, and the warmth, that come from a Preservation Hall performance. To some people, the Preservation Hall tradition is the preservation of great New Orleans jazz played by young or old, black or white. But to many people, it's those old black players. And when you change that configuration of the band, it makes a significant difference. There's no question of its "Americana" image. If there were 300 Fourth of July's in the year, I could play 300 dates every year. Our audience is white middle America, for the most part.

Jaffe looks deceptively simple to anybody on the outside. Every promoter that we have – and some of them think they're the ultimate sophisticates in the entertainment business – just think we're a lovable bunch of hicks that come to town and get what we deserve, irrespective of the amount of money that we take away and the demands that we make. All of that is calculated. It's a very shrewd operation from Allan on down, and I try to reflect it in my dealings. My clients think that we all have a warm, loving relationship. And it's true – until business requires otherwise. When you work that closely with a man you admire that much, you become of one mind together.

Two very valuable staffers also came to Preservation Hall through the "Stanford connection": namely Jane and Chris Botsford. Jane would put in many years of 12- and 16-hour days, handling a staggering amount of backroom work by day, then sitting at the gate until well past midnight. She would also accompany many of the spring and summer tours. Her husband, Chris, would serve as the principal road manager and local gopher-in-chief. He would develop extraordinarily sensitive and trusting relationships with many of the older musicians and their families.

While still a Stanford student, Chris Botsford had begun working part-time for Steve Baffrey in 1964. Three years later, when the Billie and DeDe band first appeared at Stanford, Chris had graduated, had married Jane and was no longer working for Baffrey. But the Botsfords attended the famous tent sessions, and in 1969, when Baffrey booked the band on a nine-day tour of the East Coast, he hired Chris to accompany them. A year later Baffrey hired him for a similar trip. When that ended, Jaffe not only hired Chris for another tour, but invited the Botsfords to come and work in New Orleans for a year.

Staffer Jane Botsford: efficiently fielding a plethora of phone calls and paperwork by day, then faithfully perching on a stool at the front gate by night, she logged 19 years of 12- to 16-hour days.

Chris was feeling bogged down in his graduate studies in art history, and Jane had recently completed her graduate work in librarianship at the University of California, Berkeley. So on Christmas Day, 1970, they set out for New Orleans in a Hertz van. Jaffe predicted they would stay in New Orleans at least five years; in fact they would stay 19 years, through 1989, occupying an apartment owned by Jaffe in a building a few blocks from the Hall, where Bill Russell and other members of the Hall's "extended family" also lived.

Chris quickly established a close relationship with trumpeter Punch Miller, who was in failing health. Chris and Jane helped with the making of a film about Punch that spring; and on the Hall's tenth anniversary, June 10, 1971, Chris heard him perform there for the last time – singing *Home, Sweet Home.* The veteran horn man passed away six months later.

Chris remembered:

I came to New Orleans somewhat naive about the music. It was as much the musicians themselves as their

Staffer Chris Botsford: for two decades he counted luggage, records, receipts, interviews, hundreds of plane and bus trips, and thousands of shared emotions among players and fans who loved him as a brother.

music that captivated me. I was soon as involved in their personal lives as in their musical lives.

And the musicians, I think, responded to me in that way–knowing that I was not simply a musician. Sometimes I think they're a little wary of other musicians who they suspect only want to know them because they're musicians themselves. A lot of people hang around them as musicians. Those in the bands, I think, after not too long a period of time, felt fairly relaxed with me; they sensed I wanted to know them as people – as much for themselves as for their music, which, of course, I also liked immensely.

Punch would call up in the middle of the night, scared to death, asking that I come and spend the rest of the night with him. It'd be three in the morning. I'd go down, sit with him, and he'd feel better. He was in a coma the last couple weeks, in the hospital. He had a wonderful funeral. It was the first and only funeral I've seen that had an old-time hearse, drawn by a horse. It was quite moving.

It was, of course, not the last musician's funeral the Botsfords would see, nor was it the end of their deep personal involvement with the players. Over the years Chris helped many of them get their income taxes filed, brought them refreshments at intermission, announced them to audiences, cashed their checks, shared their heartaches, listened to their grievances, counted their luggage at airports, and handled a thousand unforeseen incidents. He shuddered, recalling the time they were on a plane heading for a concert in Halifax, Nova Scotia, when he suddenly realized Cie Frazier's drums had been left on the bus. These were very old, special sounding drums, and Cie was a high-strung, excitable person. Chris began to moan, "Oh, my God. Oh, my God." Jane asked what was wrong, but all he could do was to keep saying, "Oh, my God." Finally he went down the aisle and told Cie. Cie said, "Oh, my God." A set of drums was rented until Chris was able to get Cie's back. All in a day's work for a road manager:

Around 1974, in the summertime, we were going to Ball State University in Muncie, Indiana. We drove out of Chicago, got to Gary, and heard a loud clicking noise, like a flat tire flapping in the back. We pulled off the road, and just as we made the turn into a service station the wheel fell off and rolled right into the station. The bus fell right on its axle. They sent a second bus with another driver. We exchanged the luggage and instruments. We got within 60 miles of the concert, and that bus died in a cornfield – some problem with the engine. It ended up with Jaffe and Cie hitching a ride in a camper directly to the concert, literally hitchhiking into town with the drums. The sponsor sent out two trucks, picked up the instruments and the rest of the band. And we went to the concert. That night we drove to the hotel through a driving rainstorm.

I don't think we've ever missed a job because of bus problems. Not even the time in Oregon when we had to get out and sit, sweltering, under an overpass for four hours. Or when the bus was rear-ended on the Cross-Bronx Expressway in New York on the way to Symphony Hall in Boston, with traffic consequently backed up all the way across the George Washington Bridge into New Jersey: we made it to the hall at five to eight, for an eight o'clock performance.

Then there was the time when the band went on an important TV talk show on the BBC in Birmingham, England. The other guests included some farmers who had won an onion-growing contest with a gigantic, ten-pound onion. During the show the onion somehow disappeared. The next day one of the London tabloids carried a tongue-in-cheek story

One of the earliest "revival" period musicians to become a fixture in the Preservation Hall bands was trombonist Frank Demond. On short notice the youthful Californian had abandoned his profitable home-building businesss to replace Jim Robinson, who had fallen mortally ill while on tour.

about how the Preservation Hall Jazz Band had stolen it. Everybody in the band got a big kick out of that – except Cie, who was very upset at such an accusation. It fell to Chris, of course, to try to calm him down.

Again in London, Annabels, a posh nightclub, staged a New Orleans Fortnight featuring Kid Thomas with members of the Humphrey band. Guests at the parties included the likes of Frank Sinatra, Mick Jagger, Armand Hammer and the Queen of Spain. Thomas had arrived in early September for a preliminary week of concerts, wearing his suit and long underwear. At the end of the month he left – without ever having taken off his underwear. He simply donned his clothes each night, went to the job, came back, took off his suit, went to bed, and stayed there most of the day. Many English musicians came to visit him there. Thomas preferred to do his talking late at night, about the time his roommate, Chris Botsford, wanted to go to sleep, because Chris relished getting up early and visiting London's art museums during the day. For those who knew the man, such stories were vintage Thomas.

The following letter, written in Spanish, arrived in New Orleans from Chile. It ranked as a classic in the kind of cross-cultural strangeness that sometimes entered the jazzmen's lives. Bear in mind that Thomas did not read music, Spanish, or even English. Translation by Chris Botsford:

Señor Thomas Valentine:
First of all, greetings to you and at the same time I hope you

find both your family and group that surrounds you in good health.

He who writes you is a young musician who plays trumpet, who loves all kinds of music, and who is a great admirer of your band. Unfortunately, I did not get to personally hear your group when they performed in Santiago at the Church of the Transfiguration. I ask you, distinguished maestro, to forgive me for bothering you, but since I have almost no sheet music of those precious numbers which you so brilliantly interpret, I would be grateful if you could send some because they are not available in music stores here. At the same time, I would appreciate it if you would let me know what it costs so I can send you the money.

Maestro, I hope you understand me; when someone wants something, he asks the impossible in order to get it – at the cost of whatever sacrifice, when one wants to succeed. Therefore, I thank you. May God take care of you for many years.

Saying no more, a young trumpeter who admires you says respectfully goodbye and waits for your answer.

Bruno Lorenzo Calcagno Reeves

One of Thomas' little crowd-pleasing routines involved appearing in a milkmaid's dress and cap when he sang *Milk Cow Blues*. It was always quite a sight – the very black face peering out from a floor-length, bright white outfit. Once, however, as Chris remembered:

While they were taking their various choruses during *Milk Cow*, Thomas walked off the stage to get into this costume. Well, I was being interviewed backstage and hence not paying any attention. Thomas kept the old dress in his black bag. Apparently he got into the thing – but had it backwards. He got caught in it. There was a rip, and apparently he was so caught up in it that he couldn't get back out to play. The band kept playing and taking successive choruses. Finally they saw what was happening and ended the number. Thomas never came back out. This was in Pullman, Washington – the first concert.

The next night the band told me: "Chris, when he walks offstage be sure to have his costume all ready." He hadn't done it for years, and the band was surprised. Well, I had it ready, but he somehow again got it on backwards – the second night in a row! Cheerfully, he went out and played with it extremely tight, his arms locked against his sides, so he couldn't move. The audience didn't know the difference, but I was in hysterics.

Prominent at the Hall and on tour in the 80s, clarinetist Manuel Crusto could point to half a century of professional experience -- plus a significant New Orleans jazz lineage. The famous reed teachers Louis "Papa" Tio and Lorenzo Tio Sr and Jr had been Crusto's uncles and cousin. Their lives illustrated the complex crosscurrents of early jazz influence. Crusto's research showed that the father of Lorenzo Tio Sr had been born in New Orleans but moved to Tampico, Mexico. There his daughter married Crusto's father's sister. There, also, his son, Lorenzo Tio Sr, performed with a Mexican band before moving to New Orleans, where he played with the Excelsior Brass Band and various dance orchestras until about 1892. His brother, Louis Tio, known as "Papa", who had come from Mexico with the others, was an important teacher. But it was Lorenzo Tio Jr, born in New Orleans, who played with leading jazz bands of the teens and 20s and became world renowned as the teacher of such clarinetist stars as Johnny Dodds, Jimmie Noone, Omer Simeon, Barney Bigard, Albert Nicholas, Albert Burbank and Louis Cottrell.

By the late 1960s the strings of one-night tours were developing a seasonal consistency which would remain in place for the next two decades. A basic objective was for one or two bands to be touring for short periods in every season, always leaving enough regulars in New Orleans to perform at the Hall. The mounting success of the bands, and the complexity of their scheduling, can be gauged from the summary which follows.

After playing in the Stanford tents, and at such special events as the Olympic Games in Mexico City in 1968 and in Israel in 1970, the Billie and DeDe "gang" set a precedent with their fall and late-fall tours. They visited Texas and the Middle West regularly in the years 1966 to 1968, then began ranging more widely. (In 1974, after both DeDe and Billie had passed away, this band was led by Percy Humphrey and was known as the Humphrey band.) In the late 1960s an additional fall assignment was taken on by

Although he appeared only infrequently at Preservation Hall in the 60s, and despite losing a leg in 1970, trumpet veteran Ernie Cagnolatti became a regular there and on the road after the death of DeDe Pierce in 1973. Inspired at an ealy age by Bunk Johnson, in whose band his brother played, "Cag" was a solid member of the New Orleans jazz and marching band community from the late 20s on. Like a number of the Crescent City musicians, he was partially of Italian extraction -- his grandfather having come from Genoa.

the Kid Thomas band, which initially visited the Southeast, and thereafter the Midwest and East. (This band became trumpeter Wendell Brunious' band after Kid Thomas passed away in 1987.) The Thomas band was also the first to tour South America.

From 1968 until Billie's death in 1974, the Billie and DeDe ensemble visited the Southeast regularly every January and February – Florida's boom season. Thereafter the southeastern slot was filled by a variety of groups, including those led by trumpeters Ernie Cagnolatti, Percy Humphrey and Kid Sheik Colar.

Spring was the season for touring the Midwest, usually in combination with the East, and mostly featuring the Humphrey band. Particularly during the summer months Humphrey's band was much in demand, first touring California and the West, then playing at major festivals in the Midwest and East. Included in this eastern swing were such prestigious bookings as the Wolf Trap near Washington, DC, and the Ravinia Festival north of Chicago.

Apart from this fairly regular, bread-and-butter pattern of engagements, the bands constantly jetted off to special gigs in a variety of settings – such as Ernie Cagnolatti's three weeks in a Paris theater, or the Humphreys' posh one-nighters from Venezuela to the White House, or Kid Thomas' summer weekends at the Belmont racetrack in New York, or his State Department-sponsored tour of the Soviet Union in 1979.

That 1979 Russian tour was managed by another couple who gave long and faithful service over the years – Resa, Sandra Jaffe's sister, and her husband Alvin Lambert. Alvin left the Hall in 1982 to go into business for himself, opening a successful restaurant at the busy intersection of St Peter and Royal streets. Despite her responsibilities as a mother, Resa continued taking bands on tour, working at the gate in the evenings and, when Jane Botsford was away, managing the office by day.

Touring stimulated newspaper and TV coverage – which in turn helped both the tours and the St Peter Street operation. For example, a 60-minute Public Broadcasting Service (PBS) special on the Humphrey band from Wolf Trap included shots of the Hall at night and an interview there with Jaffe. Such valuable publicity had continued unabated from the Hall's earliest days.

The overwhelming majority of articles and reviews were favorable. One writer complained that it had become sacriligious to say anything negative about the old black musicians. National press coverage during the late 1960s included articles by Associated Press correspondents, and stories in *Business Week, The Nation, Ramparts, Venture, Ebony, Family Circle, Geriatrics,* the *New York Times* (several), *Town and Country* and *Sepia.*

The 1970s brought major pieces in *Holiday, Newsweek, Travel & Leisure, Downbeat, Camera 35,* the *National Review, Horizon, US,* the *Knight* papers, the *Los Angeles Times Syndicate,* and ten or more pieces in the *New York Times* as well as those distributed by the Associated Press.

From 1980 to 1986 there were articles in *Time* (twice), the *New York Times* (at least twice), *Variety* and the *Christian Science Monitor,* and more Associated Press coverage. Prominent photographs of such Preservation Hallers as Kid Thomas and Preston

Near the heart of the Hall was Resa Lambert, sister of Sandra Jaffe. In four decades, while raising her own family, Mrs Lambert specialized in taking bands on tours to far-flung spots and in managing the Hall itself for portions of the year.

Jackson appeared over the years in *National Geographic*.

Reporting in local papers outside New Orleans held approximately even over this long period, with upwards of three stories a year about the touring ensembles in such journals as the *Washington Post,* the *San Francisco Chronicle* and the *Miami Herald*. Items published in New Orleans itself gradually slackened to about one a year. International coverage seemed to hold steady at one or two major pieces a year, not counting small, specialized publications such as the English bi-monthly *Footnote,* which from the 1960s until 1989 mentioned Preservation Hall in virtually every issue; its successor, *New Orleans Music,* maintains this interest in the Hall and its musicians.

*   *   *

The policy of non-intervention in the music did not necessarily apply to the road concerts, at least in the premier band in which Jaffe himself played. As Louis

Armstrong and other jazzmen working major concert circuits always knew, predictability is essential in such venues – even at the cost of spontaneity. Jazz buffs sometimes grumbled about the "sameness" of the Humphrey band's programming in concert after concert, year after year. Similar complaints were made in the rare unfavorable reviews. "A Predictable Preservation," was the headline the *Washington Star* over J. R. Taylor's negative coverage of the band's Wolf Trap concert in June, 1980. Two years earlier, within a more balanced piece in the *Princeton Spectrum,* Gordon Lutz wrote, "The music, alas, has succumbed to a formula, which could be the price of maintaining its historical validity. But stagnation within the formula is harder to deal with, though understandable in men playing the same music the same way for 50 years."

Such reviews comprised only a tiny minority of the total. More to the point, Steve Baffrey estimated that sophisticated jazz listeners made up less than five per cent of the large, middle-brow audiences which turned out for the Preservation Hall bands. Most people enjoyed hearing something they recognized, especially when the Preservation Hall band visited their town only once a year. They also appreciated being led through an emotional and esthetic continuity. Jaffe explained this philosophy:

> I felt that, at the Hall, I really shouldn't interfere with what the bands do. On the road, I had every intention of saying: I've been to more concerts than most of the band, and I know what I think would work. I really didn't mind putting my two cents in. I would sit down with the leader and work out sets, mainly things of pacing, and my feeling that the concert should be pretty much like a symphony or an opera: it should have a beginning, and a middle, and an end. It should really flow. It shouldn't be just a group of disjointed songs. It should have some sort of emotional impact. You should be able to change people from feeling happy about a song to having a totally different emotional response to the music. It was important to have all types of songs on the program – popular songs, and gospel songs and traditional repertoire songs. What I had seen of the bands before, they tended to get bogged down in repertoire.
>
> The songs themselves were not as important as the tempo or the feeling that was put into it: if you wanted something with a hard kick to it, or if you wanted something nice and relaxing, or something with a vocal, or whatever. And it was always important to have songs that would

feature each of the musicians. All of the musicians in the course of an evening would have an opportunity to be featured on something.

Meanwhile, Jaffe was doing what he could to counteract the gradual loss of the older generation of players. He had an abiding, longterm faith in the marketplace, believing that more and better jobs would lift the musical quality and once again attract young black New Orleans musicians back into the city's traditional music. But this, he realized, would be slow in coming, because an entire generation had been lost. The core problem was a social one: musicians like DeDe Pierce and George Lewis represented a subculture that had become virtually extinct.

Nonetheless, Jaffe tried hard, behind the scenes, to support a broad revival of New Orleans music. In the realms of both education and performance he contributed to the resurgence of the jazzy brass bands, even if they eventually took some directions he did not personally favor. He helped traditional players who did not fit the Hall formula to find work both at home and on tour. A few who might not otherwise have qualified to play at the Hall were asked to do so, especially on Sunday nights, as a tribute to their long involvement in this overall re-seeding process. Jaffe would go out of his way to help youngsters start a band in a ghetto, or put up the prize money in a contest of new brass bands in Louis Armstrong Park. (He was not the only one doing such things; the widely experienced banjoist and guitarist Danny Barker, for one, who followed an independent course after a falling out with Preservation Hall in the early 60s, did a great deal to help and encourage budding young players.)

In 1987 Lucianne B. Carmichael, principal of the elementary school attended by Jaffe's two sons, described his efforts there:

McDonogh 15 is a special place, in part because it is the only elementary school in the city that allows and encourages every child to study music and provides a full-time music teacher and instruments for any child who also wants the opportunity to play music daily in our fine jazz band.

I first met Allan when he brought his son Russell to kindergarten 12 years ago. That was in the early years of

World-class concert halls were suddenly home to players who had spent their working lives in sweltering streets and grimy dives. Here, the Humphrey band played to a packed Orchestra Hall in Minneapolis in 1984. From a sheet of stage requirements sent to all their halls by the Kolmar–Luth booking agency: "The musicians will probably appear in their shirtsleeves. . . . The front of the upright piano should be removed. . . . Six straight-back plain wood chairs are needed. They need not be alike, but must be good and sturdy. Do not worry of they are a bit beat up in appearance. . . . House lights are to remain up during performance. . . . Front lighting is important or the wonderful faces of these musicians will not be seen by your audience."

McDonogh 15. We were struggling to establish an identity, and sometimes struggling just to keep going. We had a very discouraged itinerant music teacher who came two hours a week but accomplished little because he had no instruments and no one on the staff much interested or concerned. We didn't see music contributing to daily survival.

Allan, in his gentle yet direct way, began to awaken me to the obvious truth. He began by sending us ten cornets. I was amazed. "What will we do with them?" I asked. "Play them," he replied. "But we haven't really got a teacher." "Get one." Allan was like that. His direct, empowering statements had a way of bringing possibilities to reality. We did get a teacher, Walter Payton, and the ten cornets were only the beginning.

Allan never wanted public recognition. He worked quietly. The kids sensed his care and benevolence. He often visited band rehearsals. He loved seeing and hearing the intensity and sincerity of so many kids' involvement in the music he loved. "Listen to them. They have a good sound – future musicians of the city."

Besides the hundreds of instruments Allan provided over the years, he also made possible all kinds of cultural programs, such as touring artists whom he regularly brought to the school.

He did some of his quiet work behind the scenes to see that the McDonogh 15 Band opened the Jazz Festival every

Versatile and supple, bassist Frank Fields began his career during the 30s around his home town of Plaquemine, Louisiana. After the war he made a name as the house bassist at New Orleans' famous Cosimo recording studio, taking part in hundreds of rock-and-roll recordings with such pioneers as Fats Domino, Ray Charles and Little Richard. A regular with the Papa Celestin–Papa French jazz band from 1963 into the 70s, Fields gravitated as well to Preservation Hall and appeared with many of its groups from the mid-60s into the 90s.

year. He would show up at school that magic Friday morning in April with a huge handful of free tickets so that every child could go to the festival. He loved doing it.

If the longterm results of such efforts remained to be seen, vacancies at Preservation Hall had to be filled right away. By one count, in the 26 years from 1961 until 1987, an original roster of 150 musicians shrank to fewer than 20, and the original 20 bands dwindled to four. One musician called the 1970s "the era of the big change," because so many replacements had then to be brought in. Year by year, unforgettable personalities like DeDe and Billie Pierce, Louis Barbarin, Twat Butler, Jim Robinson and Albert Burbank either passed away or retired. Ironically, this was also the decade when Preservation Hall was soaring to widespread public acceptance, the incomes of its players rising accordingly. One factor was that tourism to New Orleans increased steadily through the 1970s and 80s.

The replacements were of three general types.

Some were second-string players of the old school, both black and white. Others were black New Orleans musicians with professional experience outside of traditional jazz *per se*, such as in 1940s-style rhythm-and-blues bands. Finally, white revivalists who had moved to New Orleans, and whose style was compatible with that of the existing bands, were judiciously added. The second, and especially the third, category tended to blur the Hall's public image slightly, and subtly to shift the musical feeling, but both also introduced some needed technical strength. Not until the early 1980s were a few young black Orleanians again carrying the direct lineage forward. With the decline and death of Kid Thomas in the mid-1980s, the young New Orleans trumpeter Wendell Brunious gradually replaced him as leader.

While the overall quality of the music slipped gradually downward, not all was lost by any means. Rail-thin and leather-lunged, Kid Thomas, a founding father of the place, went on trumpeting full tilt even as his 90-year-old skin began to resemble blue-black tissue paper. Chester Zardis, Louis Nelson, Manny Paul, Emma Barrett, Kid Sheik Colar, Narvin Kimball, Emanuel Sayles and the Humphrey brothers paced men a third their age on into the 80s (of the century – and often of themselves).

Back in the 1960s, with giants like George Lewis and Papa John Joseph passing away, people had already begun asking when Preservation Hall would have to close. Jaffe gave various answers at various times. In 1973 he stated: "As far as I am concerned, there are about ten or 12 remaining musicians of first-rate quality, and as long as they are around, and still willing and able to play, then I think that Preservation Hall should remain open for them to perform there." After they were gone, he said, the Hall should close, even if the crowds were still coming. But ten years later, with many of those players gone, Jaffe remarked: "As long as there are musicians left willing to play this music, the Hall will be there. If not, it will close. But I don't think this will happen. I think a new generation will come up, maybe not the [current young] generation, but probably the next one."

One sign of his confidence was his purchase of the 726 St Peter Street premises in 1984. No one, however, could have predicted what actually did occur – less than three years later.

Cie Frazier

A Night onTour
David R. Young

David R. Young, a teacher of English at the University of New Orleans, wrote the following account in 1978:

Alexander Hall on the Princeton campus is an old auditorium with stained glass windows. The band likes to play here because it reminds them of a church. As the last of the crowd files in, the musicians take their places onstage. They sit facing the audience. Dressed in black pants, white shirts, and club ties, the band members look as though they've just finished sitting for a daguerrotype. The old-timey image, however, is soon eclipsed by the exuberance of the music. From the first notes of *Hindustan*, the band plays fiercely. This is not the speedy, corny, funny-hat-and-matching-vest Dixieland music that one hears today on New Orleans' Bourbon Street and in other peanut parlors across America. The Preservation Hall Jazz Band's music is a rhythmic, hypnotic repertoire of blues, standards, dance tunes and spirituals, all played with heart.

After the rousing opener, a typical two-hour performance will include the feisty *Bourbon Street Parade* and *Basin Street*. You might next hear *St Louis Blues* and *Panama*, a bit of *Clarinet Marmalade* or *Bill Bailey*. The piano player, James Edward "Sing" Miller, will perform the hymn *His Eye is on the Sparrow* and, for a second spotlight number, either the spiritual *Amen* or a bluesy piano solo such as *Hurry Down Sunshine*. Narvin Kimball will take a decidedly nostalgic turn with the Gus Kahn standard *Memories*, singing in a clear falsetto while the banjo rings like a bell. Several ensemble rave-ups will follow, and then perhaps a novelty number, *Tiger Rag* or *Ice Cream*, both vehicles for trumpeter Percy Humphrey's snarling, Armstrong-like vocals. The performance closes with spirituals played softly at first and then jazzed up. All seven members of the band will have taken extended solos, but there will be a nice balance of solo work and ensemble playing.

Whether at the Hall or on tour, 73-year-old drummer Cie Frazier keeps the whole thing rolling along. Watching him play is like watching a painter at work, the way he brushes the drumheads, splashes cymbal tones or lightly taps the wood blocks. An easygoing rhythm ensues, although at times Cie will really put some mustard on it. The effect is so hypnotic that the audience breaks into applause when he finally detonates a short solo on *Panama*.

"Now a lot of drummers don't listen to the melody when they play," Cie says, "but I'm always following it, and

Creative agent Steve Baffrey (right) pioneered major long-term summer bookings. At one of these – Stern Grove in San Francisco – he chatted with Allan Jaffe.

sometimes I hum along. Those younger drummers, those rock and roll drummers, they have a hard time with jazz."

Cie Frazier's explosive drumming prepares the Princeton audience for the riotous finale. He plays delicately at first, his drums whispering the opening notes of *Just a Closer Walk with Thee*, which the band plays as a quiet funeral hymn, in a slow, haunting tempo. Willie Humphrey registers deep tones on the clarinet before ascending the octaves to a trilling flute sound. The muted trumpet and trombone play softly, keeping the melody to the forefront (as is customary in New Orleans jazz) while improvising around the melody. But after several minutes of this quiet pastoral music, Cie hammers out the drum roll that traditionally signals the beginning for a New Orleans street parade, the return from the graveyard when mourners celebrate the life of the recently departed by dancing in the streets and strutting with parasols in hand while the music blows hotter and wilder.

The Princeton audience is on its feet now, clapping and stomping slightly off the beat, as the band goes from the uptempo version of *Closer Walk* into a lively *When the Saints Go Marching In*. At this point, while still playing their instruments, Willie Humphrey, Narvin Kimball, trombonist Frank Demond and tuba player Allan Jaffe descend the steps at the side of the stage and begin to swing their way through the aisles. A long "second line" of revelers forms behind them and follows the band back to the stage. The evening ends with a good percentage of the audience, young and old, onstage, shuffling and jitterbugging to this old music, this classic jazz. As the late New Orleans trumpeter Bunk Johnson reputedly said to a bebop musician, "My music's for dancin'. What's yours for?"

Sweet Emma Barrett

Tales of Emma
"Just Telephone Me"

One of the most unforgettable musicians who ever played at Preservation Hall, pianist and singer Sweet Emma Barrett continued to be asked for long after her passing in 1983. One visitor, Mrs Winthrop Rockefeller, wife of the Arkansas governor, carried a record of Emma's up to the piano and asked her to autograph it. Often a bit feisty with such requests, Emma on this occasion consented. She got her big red pen out of her red purse and, in order to personalize the autograph, growled, "What's your name?" "Mrs Rockefeller." Roughly: "I mean your *first* name." As she began to write, Emma got to thinking. She suddenly turned, looked the lady in the eye, and in a voice full of suspicion and accusation demanded, "Are you *really* Mrs Rockefeller?"

Sometimes Emma would go on strike. While recuperating from a stroke in the Jaffes' home, she got into a fight with Allan over her demand to play three instead of two nights a week and went to work, instead, for rival Dixieland Hall. Later she came back and for years sent cutesy Hallmark cards to him and his family ("to a Wonderful Boss from Sweet Emma, 1979"). Enclosed were two brand new $5 bills for his sons, which remained, with the cards, in the Preservation Hall files.

Emma had been considered a beauty in her day. In his autobiography, the great New Orleans drummer Baby Dodds, describing the Papa Celestin band of the 1920s, said: "We had a girl piano player. She was a very good looking, light colored girl named Emma Barrett. She had big eyes; we used to call her 'Eyes.' She was a very thin girl but oh my God, she could play nice piano."

Although official programs warned the public never to ask Emma her age ("A woman who will tell her age will tell anything," she said), it was publicly stated after her funeral that she had been born in 1898. Unlike most of the other surviving pioneers, she avoided being interviewed for the Jazz Archive at Tulane University. However, the archive's first curator, Bill Russell, did finally manage to sit her down with a tape machine in 1968. As summarized by Russell, Emma said in part:

"My daddy was a captain in the Civil War. Then he worked in the custom house, and he was a big politician. When my daddy first got the piano, it wasn't for me; it was for my sister, but she never learned. I just started playing. I used to play with one hand. Then I could get them both together. I always had music in me. I picked up music at seven years old. My daddy had me taking music lessons from Professor Nickerson. I used to go to his home on Galvez, below Canal Street. People never could understand how I learned to play so good because I never did practice or like to play in my house. But I always liked to go out to other places and play. When I started playing in bands, I was about 12 years old."

By 1923 Emma was playing with Papa Celestin and Bebe Ridgley's Original Tuxedo Orchestra: "Celestin was so nice, he always told my mother he'd see that I got home. When I started playing with him, that was out to Jack Sheehan's Road House; used to work every night, go out on the Kenner car. He always used to tell me I came with a little raggedy dress on. Gooby Gus Ridgley never was tops on either trombone or drums, but he played good enough to suit the public. When Celestin and Ridgley separated, I stayed with Ridgley. Jeanette Kimball took over the piano for Celestin. She's a fine piano player.

"I never did care about piano stools, always liked a straight-up chair to protect my back. I play from the wrists and always played strong for a woman, yes indeed! If the piano in the old halls was out of tune, if you get a piano that's too low, it makes the horns pull out their tuning slides too far. So I used to 'cross chord' [transpose]. That put me in a lot of sharps or flats. All pianists can't do that, but I could still make the right chords.

"I started using the bells down at the Paddock [in the 1950s]. Mrs Valenti [the manager] said I had so much rhythm in my legs and she had the waitress get me some blue elastic garters with little bells. They just started calling me 'Sweet Emma' in late years. In the early bands they didn't take any solos. It was all a general assembly – all together. They didn't fool with all that – this one take a solo, and that one take a solo, and the other one – makes things so long. They just started that here lately. On trumpet they didn't use to do all this fancy stuff they got today. They played straight. You can play the lead and all that, but you don't jazz it up and play all different stuff. That's what you call straight."

Emma remained with Ridgley until 1936, a period in which she also performed under such well-known leaders as John Robichaux, A. J. Piron, and Sidney Desvigne. A professional entertainer who, whether singing or playing, always remained keenly aware of her audience, Emma banged away on the keys with what one reviewer called a "blunt, pile driver attack." From the 40s until the advent of the "kitty halls" in the 60s she appeared with small groups at society gigs and familiar local watering holes, such as Happy Landing and the Old Absinthe House. Richard B. Allen heard her often and helped get her on Art Ford's television show on WNTA in 1958 — Emma's first recog-

nition in the East. She made a number of albums under her own name, notably a wonderful one issued by Riverside in 1961, *Sweet Emma / the Bell Gal*. Preservation Hall's all-time best seller, *Sweet Emma and her Preservation Hall Jazz Band*, was recorded in 1964 at a Guthrie Theater concert in Minneapolis (see page 235).

Remembered almost as much for her personality as for her music, Emma penetrated the Hall's family-like support system so thoroughly as to create her own sub-system.

Bill Russell went up to the spring Cotton Carnival in Memphis to help Emma with her baggage, and to help banjo and guitar man George Guesnon, who by then was having difficulty walking: "This would be about 1965. Memphis was one of the worst Jim Crow cities. Martin Luther King was killed there, and they wouldn't even allow Louis Armstrong movies to be shown there through the 50s. But Jaffe decided he was going to integrate the big King Cotton Hotel. We all went in on this red carpet. The whole band stood in the middle of the fancy lobby, and Jaffe went over to sign up. Emma was carrying a big paper bag, holding it at the top. Everybody had been wondering all day what was in that bag. We didn't have very long to wait to find out. As Jaffe was just about ready to sign the historic document to bring down the color line, there was a big bang. *Squash!* – The bottom had fallen out of the bag. There were a couple of dozen Grade A extra large New Orleans eggs all over the red carpet. I'm standing right beside her carrying the rest of her bags, and I was glad I had this bunch of newspapers

under my arm. I cleaned up everything as fast as I could. They got registered and stayed there."

Emma distrusted doctors and banks. She carried her entire savings, including old uncashed checks, around in that red purse of hers, and she was robbed on the street at least twice. Afraid to go home after the job, she sometimes slept sitting up in a chair in the Jaffes' apartment behind the Hall. She had an ulcerated leg all wrapped up in brown paper; Jaffe would call in a doctor, but she would refuse to see him. "Well, Doctor," she said, "What do you think? I'm not going to croak. Why you're here? Why you afraid of dead people?" Emma would say that, when her time came, all she wanted was enough time to yell, "Lord, have mercy!"

Dr Henry Blackburn, who looked after a number of the Preservation Hall musicians when he could, remembered: "I had the privilege of knowing her for many years before and after her stroke. When I would come in, somebody would whisper to her, 'The jive doctor's comin'!' So, she'd be ready for me. And she'd have some sharp barb to stick in me. 'There's that jive doctor. Didn't send me no postcards from Japan this year!' She'd never fail to call you on some serious breach of etiquette like that. But it was nice to hear her say good things about you because mostly she just roasted you. 'You old fart,' she would say. She had a sharp tongue, that lady."

On tours Emma would walk onto the stages of big auditoriums with her purse firmly hooked under her arm. She would move out of her own motel room and sleep, curled up in a chair, in

Emma in Memphis: neither her broken eggs nor her bandaged legs kept the band from bringing down the historic color line.

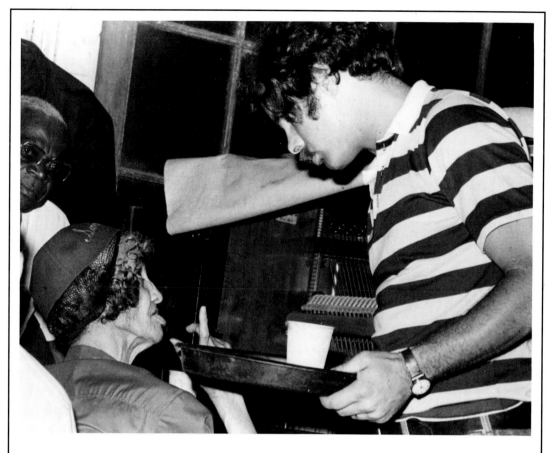

Emma with Chris: cake, twine and a felled mouse

someone else's room. And she refused to fly. Days ahead of when everyone else was leaving by plane, Jaffe would take her to the train station, install her in her compartment with a hat box full of food, and tip the conductor never to knock on the door or disturb her in any way. "Anything happens to me," she said, they'll just find out when I get there."

Following a paralyzing stroke in 1967, Emma performed from her wheelchair, reaching up to the keys to play with her right hand only. Sometimes a second pianist would sit beside her, playing the left-hand part. But the acid tongue needed no help. One night in 1976 she left a message to tell a young trombonist, known to be a womanizer,

"He might be slick, but he can stand plenty more greasin'."

Emma trusted Chris Botsford, one of the Preservation Hall staffers, more than anyone else in the world. In the last dozen years of her life he did every imaginable thing for her. "Emma wants a Sara Lee cake – a plain pound cake – no chocolate, nothing with sugar," read a typical note scrawled for Botsford. Nor was he the only recipient of her many requests. Among Emma's voluminous fan mail was this typical message from one R. A. Schatz in Minneapolis: "Dear Mrs Jaffe: The last time that I was down in New Orleans, Mrs Sweet Emma gave an autograph to a friend of mine and had asked for a certain necklace. I am enclosing the necklace for Sweet Emma;

would you be kind enough to see that she receives it."

Botsford would bring her sandwiches ("butter but no mayonnaise," underlined), twine, peppermints, a slip, "Holdmark" [Hallmark] cards, shoes. Old friends such as Willie Humphrey would carry food to her house and might or might not be allowed past the door. She insisted on being paid in brand new bills ("don't give me that fobie old money") and would nibble on soda crackers at the piano. When, for several nights running, an increasingly foul stench finally induced mild-mannered pianist Jeanette Kimball to declare, "You've got to do something or I cannot really play here much longer," a dead mouse was discovered to have been felled by the middle C hammer – just beside a little pile of Emma's crackers which had sifted down. She hated for anyone to take her picture; once, responding to a flashbulb, she threw a glass of water which landed, by mistake, all over banjoist Les Muscutt.

Emma at the keyboard: "Are you really Mrs Rockefeller?"

Moody and sleepless, Emma would spend hours a day talking on the phone to Botsford. Once he counted saying goodbye to her 15 times without being able to hang up. Jaffe once fell asleep and woke up again while she was talking to him on the phone. During these interminable conversations, which could occur at dinner time or at four o'clock in the morning, Chris got into the habit of doing something else, simply throwing in an occasional "Really?" or "No kidding."

Emma often surprised people. A well-known musician who had sat in with the band one night came over to say tenderly, "Emma, I just want to say how much I enjoyed playing with you." She snapped back, "Well, the feeling's not mutual. Who *are* you? I don't care *who* the hell you are!" Her opinions of different bands and musicians depended largely on how she felt at the moment. But even when she was sick, she would almost never cancel her performance. If a problem developed about her getting a ride to the Hall, she'd call up in tears, and a cab would be sent for her.

Emma, while unique, was also a typical Preservation Hall musician, beloved and cranky and in touch with life right to the end. "I always did love to play," she said. "The music was naturally in me... I never was timid or nothin' like that... I never was contrary or nothin' or argue... but I telling you, I been around. *Whenever You're Lonely, Just Telephone Me*: I don't know if anybody even knows that one now. But I know that from way back then."

Chapter Eight

THE LINEAGE

"My horn don't have no name."
—*clarinetist Raymond Burke*

The 1980s ushered in a surprising new trend. After a gap of more than a quarter century, some younger black Orleanians were starting to play traditional jazz. They had been born into a different world than had their fathers, who had come of age in the civil rights era and had wanted nothing to do with the "bad old days" of segregation and a profitless music. The newer players were no less individualistic than jazzmen have ever been, and no less concerned with the realities of making a living. But they were more sophisticated than the jazz pioneers. Relatively liberated from the tensions of repression as well as rebellion, they were free to follow musical paths that might have seemed heresy to the black youth of the 1950s and 1960s. Reaching back to discover their own roots, these young jazzmen began to revalue and relearn styles laid down by the generations of their grandfathers and great-grandfathers.

While that cool technical wizard, New Orleans-born trumpeter Wynton Marsalis, was off conquering the world with his fastidious classical and modern jazz sounds, and crediting his bluesy roots, several of his contemporaries were beginning to appear at the city's traditional jazz spots, including Preservation

Trumpeter Punch Miller taught his student Tommy Sancton at the Hall by day in the 60s. En route to one successful career as a "Time" magazine reporter and editor, and to another as an accomplished part-time jazzman, the budding writer and clarinetist published a long, loving portrait of his mentor in "Downbeat" magazine. Their relationship illustrated one of the Hall's most important byproducts: the passing on of a noble lineage.

Hall. By the mid-1980s trumpeter Wendell Brunious and clarinetist Michael White, in particular, had become regulars there and were touring widely. Bassist Walter Payton was seen at the Hall with increasing frequency. Some others, such as trumpeter Gregg Stafford, remained inexplicably absent.

Newer drummers included Frank Oxley and Bob French, both sons of prominent New Orleans musicians. Another was Stanley Stephens, a broadly based professional from a jazz lineage that included his grandfather Alfred Williams, a parade-style drummer who had worked at the Hall before his death in 1963 (see photograph on p.40):

> My grandfather was a very, very good snare drummer, and it's a pleasure walking in his footsteps, playing with some of the guys he played with that are still around. It's just an honor to play here at the Hall.
>
> When I was around four or five years old, I would be in the parades with him. So it's kind of a culture thing that I grew up with. He showed me. These parades used to pass right in front of our house. And he would be in the parades, and I would go out there and walk with him, three blocks or so. And it was really fantastic. I relate to what was happening from the street. My grandfather stayed at my house, and I was messing around with his drums. I wish he could be around now to see how I done really followed in his footsteps.
>
> When I got into this business, I figured I would just cover it all, different styles, different bands. Playing the traditional music that it all started from is really a big help. And to have a place to come and play it. And to have a city like New Orleans to play it in. This is where it all started. But it died for a long time. When I am working on Bourbon Street, people come in and say, "Where are the rest of the black bands? This is what we came to New Orleans to see, what's written in the history books." They need more halls like this around the city.
>
> I been comin' here to Preservation Hall since I was 15 or 16 years old. And Preservation Hall musicians used to come to my house. I listened to my grandfather's records, and I studied with James Black, and I went to the New Orleans Creative Arts Center. My instructor was Ellis Marsalis [father of Wynton Marsalis], and he stressed that we learn New Orleans jazz. To pass, we had to learn all styles of music. I thank him again.

Wendell Brunious, born in 1954, was another well-trained, versatile young professional. At one jazz festival he was seen performing with eight

The grateful inheritor Stanley Stephens has joined the present generation of professionally trained, widely experienced black musicians. His business card had been meant to say "international drummer" but was erroneously printed "internal" drummer. Stephens left it that way.

different groups, from traditional to bebop to Latin to reggae, rushing from one stage to the next. His trumpet work at Preservation Hall miraculously blended elements of the rugged Kid Thomas and polished Clifford Brown styles. Jaffe chuckled when he remembered that Wendell's father, John, a relatively sophisticated trumpeter, pianist and arranger, was considered too young to play at the Hall when it started.

In the years preceding Thomas's death in 1987, Brunious was eased into the role of leader of the Thomas band. His ability to pull this off smoothly among men two or three times his age derived not only from his talent and personality, but also from his jazz family lineage, which included, on his mother's side, pianists Lester and Burnell Santiago and banjoist Willie Santiago. Wendell had been named after trombonist Wendell Eugene; saxophonist Harold Dejan was his uncle; and bassist Frank Fields and his wife had looked after Wendell and his seven brothers and sisters after their parents died. Such are the clannish support systems that continued to lend the New Orleans music scene a special continuity.

Crisp, creative, witty, soft-spoken, yet firm and professionally ambitious (with a degree in marketing), Wendell brought a fresh breeze into the Hall. Although he literally worshiped the ground Louis Armstrong walked on, he had a different outlook than either the flinty oldsters or the out-of-town revivalists. Under Brunious, the former Thomas band began to be shaped more consciously, with more sensitive dynamics and backings, and an expanded repertoire including songs featuring Brunious himself on quiet vocals. If the playing of the new generation lacked the hell-for-leather drive and sincerity of those for whom the Hall had been established, one reason seemed to be that the younger men faced wider-open doors of possibility in their lives. No longer did a black musician need to pour everything he had through a keyhole-sized opening.

Few of the younger local traditionalists played stringed instruments, in part because their chief proving ground had been this city's bubbling resurgence of brass band activity. By the mid-1970s venerable marching ensembles such as the Olympia, the Young Tuxedo and the Majestic were accepting and shaping younger players. Two other groups –

A gentle handing-over of the leader's baton occurred in the mid-80s as the redoubtable Kid Thomas (left), having led groups under his name for nearly half a century, was joined by the skillful and sensitive Wendell Brunious (right), who, as Thomas's strength finally ebbed, gradually took charge.

Doc Paulin's Brass Band and Danny Barker's Fairview Baptist Church Christian Band – made a specialty of doing so. High school band competitions played a role, too; the 1980s brass bands, composed mainly of teenagers, were performing in the streets in many parts of New Orleans. The best known of these was the Dirty Dozen, but there were many others, such as the Rebirth, the Pinstripes, the Chosen Few and the All-Stars.

Jaffe's sons Russell and Benjamin played several instruments. They became part of the scene of young musicians in Jackson Square and elsewhere. Anthony "Tuba Fats" Lacen was, as one magazine put it, a "gentle giant in the neighborhood of 6′ 5″ and 350 pounds," who "makes the sousaphone he plays look like a toy." A relatively young Olympia regular, he also played jazz jobs at the Hall. Tuba Fats was one of those who introduced syncopated rhythmic patterns to the traditionally more sober brass band bass style. By 1980 he was already being idolized by younger players, who vied to outdo him. For those not enjoying other advantages, such as a musical family background, this type of role modeling can be important.

Thus a highly visible street band resurgence was helping to re-seed traditional jazz. Besides the "push" of training and inspiration, there was the "pull" of good jobs, starting with feed-the-kitty sessions serenading the tourists. The local neighborhoods, with their street parades, social clubs and gospel churches, remained important spawning grounds as well. Adaptability, and a sense of roots, remained part and parcel of New Orleans music – plus staying alert for the main chance. In 1986 a 19-year-old tuba player in the Rebirth Band, Philip Frazier, told Vincent Fumar of *Dixie* magazine:

We all started together at J. C. Clark High School. One of the band member's parents was asked to form a jazz band to perform at the Sheraton Hotel. We got about ten or twelve people to join, and afterwards someone decided to go to the French Quarter. We started making money off tips. We liked the idea and decided to keep it together.

Like every other teenager, I listened to a lot of disco music, a lot of pop stuff. But when we moved into the Sixth Ward – Treme on St Ann, it was the second-line area where a lot of people like to hear this kind of brass band music. The Sixth Ward High Rollers was the first second-line club to give us a start. We heard the Dirty Dozen, Tuba Fats and the Olympia Band. Then we heard the Majestic, Doc Paulin and the Pinstripes. We're still learning.

Some people say it's the sound of a school band mixed with a jazz band. I'd say we have a jazz be-bop sound – rolling music. People like to dance off it. In the French Quarter we play a lot of traditionals. On second-line tunes we mix the traditionals with a lot of pop tunes. That's what the Rebirth is all about – having fun and being versatile.

I think that a brass band can take any song and change it to a jazz song. We do *Shake Your Booty* and *Billie Jean* and make them sound like second-line songs. We play *Killer Joe* and *Don't Drive Drunk* by Stevie Wonder. We also want to learn a lot of traditional songs – to be prepared when the older jazz bands decide to break up.

Somebody will have to carry on. When I first started, I didn't know anything about the history of brass bands. At Clark, in my senior year, I just happened to stumble on a book that listed all of the old jazz bands. I just told the other members that it's something great that we're doing. That we should be proud to continue on with this tradition. Some day we're gonna be in history.

I wish that more young people would try to form jazz bands. We're also looking forward one day to playing in Preservation Hall, which is one of the biggest dreams any band could have.

*At a neighborhood social club
in 1985 the Doc Paulin
ensemble serenaded the
membership after marching in
their annual street parade.
Paulin's long-established band,
favoring teenage musicians,
exemplifies New Orleans'
ongoing system of nurturing
grassroots jazz talent.*

Exposure, recognition and expectations of "being
in history" had been accelerated – some would say
too much so, along with the tempos – from the brass
bandsmen's stately pace of 40 years earlier.   The
change mirrored the value shifts in the wider society
in which the youths were growing up. Now, public
school music instruction and a decent horn were
generally easier to come by. But, on the other hand,
there was less willingness to delay gratification. There
was less of the measured depth and respect long ago
imbibed by a more traditional player like Percy
Humphrey:

I started tambourine when I was six or seven years old,
and I got on drums when I was nine or ten, because my
granddaddy did nothing else but teach music, and we had
to learn music, and I had to play with his different groups.
I was in his number three group, and I worked up to
number one group. We had to read, because to play these
overtures and things like *Aida* and *Poet and Peasant* the
drummer had to count, and if you made the lick in the
wrong place, Grandpa would chew you out.

If it wasn't in you, he would tell your parents, "Don't
be throwing your money away. He'll never learn it. He
don't practice, he don't listen. Keep him at home, or find
another teacher." He wouldn't want to waste his time.

On trumpet, my granddaddy taught me, my brother Willie taught me, and my brother Earl helped bring me out on the numbers that he knew that people liked to hear, kept popular with Chris Kelly and Sam Morgan and all them.

Even after I came out of high school, my granddaddy didn't want me to leave town. I used to have to get special permission to go over the river to play a job. He didn't want me to go. Said the ferry might be moving and I try to catch it and fall in the river.

Later, I was a member of Willie Cornish's orchestra. And he invited me to the rehearsals of the Eureka Brass Band. They had a professor to teach them, and I needed it. I welcomed a teacher of brass band music. I stuck with them, but I had to do like everybody else: wait my turn to go out and play with them. When my turn came, I would do what I could to assist the leaders. They played all types of hard music, and they contracted to do a whole lot of hard jobs. And in the evenin', when that sun was gwine down, in the heat of the day the older men was weakening, and being on the instrment myself, I'd go ahead and grab that lead and go ahead and continue to play it. And when they felt able to come back to it, they'd pull up. Then I'd get my rest and get back on my second or third part. I was trained to do with them, and I kept that up.

Until they got so they commenced to either quit playing or became ill with something. Every once in a while I would go in on a regular job, and I had to take charge, leadership, of the band, temporarily. When I got a regular night job, I'd turn the leadership over to some other trumpet player, because I felt it a little hard playin' day and night and carryin' on my other work, too, during the day.

I can't remember what year it was, but we were on a Carnival Day job, and the two oldest members of the band told me when I came out that mornin', said, "Now listen! We's tired of this foolishness of you puttin' us in charge of some of these other guys that don't know what they doin'. We want you to stay with us all the time. Even if you go on another job, you our leader. We don't recognize nobody else but you." And when those two men told me that, and the rest of the men agreed, I said, "Okay." And I been recognized as the leader of the Eureka Band ever since.

To one well-educated young black Orleanian, Michael White, traditional jazz was not a means of outgrowing his origins, as it had once been for so many – but a way back into them. Born in 1954, White had grown up unaware of his city's musical heritage. Not until he was 21 and well begun on a career that would earn him a Ph.D. in Spanish and an associate professorship at Xavier University did he realize that he had overlooked a vital tradition that was still all around him. From then on, he pursued it tenaciously:

I had to go back to the origins and the roots and the history and the development, and look for a meaning in it. I found out that my family people included bassist Papa John Joseph, who played with Buddy Bolden; his brother, clarinetist Willie Joseph, who recorded in 1927 with Louis Dumaine; and Earl Fourche, the alto player with the Sam Morgan band.

I came into traditional jazz much the way a European jazz fan would – I went to the Jazz Festival and haunted the Jazz Archives at Tulane. When I heard Sidney Bechet and Johnny Dodds, I said, "Hey, that's me. That's where I'm from. That's home." I didn't even know of George Lewis until 1979, but the first time I heard one of his records, I said, "That's it!" It was like a light bulb went on in my head. That was it. Instead of just hearing music, I heard what I had inside of me. And I said, "That's what you have to find and bring out."

A hard-core New Orleans person who would understand what's going on in the second line of a street parade, the perception they have of Bourbon Street and the French Quarter is negative to what they're feeling. Some bearded, pot-bellied guy standing there blasting loud, imitated choruses of Louis Armstrong at 90 miles an hour is not what people down here feel. And to a lot of people Dixieland is a racist turnoff. Of course, if I had found those things in the music, I wouldn't be playing it today. What I found in the music was this spirit of pride, a high degree of intelligence, an acute sense of survival consciousness and of individuality.

New Orleans people are different. We have different ways of thinking and being and acting and talking, and the music is one part of that. If you can please a local crowd,

Trombonist Freddie Lonzo appeared with fair frequency at Preservation Hall in the 80s. Among the best of the handful of younger black New Orleans players drawn to the music of their ancestors, he was born in 1950, played in Doc Paulin's band in his teens, and thereafter worked steadily in the internationally prominent Louisiana Repertory Jazz Ensemble as well as in the pit band for the highly successful musical comedy "One Mo' Time."

*Clarinetist Michael White,
though born in New Orleans,
only began discovering his
musical roots at the age of 21.
Thereafter he divided a busy
schedule between serving as
Associate Professor of Spanish
at Xavier University,
appearing regularly at
Preservation Hall and
concertizing throughout the
world. Such were the striking
social and professional changes
which had overtaken New
Orleans.*

you've done something. Initially I played for local crowds, church parades, jazz funerals, club parades. All of these were primarily in the black community, but there were also parties and dances and weddings and clubs and all these things that we played in the white community, too. At community events you have people that understand. At least they have a feeling for what you're doing. Not that the tourists don't; but you don't really feel that they understand. They're just sitting there, observing.

Some of the best times I've had playing were in the street parades when the attention is not on you, and when there is a meeting of the souls, a spiritual union between all the people that are there – the club people, the second-liners, and the musicians. Your thing is the music, and you play. The second-liners' thing is dancing, and they dance. And their dances become creative. Your music generates more exciting forms of dance for them, and their dance does things to you.

Sometimes out there, you're transformed. The streets start shaking, and you see people doing things that are hard to believe, like down on the street dancing on their stomachs without any problem. You see all kinds of gyrations that might look obscene in another context. There was one guy that would be on rooftops, and every block, by the time I looked up, he was there. How he crossed streets and all, I'll never know. But it was just incredible. That kind of thing was the best – where you had local people that understood, at least on the spiritual level, what was going on, and all participated. No one can tell me that what the second-line dancers and the club people with all their beautiful costumes were doing wasn't equally valuable to what the musicians were doing.

Every time I play at Preservation Hall, it's quite an experience for me. I go over to the spot where my ancestor died, Papa John Joseph, and I say to myself: "This is the place where he died." I look at the clarinet chair and I say: "This is really it." I'm going to be sitting in George Lewis's chair, Burbank's chair, Willie Humphrey's chair, and it makes me shake inside. When you sit in that chair, you think of all the great players that have come before you, and you think about yourself and how far you got to go, and it's really a scary feeling, but it makes you feel good.

That enduring respect, plus plenty of fresh ambition and articulateness, earned Michael White a conspicuous place in the international classic jazz scene. In 1989, for example, he took a well-rehearsed band that included his former mentor, the banjoist, singer and commentator Danny Barker, north to Manhattan to play the music of Jelly Roll Morton at

Double troopers, leader-trumpeter Kid Sheik Colar and pianist-singer Sadie Goodson were married when nearly 80. Both possessed impressive track records with New Orleans bands from the 20s on. Colar had been among the very first regulars at the impromptu sessions at Larry Borenstein's art gallery – the forerunner of Preservation Hall. Goodson was the sister of Billie Pierce. Approaching their ninth decade, Sheik and Sadie were still blasting away at the Hall– testimony to a remark made by the great banjoist Johnny St Cyr: "Jazz rejuvenates a person."

Alice Tully Hall. The August 7 concert drew a six-column advance spread in the *New York Times* which was followed by a glowing review.

* * *

Not merely in New Orleans, but around the world, the original style had been reseeding long enough to have produced a number of second-growth players with something to say beyond the imitative stage. Having furthered this internationalization of the music and its audiences, the Hall found itself no longer an isolated outpost dedicated to a parochial form. By the mid-1980s, jazzmen were hurrying from their nights at 726 St Peter Street to worldwide tours, festivals and other gigs with a fluidity unheard of in the 60s. Not that it was easy to make a living playing traditional New Orleans jazz. But for some it had at least become a realistic possibility. Regulars at the Hall now included a number of transplanted jazzmen of the revival generation, including trombonist Frank Demond (from California), reedman Jacques Gauthé (from France), banjoist Les Muscutt (from England), banjoist Neil Unterseher (from Lincoln, Nebraska), pianist John Royen (from Washington, DC), and pianist Steve Pistorius (from Port Sulphur, Louisiana).

The outlines of the old form might be blurring, but public awareness of the Hall remained sharp. Coverage in the 1987 edition of the popular guidebook *Let's Go USA*, for example, was much like what the *New York Times Travel Section* and other tourist guides had been saying for two decades:

> Jazz began in New Orleans, and is alive and kicking today. A lot of the jazz is played in bars where innocent customers are lured in and pay huge cover prices. Most of the jazz is loud enough to enjoy from the streets, where you can usually see the bands as well. You might want to bring your own provisions and listen from outside . . .
>
> The city nurtures its artists. Tiny Preservation Hall, 726 St. Peter St. (523-8939) hasn't changed in 50 years [actually 26 years]. Nothing distracts from the aging musicians of the Preservation Hall Jazz Band and the outstanding traditional jazz they play here every night. When the band is away touring the world, other classic groups perform here. Admission to the small, dark hall is $2, and no drinks are sold, though you can bring your own soft drinks. Doors open at 8 pm and the music goes on until midnight [actually 12:30]. Chat with the musicians between sets. There is a big jazz festival around the end of April and beginning of May each year.

Such thumbnail sketches missed the churning groundswell of jazz activity going on at such places as the French Market (three outdoor locations), the Meridien Hotel (nightly plus Sunday brunch), special spots like tiny Fritzel's and huge Storyville Hall, and two major new tourist-related shopping malls, Riverwalk and the refurbished Jax Brewery.

Following Louisiana's oil slump, and a steep decline of the once-important port of New Orleans, tourism had become the city's number one industry. With the river excursions, historic buildings, famous

A new-old face in the 80s was that of Pud Brown, a versatile reedman born in California. Brown's far-flung career had included long stints with trombonist Jack Teagarden and with straw-hat Dixielanders around Los Angeles.

Rock-solid, British-born Les Muscutt was one of a handful of transplanted "revival period" traditionalists who gradually earned a regular weekly slot at the Hall as the oldsters faltered or disappeared during the 80s.

cuisine and huge new convention facilities, steadily mounting numbers of visitors were drawn by the city's reputation for original jazz. In the background were 20 years of slow integration and the "greening" of America. The new ethics of pleasure and consumption impelled the rest of the nation toward the good times for which this city had always been famous. For the first time in nearly a century, the New Orleans jazz scene in the late 70s, 80s and early 90s was lively and expanding.

The change in the jazz environment was most vivid along the riverfront. On the eve of World War II, when Bill Russell first came to town, musicians of the calibre of George Lewis and Jim Robinson heaved gunny sacks along the docks as stevedores, hoping to play the occasional evening dance or long, sweltering Sunday parade. Now, for better or worse, most of those docks were gone. They had been replaced by tourist facilities where strolling jazz quartets wended their way among glittering, air-conditioned shops. Someone else bleeped away at a calliope on an antique sternwheeler, and a brass band was getting a high fee to blast away for five minutes in an immense convention hall while the flaming baked Alaska was being wheeled in.

* * *

Continuing to serve as a gateway between neighborhood New Orleans and the mass society, Preservation Hall thus oversaw a two-way traffic of growing complexity. Musicians old and young, black and white, local and transplanted, were relying on the city's resurgent traditional jazz scene in general, and on the Hall in particular, for steady professional work.

One price of this kind of progress was that the crisp edges of the style were softening. While Jaffe usually avoided direct comments on the music, he did mention that he missed the old roughness. Another staffer admitted that she missed the fire and drive. Part of the problem was that genuine new talent was not appearing at anything like the rate needed to replace such steadily disappearing stalwarts as clarinetist Raymond Burke, banjoist Manny Sayles and trumpeter Kid Thomas. While he remained a

The French reedman Jacques Gauthé (above), after arriving in New Orleans as a master chef, segued into the role of a very active full-time jazzman. During the 80s and 90s he was featured not only at the Hall but also at many jazz spots around town, notably the French-owned Meridien Hotel, where he served as overall musical director. Nebraska-born banjoist Neil Unterseher (below) moved to New Orleans in 1964 to perform at Your Father's Moustache. Before long he was to be heard in a number of riverboat and nightclub settings, sometimes leading his own band, the Razzberrie Ragtimers, at others being featured as a Flamenco guitarist. He was a regular at Preservation Hall from 1984.

vigorous participant in, and supporter of, the neighborhood-based marching band resurgence, Jaffe admitted that its increasingly riff-oriented melodies and shuffle-beat rhythms sometimes degenerated into "brass band disco." Others, who had long loved the inspired handful of traditional jazz recordings from the 1940s and 1950s as well as the unparalleled "classics" of a generation earlier, could only shrug at the veritable flood of mostly indifferent records pouring out of New Orleans and elsewhere from the 60s through the 80s.

To some, detecting an occasional bebop phrase in Preservation Hall was like seeing a shrine desecrated. A few felt performance standards were declining on the tours as well. Others replied that such fastidiousness was like trying to straighten out the meandering Mississippi. Cross-fertilizations between rhythm-and-blues, brass band music, early jazz, pop influences, gospel, Cajun and other forms had marked the New Orleans music scene since the 1940s and before. New standards of performance and acceptability had always been coming in; jazz was a hybrid breed. Writer Marcel Joly made this point in 1986:

The ideas of purity of style were made by critics and writers. Very few musicians share them. Try to ask one of the old-timers to describe what kind of music he was playing 40 years ago. You'll be puzzled by the answers you get! "We had a good band, we played all kinds of stuff, you know." "Did you play traditional New Orleans music?" "Sure we did, we played Dixieland like they play today, we also played some Jimmie Lunceford arrangements and some Duke Ellington, you know, well whatever was popular during those days . . ."

Didn't George Lewis base his famous *St Philip Street Breakdown* on Woody Herman's *Chip's Boogie Woogie*? Wasn't Tommy Dorsey one of Louis Nelson's favorite trombone players? Didn't Albert Burbank at one time try to sound like Benny Goodman? To hell with purity! It's a small miracle New Orleans music retained so many characteristics that set it apart from any other music in the world. Could, to take an extreme example, the Dirty Dozen Brass Band, with their mixture of rhythm and blues, modern jazz, Mardi Gras music and traditional New Orleans brass band music, come from anywhere else than New Orleans? . . . New Orleans music today is not a museum piece but a living, changing and evolving music, just like it has been for almost a century.

Despite this natural evolution, longterm continuity of style did remain a goal at the Hall. The place might be dedicated to the musicians, but management did the hiring. Many factors had to be considered. There was an evident effort to balance bands containing older players who had grown weak with younger ones who might look less historic but had stronger "chops." Only the Humphrey band preserved a fairly steady roster of players. On any given night it was hard to predict who might appear in the Kid Sheik, former Kid Thomas, and various pickup bands. Being open every night of the year except Mardi Gras, the Hall necessarily ran in a fairly routine manner.

More and more, during the 1980s, Jaffe delegated the hiring of individual players to Jane Botsford and Resa Lambert. Not being musicians themselves, they simply worked down a mental list when a regular couldn't make it – often on short notice. One or two of the better players complained privately of this "interchangeable parts" atmosphere, although it is doubtful they fully realized the problems involved. Certainly, frequent variation of personnel and leadership did not favor the kind of settled-in chemistry that continued to mark the Humphrey group.

The music played at the Hall may also have been affected, in subtle ways, by the fact that the younger local musicians were coming to maturity in a divided culture. Linguists speak, for example, of "code shifting" between Black English and standard English – the tendency of the same person to use different accents and expressions in the different worlds of the local neighborhood and the mass commercial society. An experienced jazz listener can detect similar shiftings of expression in musicians who have acquired a certain level of sophistication. Bourgeois surroundings have a polishing, restraining effect on the way one expresses oneself.

"Bifurcation" between the local and tourist cultures showed up in other ways, too. Most established Orleanians were less and less willing to set foot in the teeming French Quarter. Yet they turned out in droves for the annual Jazz and Heritage Festival, which was quite profitable, drew much of its talent from out of town and resembled a big state fair.

This kind of "shift" between the viewer and the

Swinging along the 1100 block of Decatur Street, the Young Tuxedo band took its spanking-fresh energy into the French Quarter for the First Annual McDonogh 15 School's Performing Parents Review, circa 1984; musicians include (from left): Awood Johnson and ?Lester Calliste (trombone), John Simmons (trumpet) and Gregg Stafford (cornet).

viewed is by no means limited to New Orleans. Historian Daniel Boorstin touched on it in the context of a visit to Istanbul:

> Out-of-doors the real Turkey surrounds the Istanbul Hilton. But inside it is only an imitation of the Turkish style. The hotel achieves the subtle effect, right in the heart of Turkey, of making the experience of Turkey quite secondhand.
>
> The museum visitor tours a warehouse of cultural artifacts; he does not see vital organs of living culture. . . . Tourist attractions serve their purpose best when they are pseudo-events. To be repeatable at will they must be factitious. . . . By the mirror-effect law of pseudo-events, they tend to become bland and unsurprising reproductions of what the image-flooded tourist knew was there all the time. The tourist's appetite for strangeness thus seems best satisfied when the pictures in his own mind are verified in some far country.

In 1987 Hall staffer Dodie Simmons, having toured Japan two years earlier with the Kid Sheik band, observed that "There's a great appreciation for New Orleans jazz all over the world – except in New Orleans. They teach traditional jazz and grand marshalling at the University of Waseda. Most

In a tradition-blessed burst of gaiety, crowds swirled among members of a brass band during the kind of celebration that would continue to inspire and shape young New Orleans jazz players.

musicians in Japan learn the music in school. Girls are taught to be grand marshalls, with umbrellas. It's incredible that we don't have anything like that here."

But of course who in New Orleans ever needed to go to school to learn to twirl an umbrella? What the still-seminal city neighborhoods continued to have in abundance was the very thing that was drawing a sophisticated young man like Michael White back to its bosom. The seedbeds could seem a long way from the lavish brunches and insouciant shopping malls. But the soul was still there. While New Orleans continued to suffer from chronic problems – illiteracy and unemployment, among others – its virtues were harder to quantify. They included a strong maternal feeling, a sense of belonging, people taking care of other people in a personal way, and a locally determined sense of what life is about, that set this city apart from every other one in the United States. The jazz community remained a special womb within this larger womb.

Creaky and unimproved, the Hall had earned its own niche in that community. As the vocalists still sang of legendary Basin Street, this was a place where all the folks could meet. In earlier times some of the musicians, given a choice, would have preferred to play in more gussied-up surrounds than Mr Larry's dingy old art store. But in the end these modest surrounds turned out to be better theater, and a happier place to work, than, say, the Hilton. Noting that New Orleans was in danger of becoming a caricature of itself, author Calvin Trillin pointed to Preservation Hall as an exception.

The continuing miracle, as drummer Trevor Richards put it, was that, "Whatever the music produced in this city, they always play it as if they mean it."

Inner simplicity – the music of the heart – was still proof against life's outer complexities. Clarinetist Raymond Burke would occasionally utter statements which, like his playing, had an aura of mystical truth just because they were so down-to-earth. As he did one evening in the carriageway when he confided in his thick drawl: "My horn don't have no name."

* * *

Jaffe made various statements at various times, to various people, about the likely future of the Hall. The underlying theme seemed to be that the place should remain open as long as musicians existed who wanted to play there. In 1986 a person intimately involved with the Hall for many years remarked that he believed Jaffe, who did not depend on Preservation Hall to make a living, would long since have closed it had that not meant turning so many musicians out of well-paying jobs. A close friend of Jaffe's remembered him addressing the issue from a different perspective:

Allan said he didn't know how long the Hall could or should continue, but that musicians hadn't stopped turning up in 25 years.

I remember telling Allan that I didn't want to renew the ties I'd had ten years previously with musicians at the Hall, that too many of those I'd cared about had died, and I didn't have the courage to get close to the survivors. He said he did give thought to the fact that the majority of those he considered close friends were aged enough that death needed to be anticipated, and that each death hurt differently. He didn't look for a way to avoid the losses; he speculated that he'd grieve more frequently than other

Steve Pistorius was most audible in his continuing role as a calliope player on the steamers moored along the levees and plying the Mississippi with thousands of nostalgic tourists. But he was also in constant demand as both a ragtime specialist and a fine jazzband pianist.

John Royen, a pupil of Don Ewell, deftly fused the influence of several of the great jazz pianists, from Jelly Roll Morton through boogie-woogie and beyond. His energetic style lent a clear harmonic backbone to many Preservation Hall bands.

men his age. Then, after one of his overly long pauses, he said he wondered if he wasn't, in ways he didn't recognize, affected or hardened because of his proximity with death, and that he'd be sorry if that were so.

I don't think Allan heard the music as a thing apart from the musicians who made it. I never heard him criticize music the way some of the jazz buffs who visited did. He didn't expect his friend whose false teeth pinched to sound like a 1940 recording. He could hear fatigue, boredom, enthusiasm, renewal, inspiration – ups and downs of the musicians who were true to their sound, or changed to please crowds. Allan forgave them much. He indulged the bandleaders who hired lesser musicians than Allan might have. He let the music happen to a greater extent than some jazz lovers would have. Where he could have gone after the sound, he deferred to the humanity. That's what audiences experienced: company with musicians playing old-style music, New Orleans-style jazz, sometimes imperfectly executed but dazzling with remembrances. Some of the younger musicians played old music new style, new music old style, and old music old style, but I don't think Allan or Preservation Hall audiences could settle in comfortably with the newer players – the difference between a thing remembered and a thing newly learned was too great.

Allan gave me the impression that he hoped the future of the Hall would be clear enough and that he'd be sensitive enough to follow its lead. I don't think Allan shaped the Hall so much as he served what he discerned was fitting.

Enduring the criticism inevitably leveled at one who is good at getting a lot done, but who rarely explains his motives or decisions, Jaffe grieved silently over the Hall's human and musical losses. The fact that life is always imperfect did not greatly trouble him. His way was not one of refined esthetics, but of steady effort, of continually giving and receiving in the family-like atmosphere he set around the Hall. Below the surface of his conversations there simmered a kind of deliberately unsystematic philosophy, dosed with virile, coarse-grained love, sometimes laced with bitterness or resignation. As regards problems of musical quality, he might have agreed with an acquaintance who observed that "an exaggerated purity lacks vitality." Wondering what lesson might lie hidden behind yet another faltering version of *The Sheik of Araby*, a listener might have found an answer in T. S. Eliot's words, "Teach us to care and not to care."

A fresh generation of pianists graced Preservation Hall, its tours and New Orleans generally from the late 70s onwards. Swedish-born Lars Edegran (above) had been a fixture since the 60s, playing several instruments in a host of venues and acting as an intelligent arranger and leader of many bands including the New Orleans Ragtime Orchestra.

The cavernous rooms above the Hall proper, and in the rear beside the patio, were stuffed with memorabilia, voluminous files, musical instruments, pictures, collections of piano rolls, folksy clay dolls and hundreds of other odd and intriguing items – all barely kept from intruding on the heaped-up desks where the phones never stopped ringing. Frank Demond once asked Jaffe what he would ever do with all this memorabilia. "One day," he replied, "I'll just walk away from it." Conversations with Jaffe in the Hall, while walking up and down the hills of San Francisco, at table in Allan and Sandra's modest yet distinctive French Quarter home, and while churning across the landscape of America in Greyhound buses yielded countless hours of cassette tapes. Some gleanings of his thoughts about the Hall and its future:

Some of the musicians introduce my two sons to people as, "This is going to be my boss." But I think that assumes an awful lot. Parents like the idea of the children following in their footsteps. It gives a certain amount of assurance in their own life that what they did was worth copying. It assumes the Hall is going to continue that long. I'd certainly like to think that, but when I start to visualize it, it's hard to visualize who is going to be playing there.

There's a difference between black style and white style. I'd rather have black musicians than white musicians playing. I don't mind white musicians who are playing in a black style. I would rather have an older musician than a younger musician. That's what the Hall was started for. It was really for the older black musicians. One of the fringe benefits was that the young white musicians would have a place to hear them and learn to play. I would certainly rather give an older musician a job, not necessarily one or just all of them, but one who has made a serious contribution. If Harold Dejan didn't make the contribution I think he's made, there would be no reason. There are a dozen other musicians that could be playing in his place. I think that he is entitled to play. Kid Thomas is entitled to come in and be paid for a job, even if he only wants to play for one set. There are other musicians, both black and white, who we send checks to who don't come out and play.

I think that the idea of the groups staying together and still mingling is basically what this country is starting to revert back to. The idea of the melting pot: being able to get along and still keeping your own traditions.

Your ears are listening to something with your own prejudices. Just like all the people who wouldn't listen to George Lewis because he didn't sound like Johnny Dodds.

The jazz buff's jazz buff,
musician, composer, historian,
self-abnegating yet crusty
helper-out of thousands of
jazzmen and their friends, Bill
Russell muses on his obscure
perch near his longest-lived
companions – records, brooms
and the carriageway cat.

You set your own period and say this is my standard. Everybody has a period that they're tuned into. This is what they've heard for the first time, and it's difficult to hear something past that, other than that. I don't like the King Oliver band. I'll say it doesn't sound like a New Orleans band. Who am I to say that, but in my own mind I say that's not the way the bands ever played here.

Today, when people talk about traditional musicians, they lump Armstrong and Dizzie Gillespie in the same group. I wonder if Gillespie's older than [Preservation Hall drummer] Frank Parker? He very easily could be. Gillespie's a traditional musician! So that generation that saw that conflict [between modern and traditional jazz] doesn't really see it any more. Where I would see it come up today is like with Wynton Marsalis. His conflict is between guys that have sold out commercially and himself who has kept pure. I like his playing, but I think that either he or the press has made him into something. He has to be commercial, maybe more commercial than any trumpet player right now, because he's getting more work. But he's really talking about musicians who pander in what they play to the lowest level of an audience's taste.

I'm not about to paint the front of the building, and I don't mind a couple of boards that give. When we wash the windows, I only do one side at a time. This year I did the back, and next year I do the front. I don't want the windows so dirty that you couldn't see through, but I certainly don't want them clean, either. I'm not kidding. That's what we do. I've got to make some contribution.

I think that people should have the privilege of making the discovery. I think that still, today, people come in and discover Preservation Hall, and that's the way it should be. People should come in and I don't want it to be clear-cut on what you're supposed to do. You've got to come in and figure it out yourself; there are no big arrows and signs that say: this is what to do. Here's someone who stood in line for 20 minutes, and he still comes out with that feeling that he discovered something. It's exciting.

I think one of the important things that bands can learn from coming to New Orleans is seeing that the music is not static, that it's changing, and that it's functional, and that it's not terrible to try a new song and if you don't play all the old songs, it's not terrible either.

There are so few younger musicians. Last year [1985] there were 75 musicians who played at the Hall. In some of the early years we had 200, even 300 one year. If one musician comes along to replace 20 or 50, that's not enough. It's hard to visualize who is going to be playing there.

I respect Bill Russell's opinion more than anyone else's. I would like to talk to him about what he sees as the future for the Hall, whether he thinks there is a future for the Hall. But it's a long, painful subject and I don't want to put him through it, and I don't know if I'm right or wrong in not doing it. Anyway, I would like to sit with him and spend a couple hours a day for a month talking about it, or not talking about it, letting him listen to me or listen to him, or whatever. I think both of us talking about it long enough, it's going to come out, maybe not the same decision I have now, but at least I'd be satisfied with my decision.

My decision now is, as long as the musicians want to play there, the Hall should be available for them to play. As long as Percy, or Willie, or Nelson, or Thomas wants to play at the Hall, I think they ought to be able to play. And the Hall ought to be able to stay open so that they have that venue to play in.

I saw a bigger role for the Hall in getting young people to play and, although these have come along, I don't always like the music they're playing. It's like the old civil rights story, you know, "I sat at the lunch counter for six months, waiting for them to serve me, and they finally served me and I didn't like the food!" I waited for 20 years for the young guys to start playing the music, and I don't necessarily like the way they play.

The purpose of the Hall was never a profit motive. It's always had other purposes before that. I've never lost sight of the fact that it has to make a profit to stay open, but that wasn't the purpose. And so a lot of these considerations are serious to think about. Bill Russell was not satisfied with this drummer, that drummer. He says it should be at a certain level. And the problem is, what if it's not at that level – then what? Bill has an answer for that somewhere inside of him. He has an answer to say, you should keep looking, it's something that's maybe gone over, or forget about it. That was a golden period that's not going to happen again.

But I don't think that's the answer. That didn't happen in any other music. Maybe with the waltz or something? There have always been great violin players, and there will continue to be great violin players. You say, they emerge from a big wide substratum, with the soil being enriched, and then a few outstanding people come out. Well, for the first time, there is a possibility of that large group. Is it worth hanging in there and hoping it happens? Are you doing any damage by hanging in there? I don't know. I'm not claiming there is damage being done. I certainly could make a good argument there is. That by popularizing the music, if it's no good, the bad drives off the good and becomes a standard.

As I said, the purpose of the Hall wasn't a profit motive, and I also don't have to do it to make a living. My other interests have actually proved more profitable than the Hall. I've been fortunate with my other investments. But if I'm going to spend my time doing it, I'm going to do it as well and as successfully at every level as I can. I want the music to be as good as it can be. I want the profits to be as good as they can be.

Willie Humphrey doesn't have to be out on the road playing because he's hungry. He doesn't have to work any more. He has enough to take care of him. So, he's doing it for another reason. As long as he's doing it, he wants to be paid as well as he can, and he wants to play as well as he can. That's fine.

I don't want to say, hey, here's a job, come do an adequate job and get an adequate day's work. I want it to be better than that. The music ought to be better than that. It's got to be better than adequate, and if it's not better than adequate it has to at least be going in that direction, saying, yeah, there is potential of having some great music. There still is. There might have never been a night that something spectacular hasn't happened with any band, not all night for sure, but in four hours it certainly has. And some nights it's all night. In the poorest night's music we have something that, if it were on a record, I would cherish forever, and so would everyone else.

Lifetimes of commitment:
Allan Jaffe saying goodbye to
trombonist Jim Robinson,
1976.

But, it's being done by a group of people that there's no call to replace. There's a whole lost generation of musicians. And what's lost more than anything is the social context of the music. We might end up with one band, and from that band, maybe three or four would emerge. Maybe it's going to have to get down to that before it gets better. If there are going to be any younger musicians playing, it's going to be those that survive and decide and make the commitment to do it.

I'm certainly going to hang in there. As I say, these are things I would like to talk to Bill about. But they're tough things to talk to him about, because, for him, it's his whole lifetime of commitment.

*   *   *

Jaffe had no way of knowing that that "lifetime of commitment" would soon apply to himself. The month-long conversation with Bill Russell never occurred. In late 1986, at the age of 51, Jaffe was discovered to have incurable melanoma.

"Where he could have gone after the sound, he deferred to the humanity," one friend said of Allan Jaffe. On the facing page the owner-manager is shown performing on helicon in Preservation Hall with (from left) Frank Demond (trombone), Frank Parker (drums), Percy Humphrey (trumpet), Willie Humphrey (clarinet), Sing Miller (piano) and Narvin Kimball (banjo). Jaffe's vacated place was filled, first at home and from 1987 on tour, by James Prevost (right), a reliable, broadly experienced New Orleans string bass player.

He bore the news as he had lived so much of his life – with noble equanimity. Family, friends and musicians came to visit, remained close. Concerning this book on the Hall, he continued to feel it should be about the musicians. He stressed the positive contributions of Larry Borenstein and said softly, "the music itself is what is." On Monday, March 9, 1987 – barely three months after having been diagnosed – Jaffe passed away.

Shock waves rippled around the world. The nation's press eulogized Allan Jaffe as the man who had saved New Orleans jazz from extinction. Many quoted Harold Dejan, leader of the Olympia, that jazzy brass ensemble in which Jaffe had done so

much tuba playing: "He believed in helping people out. If you didn't have no horn, he'd try to get you one. I don't know what would have happened to a lot of musicians without him."

It was announced that Jaffe had donated a building to the New Orleans Jazz and Heritage Festival Foundation for a planned School of New Orleans Music. The forthcoming festival itself would be dedicated to him. George Wein, the promoter of this and other successful festivals, echoed the feelings of many: "If it were not for Jaffe there would be no festival. When I first came to New Orleans, he was my guide, my teacher, my friend. To say I will miss him is an understatement."

On Wednesday, March 11, a standing-room-only crowd pressed into the small, hushed chapel of the Tharp–Sontheimer–Laudumiey Funeral Home on North Rampart Street, bordering the French Quarter. Beside the closed casket, the Humphrey band members wept as they played *Precious Lord, Lead Me On, Just a Little While to Stay Here* and *In the Sweet Bye and Bye*. Rabbi Raphael Adler spoke. He referred to Jaffe as a "rebe," or spiritual leader.

Then, outside, Percy Humphrey stood alone near the driveway. Softly, under the cloudy sky, he blew his trumpet in the direction of the three brass bands, the hundreds of musicians, relatives, friends from around the world, and so many others who felt a direct relationship to Jaffe. Gaunt, 82-year-old Bill Russell, feeling chilled in the gathering drizzle, shook his white head in stunned disbelief.

The crowd followed the hearse as it wound through the French Quarter, pausing at the Jaffes' home on St Ann and at the Borenstein residence on Royal Street. Local jazz buffs who had attended New Orleans funerals for decades said they had never seen such a sendoff. The streets became choked with people, including tourists who joined in. Umbrellas twirled; red and white carnations showered down from balconies. The procession halted in front of Preservation Hall, where *When the Saints Go Marching In* was played as a dirge. Many of the mourners held long-stemmed white carnations which they had gently lifted from the roof of the hearse.

Later, at a private internment at Chevra Thilim Memorial Park, the Olympia Band played a single number at the graveside. Finally, family, musicians and friends gathered at the Hall for red beans and rice. The Humphrey band performed there that evening as scheduled – and as Jaffe would surely have wished. And, in another fitting coincidence, they left the next day on a long tour of the Midwest, with Chris Botsford as manager, and James Prevost replacing Jaffe on bass.

In the years that followed, Jane, Chris, Resa and the other staffers continued to operate the Hall and the tours largely as before. But, of course, a major presence was gone, which brought another change: Sandra Jaffe, seen only infrequently around the Hall after the birth of her sons, was now its sole owner, and she returned to a more active role.

As the 1990s dawned, the future of Preservation Hall seemed as challenging as ever. The years under Sandra had been marked by staff shifts and by scheduling changes such as the occasional closing of the Hall on Sunday nights. Most poignantly, the loss of the original players continued apace: gone from under the Hall's gentle spotlights were such key men as Kid Thomas, Louis Nelson, Father Al Lewis, Sing Miller and Chester Zardis. But, like so many others, they would never be forgotten.

Sandra Jaffe, 1985: in the early 60s, as co-partner with her husband Allan, she had collected money at the door and attended to a host of physical and personal details. Then, after the birth of her two sons, she withdrew to a less active role. In 1987, after Allan's untimely death, she found herself sole owner of Preservation Hall and returned to its active management.

Milton Batiste

Report from New Orleans
by Tom Dent

Tom Dent, a well-known New Orleans poet, directs the yearly New Orleans Jazz and Heritage Festival.

New Orleans is a weird town, wavering in the breeze of history. An old place, one of the few towns in this country where one can look at the layers of two or three centuries in one glance. Then there is also the poised wrecking ball of "progress."

One hundred fifty years ago New Orleans was primarily a black city, as it is becoming again now. The city was largely built by black people, skilled and unskilled, slave and free. It was, and has always been, a river city, a seaport that made it on the sugar and cotton trade, and later on oil. But all that is changing now. Now the city wants to make it on reputation, that is tourism, and if possible on the grand scale. This is the reason for the domed stadium, the largest in the world, with all the problems that white folks have when they decide to build something too large. It is also the reason for new hotels and

office buildings and even the current obsession with Preservation.

And as New Orleans wavers, like a rickety old building, in the winds of time and change, a young black dude thinks about it all and he thinks about his plans to leave. He is any young man, just turned twenty, married or getting married; and he can't get a decent job, if he can get one at all. He's heard things might be better in LA or Chicago or Detroit or wherever in California his family has relatives.

As for New Orleans, he wonders what "progress" means for him. He even wonders about the new black politicians, and what they are doing for him. He sees them on TV now and then talking about this and that but they don't touch his life as anything real. He also wonders about the rash of new movies on Canal Street with his people running around pushing dope, or breaking up dope rings, or being beautiful secret agents, or cowboys; he wonders what that has to do with his life and livelihood. He wonders about the two soul radio stations, "your black giant booming you the latest in news and sounds" with steady advertisement from Mr Tee's jewelry store offering beautiful diamond rings with nothing down if you're getting married. He has a buddy who got one of those rings and they sat down one night and figured out that he will be paying for it for at least four years. But the music is good . . . when they play music.

And as he strolls past the downtown Howard Johnson's he notices that it is open again with the same stupid sign outside, this time SUPPORT YOUR SYMPHONY ORCHESTRA, BEAUTIFUL MUSIC . . . As New Orleans wavers in the winds he wonders what will happen to the *niggers* of New Orleans, will it be their city too, will it be a good city for niggers. Or whether there will come a time when there are his people and his music but no more niggers.

Suddenly he hears Batiste's trumpet sound the call. He feels the excitement run through his body as always; the Olympia is ready. The beat, the jump, the swift movement of rhythm, the entire crowd of his people carried away into unity of motion, singleness of purpose, individuality of motion. The second line is everybody's thing together and everybody's thing for themselves.

Umbrellas raised, the huge throng moves before, behind and with the band as if convulsed into it, become a part of it, reunifying movement and sound. The drumbeats echo like shots underneath the Claiborne Avenue overpass. Traffic stops before the black throng. Our dude feels like he is a part of an irresistible and undeniable force. He has heard people condemn the parades, the music, the

funerals, the dance, but he realizes there is something deeper, and he is a part of it, something old and certain about what it means and what it celebrates. Something he cannot put in words.

And for the first time in a long time he really doesn't want to leave New Orleans because, as the trumpet of Wallace Davenport darts out, echoing off sunrays, he knows there won't be anything like this in LA or Chicago or Detroit, there is something about this moment that can't be defined by money or jobs or progress or new buildings.

Quickly our dude moves closer astride the band, his umbrella up high bobbing with him. And he imagines that this parade never ends – it marches right on to City Hall and through it on Monday morning, through the courts, through Parish Prison and Central Lockup, then winds its way through the library, up and down Canal Street, through Maison Blanche and Holmes [department stores], through Mr Tee's taking a few diamonds along with it, and right over to Tulane and Broad to the police station bursting the eardrums of the police so that their brains fly right out the side of their heads in both directions and the music oozes in to impart finally some sense.

And then there were no more niggers because the niggers *were* the city: what his people had learned long before him was the order and the music was the law.

But he noticed that the Olympia had stopped playing, the excitement had cooled down, and the good dream got lost. Soon, when the parade was over, he would have to get back to his plans to leave.

So much for the weird town, this nineteen hundred seventy-fifth year of the Anglo calendar, wavering in the wind of history.

On the Road with Preservation Hall

A Postscript

NEW ORLEANS. Departure day. Morning. Sidewalks getting scrubbed down. Crowds and debris missing from the French Quarter. Sunshine on ancient patinas. Ironwork patterns repeated as shadows. Streets around Bourbon reopened to vehicles for a few hours so trucks can make their deliveries. Fresh, clear, peaceful air – as it must have been in the days when more of the musicians could afford to live in the French Quarter (but only a meagre living could be scratched out).

Suddenly, the crooked strings of second-story balconies are dwarfed by an immense, stainless-steel Greyhound Americruiser. Shouldering its way along narrow St Peter Street, it groans to a stop beside the Hall. Belly hatches begin gulping in tall stacks of record boxes hand-trucked out through the frail-looking French doors. Hundreds of these records will be peddled nightly from blazing stages across the continent. The musicians' suitcases accumulate in a modest line along the curb. Into the cavernous belly of the gleaming silver whale go the stout black drum cases, plastered with travel stickers.

Sauntering up one by one, given a hand at the door by driver Bill Sones (a plump good-old-boy from Mississippi who has been doing this for many years now and really loves these slow-going oldsters), each with his own character-istic gait, greeting, figure, hat and horn case, the musicians haul themselves up the stairs and scatter their presences more or less evenly around the comfy interior.

Bill reminisces about the special needs and habits of some who have passed away: where blind trumpeter DeDe Pierce used to sit, and where his intravenous feeding bottle hung, and how much he liked stopping in earlier days at O. T. Hodges Chili Parlor in St Louis. "Even though he was blind, he'd always know if the weather would change. He'd say, 'It's raining outside,' and I'd say, 'How do you know?' and he'd say, 'I can hear it.' DeDe's health used to be my responsibility. Or seeing he'd get off the bus okay. When he'd get ready to go on stage, I'd usually lead him up to the stage to where one of the musicians'd get him. He really wanted to play. When he got so bad he couldn't, he'd sit back and cry. I knew from Dr Blackburn that he was in extreme pain."

We snake through narrow streets toward the freeway. Checking a map of New Orleans can help a person under-stand something of the anatomy of this music. The streets are curved, rather than straight. Or *are* they? In a strange way, the New Orleans arteries appear both structured and free. Partly, this has to do with the meandering yet straight Mississippi. Through New Orleans it makes a huge loop, actually flowing north as it passes the Central

Business District and the French Quarter. But on a big map it comes straight down from the loamy soils of those four-square prairie towns into whose perfectly sterile auditoriums we are going: Marymount College in Salina, Kansas; University of Wisconsin, Whitewater; Iowa Central Community College, Fort Dodge; Minnesota Orchestral Hall, Minneapolis; Auditorium Theater, Chicago: one-nighters extending across the Heartland and up the East Coast into Canada.

BATON ROUGE. Humming along the Interstate, the jazzmen are in an upbeat mood. Laughing and joking, they have begun trading horror tales of the bad old times on the road in the 30s and 40s: of fumes and freezing winds pouring through the rickety buses, of desperately scanning the bare Texas horizon for an outhouse (or a tree), of being told to keep playing in a park in Georgia where a guy was being tarred and feathered. "Not like this," one tells me, "this heaven." Most of their stories whizz by in such a marvelous, thickly accented gumbo-speech that I can't quite keep all the ingredients straight.

Manny Crusto: "Playing out on the lake, I'd remember the waitress's friends' favorite numbers and play them when they came in, like a guy off an oil rig on certain days. So I'd get a tip *and* some wine."

NORTHWESTERN ARKANSAS. False-front shacks and stores. Outhouses. Steeply rolling forested country – the Ozarks. Log houses, buff grey expanses, plowed green river valleys along toward Fayetteville. Bare trees. Quilts. Two-strap jeans. Next to the log cabins, TV satellite dishes.

It often happens that, seeing this silver whale nose up to a roadside cafe, the waitresses's eyes fill with panic – until they realize no more than half a dozen of us are coming in.

Some of the musicians avoid spending money in restaurants. In the mornings Sing Miller munches on sweet rolls out of a paper bag. In the late afternoons he unpacks his electric frying pan and cooks red beans and rice and hamhocks in his room.

Words sometimes seem more an obstruction than an aid to what Sing is trying to tell you. His message comes from somewhere below the level of linear speech. He is not about to let it get lost in translation. His is the blues gift. He is all soul, and heart (and belly). The way he shakes his head sometimes, overcome with the inexpressible, makes me think of what the Indian poet-saint Kabir called "the unstruck sound." And the way he casts a chubby hand skyward, in tribute, every time he sings "I know He watches me." Stubborn, sensitive, outrageous, moving, nutty and the butt of private jokes, Sing is nonetheless the one I feel most like sitting with the evening I get the news that an old friend has suddenly died.

On the bus, each morning, during this non-playing part of the tour, there is talk of the TV programs they watched the night before in their separate motel rooms.

SALINA, KANSAS. Bright ice on trees, blown glass beauty. It scrapes fiercely on the sides of the bus as we inch toward the concert hall. Descending, the guys step very carefully. The piano turns out to be a resonant old upright.

"I remember this place."

The stage is still dark. Allan Jaffe shouts down from somewhere to his assistant, "Hey, Janie, tell Percy to wear a sweater." She does. He does. She admires it.

"How we goin' on? Coats or what?"

Jaffe: "Any way you want."

Backstage, one devotee tells another he closed down his truck stop at 5 p.m.

to come 60 miles on an icy road to hear this band.

Full house. Frank Demond's dance-like movement out across the stage and back. Percy showing mock anger at this, gesturing him to come back, pointing to the seat. Buddha-like, immovable, Percy gets ponderously to his feet for his solo. After that, settling back down, he pulls his black trouser legs up a little, exposing thin, ribbed, white socks.

Demond is one of the younger players who have gradually been filling the gaps left by the departing pioneers. He has advanced from being an imitative disciple of gruff-sounding old "Jim Crow" Robinson, complete with Jim's leg kicks and other mannerisms, to playing a sweeter, sliding style more natural to himself. He still repeats many of Jim's phrases. I like Frank's tone.

Iowa. The storm worsens as we head east. Heavy snow, the road a sheet of ice, cars and trucks littered in ditches. Jaffe hands Bill, the driver, a timed-release aspirin. Nothing but whiteness beyond the windows all day long. Tramping ankle-deep through fresh snow into a truck stop only to find the electricity out, no food available except cheese sandwiches to go. We barely make it to that evening's concert on time. But there's a special warmth about it. Co-singers Narvin Kimball and Sing Miller get an appreciative response from the audience when they do *I Get the Blues When It Rains.*

In the morning I notice Sing sitting alone in the motel lobby, staring out at the snow and sun for over an hour.

"Definitely in the top ten" of all their concerts, says Frank Demond, were two nights in a new, huge, beautiful auditorium in Caracas for Venezuela's bicentennial. People were dancing up and down the aisles. The second night it was more subdued because the President was there.

Never will Jaffe get a phone in the bus. He goes on tours to get away from the phone. His assistant, Jane Botsford, perches on the arm of the seat across the aisle by the hour, feeding him envelopes one at a time, arranged in order of importance, out of a cardboard box stuffed full of mail which has been forwarded from New Orleans.

"When do you plan to retire?" I ask Jaffe. "I don't plan to start working," he replies. In the back offices at the Hall, despite what Jane considers a crush of absolutely imperative work, he keeps an air of blithe freedom, coming and going and letting her do the worrying about all the important people he absolutely must see, while he has suddenly disappeared to eat oysters with some friends for three hours. Returning, he randomly checks this or that bit of paper, ignores others. Somehow the enterprise lurches on.

Percy describes a free-for-all that started years ago at a parade. A guy came at him with a beer bottle. Percy ducked, the guy hit his leg, Percy hit him with his trumpet and broke it on the guy's neck. "A good Buescher horn, too." The guy charged on, and a big tough drummer finally nailed him.

What can a drummer do if others have unsteady tempos? Frank Parker: "You got to act like you don't hear it." Tapping on his right bass drum foot: "The buck stops here. You got to be strong. You got to call on the Almighty."

At an upper-middle-class chit-chatty cocktail party, the old jazzmen sit silently, politely lined up in a row of chairs near the food table.

The critical faculty interferes with the jazz event much as a theology lecture would with the giving of communion (which is not to say one should dispense with theology).

"It's not always the quality of music that counts," a folklorist tells me. "Somebody who might have played better 30 years ago might still do it in a way no one else now does it."

Says Dick Allen, who was curator of the Jazz Archive at Tulane for many years: "I'm easily annoyed when I think of music as precious." And: "Jim Robinson was very unsophisticated musically – and I loved it. I loved his mistakes. I loved everything about Jim's playing because it had that frisky spirit. Never lost the beat. He could play the same break again and again, but it didn't matter, it was a good break and he still had fun playing it. Jim was a guy who could enjoy the simplest things in life or the complex things. Jim would dip into my pouch and chew aromatic pipe tobacco. Wow! He could do that! What there was in life to enjoy, Jim was gonna enjoy." But finally: "If you love New Orleans music, you're gonna get awful sour after a little while. Because it's a very painful thing to love New Orleans music and live in New Orleans through the 40s, 50s, 60s, 70s, 80s. Such losses, such a decline. It's a painful experience." On the road two weeks so far. Three to go.

Manny: "No excuse to be late to anything."

Sing: "That school teacher whupped me for being late. No reason to do that."

Percy: "She did too."

They argue about this. Percy: "I'd get whipped by that teacher *and* my daddy *and* my granddaddy."

Jaffe: "Uh-oh." He stops in the aisle between them, jokes with Sing: "What did you do *after* school?" Ratty vibes in the bus at this moment; Jaffe has stopped an incipient "humbug."

Paunchy, shuffling Sing takes bows onstage like a Metropolitan Opera star, points at high balconies, one side then the other, sweeps the orchestra pit, touches his forehead. He couldn't care less that the applause is beginning to sound ironic. The band has to start the next tune to induce him back to his piano stool.

NORTHERN MICHIGAN. During intermission Frank Parker gives two wide-eyed little boys a drum lesson backstage. After the concert one of them comes up onto the stage. Frank hands the boy the drumsticks he's just used and says forcefully, "Next time I come here I want you to *show* me something with those." The boy is transfixed. His parents have to call him sharply from the back of the auditorium to make him come home.

I remember. Something comes alive in you. It might work its way out as music or in some other form. Who knows where all the seeds will take root?

He who hears only the notes hears not this music.

INDIANA. They often eat at Shapiro's, a Jewish cafeteria in Indianapolis.

Manny swings his arm around to get rid of the pain in his shoulders before going onstage. Old guys have lots of pains. Narvin tries to give him advice. Manny won't listen.

After a day off, everybody's feeling peppy. Very audible in the way they're warming up in the dressing rooms. Percy high and vigorous. Later, he unexpectedly launches into a little dance during the trombone solo in *Ice Cream*.

Allan plays long, sustained tones on his tuba accompanying the banjo solo on *His Eye is on the Sparrow*.

Afterwards, road manager Chris Botsford, his wife Jane, and driver Bill Sones are selling records at the edge of the stage:

"I have your other record, not this one. I'll take it."

"I was nine years old when I heard this band the first time."

Sometimes you forget which state you're in. Once a stewardess on a plane asked Willie Humphrey where he was going. Willie couldn't remember. I'm half his age and right now I can't, either.

Backstage at a Catholic girl's college, after everyone else has left, two girls are playing a classical cello and piano concert for Jaffe, Percy, Jane and me, the four of us hovering around them like silhouettes in the crepuscular gloom.

The antiseptic environment of auditoriums and motels is brought alive by these frail-seeming survivors.

Percy is the only one you see regularly in the motel restaurants, eating early suppers before getting his teeth glued in and having a rest ahead of the concert.

Some of the bands' favorite barbecue joints: McKeska's in El Campo, Texas; Jack and Eddie's in Fort Myers, Florida; and Arthur Bryant's in Kansas City. Other places where they often stop: the Ocean Grill in Vero Beach, Florida; Blackie's in Chicago; and a boarding house in Savannah with great bisquits that was mentioned in a *New York Times* travel section but whose name nobody can remember. Also the musicians like the Heritage Houses, where you pay one price and eat as much as you want, including pastries, and ice cream out of a machine. In the late 60s and early 70s they often stopped at Club 64 in Council Bluff, Iowa. "Me and Mr Percy'd drink that Wild Turkey," fondly muses Bill Sones.

MINNEAPOLIS. A hilarious foul-up about the room reservations in a fancy downtown hotel. The lobby is on the third floor. There seems to be something wrong with the elevators, and the musicians are confusedly carrying their instrument cases up and down in different elevators, not knowing whether to get in or out, their bewildered

faces appearing and reappearing as the doors open and close. Sing shakes his head and mutters in his nearly incomprehensible accent, "I want a hotel on the *ground*, man."

AURORA, ILLINOIS. As usual, various friends show up in the dressing room. They point to their kids, a year older than last time the band was here. The band guys seem to recognize them, taking easily and naturally to this far-flung family role. It's a wonderful old vaudeville theater from the 1930s. People are sitting on the stage. The musicians like that. Marching out in their little one-by-one routine on the first tune, Frank Demond plays to this and that individual among them. Lots of eye contact.

I find myself seated in back of the band, right behind Allan Jaffe's tuba. There are those who object to his having injected himself into the group among the "authentic" oldsters. But I enjoy his playing; it carries simple, jagged street-parade cadences, dovetailing with Parker's tom-tom and bass-drum accents. At home in New Orleans Jaffe plays mainly with the Olympia Brass Band. Like most of the musicians, he has been playing exactly the same notes for more than 20 years. And meaning it every time. I chart his movements while playing:

1. Basic left and right rock, as when the tuba opens *Joe Avery's Blues.*

2. Bounce on toes and heels.

3. Lean on one hip so the other goes up and down.

4. Simple knee wiggle.

5. Tiny steps (in place).

6. Combination rock and bounce (moving left and right while at the same time up and down).

7. Several small steps forward.

8. Knee squat as in German oompah music.

9. Also, he moves all over the back of the stage behind the band, turns to different sides, alternately closes his eyes and keeps them peeled on everything going on, turns completely around to check the audience behind.

10. During the drum solo, a complex dance impossible to describe.

Once, Allan's tuba bangs Sing's head when Sing comes backward to take a bow. Allan pats Sing's head, points, laughs with Frank Parker and the audience. All sorts of little winks and laughing between Demond and Manny Crusto, pointing at funny things, keeping it all light and upbeat, which the people love.

For some reason Percy has been stomping off *Panama* slower and slower as the tour moves along. Tonight he again dons his gray cardigan. Frank Parker keeps his jacket on – he's cold, there are even a few fur coats in the audience – but everyone else is in their shirt sleeves. All are wearing their red or blue Preservation Hall ties, some with unbuttoned collars.

Before they start Narvin's feature, *Memories*, he tells the rest of the band: "Very soft and very sweet." Because this can be faintly heard through the mike, a ripple of warm laughter spreads through the audience. He previously announced he is playing it in memory of a banjo player whom he met last time they were here, and who has since passed away.

Manny, after his solo, does a nice accompaniment standing next to Narvin, who resumes singing "Memories of love so true." This kind of sweetness in the New Orleans tradition is so often missed by the "revivalist" generation of younger Whites. Why? Something to do with the difference between receiving this music with your mother's milk and struggling hard to master it later.

Afterwards, while the band is driving away past the marquee advertising it in bold letters, a couple who had been at the concert turn and wave excitedly to the bus like old friends. INDIANA. Jaffe rarely aims his mean streak directly at any of the musicians, except in the way of sarcastic kidding with some practical purpose behind it. But he can be fierce in keeping would-be exploiters away, or in silencing a player who really gets out of line, which the others appreciate.

MINNEAPOLIS. A resident who has known the musicians for 30 years muses, "There is a lot of wonderful humor. And a kind of unified story-telling among themselves. Those guys have their own folkways in describing things, but you know very well that they have pretty strong feelings toward each other. Just the way they tell stories, they remind each other of what happened at this point in time, to this fellow or that fellow, many of whom have been dead and gone a long time. The feeling they have about their shared experiences, the lives they've all had to lead, are so different from ours and the other people they are playing for. As they're playing, they're kind of telling a little story with a feeling that gives the music such a uniqueness. The music continuing in the Hall with newer players will never be quite the same because they will not have shared the same life experiences.

"Like when they would stay in the different homes here, the stories they told of trying to survive during the Depression. After they got through playing a job, they'd all end up in the kitchen for sandwiches and milk and ice cream, and that's when the stories would start. And they were all told with a great deal of affection and good humor – you never saw any bad humbugs. It's that feeling of a shared community experience that is so unique to New Orleans musicians. And if you enlarge upon that, it's true of the overall black experience. It comes through in much of the black music."

Driver Bill Sones: "The only thing about Kid Thomas is you have to watch what he eats. He likes his eggs in the morning. He likes meat balls and spaghetti real well. Take him to a really good place, and he'll hate it. A mediocre place, he'll probably like real well. He never carries anything in his bag. Usually a couple pairs of shorts. You pick up his bag and almost throw it over your head. One bag he had, there was nothin' in it, not one thing.

"Some of the guys wash their undershirts, drawers and stuff, hang them out every night to dry. Reach over the bathtub, put a little Cheer or Tide or somethin' in. Do their own scrubbin'. Shoe shines. You go in their room and laundry hangin' all around, you think it's a laundry rather than a hotel."

OHIO. Sitting in huge concert halls full of people, I feel: this is a great gift to the world.

The feeling of hush, almost of worship, during *Closer Walk* and other soft numbers, broken now and then by applause.

Cutting a swath across the broad Midwestern landscape, the bus does resemble a mother whale, its belly full of records and instruments, spewing notes over the prairies and towns, hatching again and again this precious cargo of old troupers.

More stories about other musicians they've all played with for years. The aloofness of one is a standing joke: "How you feeling?" "Poca poca." "How's the family?" "None of your business." "Heard you're going out on tour next week." "So they say." The same jazzman would lie on his bed and practice his imaginary banjo in the air, exercising his fingers. He would also get up in the middle of the night and start tuning up or washing his laundry – neither of which thrilled his roommates. He had a habit of formally announcing himself in stentorian tones before entering any room, day or night, as his mother had long ago taught him. Once, called at 2:30 a.m. for an unusual job an hour later, he replied, "Just a minute, I got to check my book." If there were any group decision to be made, he would immediately raise his hand and say, "I'll go with the majority."

MILWAUKEE. The bus breaks down. As it limps into the Greyhound terminal, there, stuck up on the glass window of the dispatcher's office, is a picture postcard of the Kid Thomas Preservation Hall band. Only Frank Demond seems to find that remarkable. Everyone is tired, bedraggled. But, despite their ages, and the managers' telling them not to, all pitch in to shift the mountains of stuff from one bus into the other.

"We play for free," says Jaffe. "We get paid for traveling." He buys everybody a big dinner at a nice German restaurant called Ratzsch's. Here Percy tells of the time they flew to London for one night to play a super-fashionable party given by financier Sir James Goldsmith. "For them elite," says Percy, "we was the *delite*."

Willie Humphrey's wife, Ora, told me about another time they were in London, and Willie was a featured guest star. Every night a long limousine appeared at their hotel to take him to the job and bring him home afterward. A special chef was provided to cook for the New Orleans people. "Ain't nothin' wrong with this job," said Willie. "But it ain't New Orleans." (His "grand-mama" used to take in washing.)

What a wonderful way these guys

have of celebrating and weaving stories around all the small details of life. Sing comes up the aisle to present me with a styrofoam cup carried from the motel. He tells me it's a much better one than identical cups stacked high in the back of the bus. Forget logic; he wanted to give me something. He's always bringing Bill Sones cups of R.C. Cola or Orange Crush. Bill loves him for it.

PENNSYLVANIA. Sing bitches at Jaffe for hiding the bottle of Old Crow the auditorium management put out in the back room for the band. A whole volume could be written on this subject.

Jaffe's father comes to the concert in Philadelphia. Backstage he says to me, "Isn't it wonderful to think that a child of yours can make a living from making people happy the way he does? Just imagine, a doctor gives you a medicine prescription and hopes maybe it's gonna do you good. They play the music and see everybody excited and happy. What could be better? I'm proud of that."

Chris Botsford has noticed that the more the people spend for tickets, the more records they buy. Especially, they buy a lot at benefit concerts.

Bill Sones again: "After Jim Robinson was sick, the last trip he made, we got out at a Holiday Inn. It was real windy that day, and his hat blew off his head. As he was goin' to get it, he stumbled and fell. He skinned his arm a little and skinned his chin, and Jaffe and I grabbed him and picked him up, and I went and got his hat, and we went and took him on to the room. I got stuff off the bus and put some methyolate on him. And we had him sittin' in a big chair, and I picked at him a little bit, try to take his mind off of what had happened, 'cause it had kind of unraveled him a little bit, the fall. I got some pictures of him sittin' in this chair, and in my mind I remember he was real appreciative of me helpin' him, and putting the stuff on his arm and cleanin' it, 'cause it had a little dirt in it, you know, got a rag and cleaned it up. He seemed like he really liked that, he really appreciated that, and that always sticks in my mind, every time I look at that picture."

DELAWARE. Lots of extra friends on the bus tonight. The spirits of the musicians are rising: "Wait till we get to Philly and especially New York. Once we had a party on the bus and sidewalk in front of the hotel all night until morning."

Out on the road, in motel and freeway and fast food land, the citizenry's hunger for the organic and personal. This Americruiser is bringing it, and the people are eating it up. Some of them point to individual musicians and say, "There's So-and-So." Others ask after someone who's missing. Some bring gaily painted parasols for the dancing in the aisles.

NEW YORK. The Lincoln Center audience is extremely responsive – far less cool or inhibited than most of the Midwest audiences. Also the New Jersey working class area audience was tremendously responsive – open to their own feelings.

Interviewer: "Who taught you to play piano?"

Sing: "Nobody taught me to play piano."

"What does New Orleans jazz mean to you?"

"It mean everything to me."

"What did you do in the war?"

"All I did was shine shoes and play piano and shake dice."

"Weren't you a feature attraction in Europe?"

"Sho. A woman brought a picture to me to sign and said, 'I'm the cause of you gettin' this job.' I tore up the picture and said, 'You ain't the cause. *I'm* the cause. My piano playing.'"

A man writing an academic dissertation on the blues gravely asks Sing where the blues began. Sing: "I'll *tell* you where they began. Blues began with fish fries."

Twentieth-century America can package anything. In a world of mass distribution, you learn to prize the earthy, the unglossy and unvarnished, as being closer to the inner truth of your own heart.

The Indian saint Ramakrishna said, "The world is indeed a mixture of truth and make-believe. Discard the make-believe and take the truth."

Part of Jaffe's wisdom has been to leave creaky old Preservation Hall as is. Once, my stepson, drummer Jeff Hamilton, trying to be helpful, oiled a squeaky hinge on one of the ancient French doors; Jaffe made him painstakingly remove the oil until the hinges squeaked properly again.

"Who are those guys?" people wonder. They look different. They are different. New Orleans is one of the few really "different" cities. Part of what sells these bands: a city that has never been co-opted into the Anglo system.

A kind of anti-show-biz show-biz, the way these old characters are non-staged, strolling out in their sometime caps and baggy pants. A period piece. How much of it was accident? Jaffe does run his power trips, but at least he had the sense to leave people and things as they were, genuinely respecting them. He also has that green thumb, that intuition for making the right everyday decisions, small and large – and his special fondness for the off-beat. Such as the time he sent Sing to represent the band on an important live radio show in Alaska. Packaging the perverse.

Having to leave the tour, I feel a sudden emptiness. No wonder so many fans adopt Preservation Hall as a kind of surrogate family.

NEW ORLEANS. Trombonist Worthia "Showboy" Thomas won't talk to me for my book. Instead, he wants me to do a whole book about him. *With* him. "I was livin' under the same tent the elephants were. Barnum and Bailey. I had the sideshow band. I was the bandleader. I been around. I have a hell of a history behind me – if you – *we* – want to make some money. I don't go around looking for publicity."

"Enjoy" is as big a word around New Orleans as "achieve" is in the rest of the USA.

The *Washington Post* recently carried a story about Preservation Hall entitled "What's Right with America."

I say to Chris: "It must drive the musicians crazy when the TV people come into the Hall and set up all those lights." Chris: "Not if they're gettin' good money."

Sweet Emma Barrett's comment on Steve McQueen when he was filming a segment of *Cincinatti Kid* at the Hall: "He's a nice little fellow."

Percy Humphrey's comment on Emma Barrett: "Disagreeable, but a good mixer."

Australian trumpeter Maurie Garbutt remembers one night in 1971 at the Hall when Kid Thomas deliberately and repeatedly played one of the notes of the opening bar of a certain tune in the wrong key. Each time, he got the oddest look from Louis Nelson and Emanuel Sayles, which broke up the audience.

Another visitor remembers the night in 1969 when the rail-thin Jim Robinson, in a humorous mood, wore a false pot belly. This so disgusted Polo Barnes that he got up and walked out, refusing to play as long as Robinson kept that monstrosity on.

When people asked Thomas how old he was, he would usually say, "I'm a hundred." One night, seeing the shock on a woman's face, he corrected himself: "No, no. I'm two hundred."

For years film star Woody Allen played his clarinet at home with records of his idols, George Lewis and Albert Burbank. Not long after George's death, Woody went to Preservation Hall to record the sound track for his film *Sleeper* with Percy's band. They received $12,000 for this. "He has a wonderful ear," Percy said afterward. "He did what you should do when you sit with another man's band. He played along with what we played. He didn't try to be a celebrity." Albert Burbank congratulated him. So did Jim Robinson. "Did anyone ever tell you you sound like my old friend George Lewis?" he asked the actor. "What's your name again?"

"Woody," mumbled Allen shyly.

"Willard? You're real good, Willard."

Cornbread Thomas played a clarinet in which all the pieces had come from different horns.

London. Alyn Shipton, an accomplished English jazz bassist and publisher, praises banjoist-singer Father Al Lewis: "I think Father Al is one of the great original banjo players. He has the ability to build up a carefully constructed solo. He'll play four bars of vamp; then he'll perhaps do a few bars of single-string work; and then he'll conclude with some chord work. It's very interesting listening to him over a number of evenings. He's rather past it now, but he was recorded enough in the early 70s to have that style put on tape for posterity."

Shipton goes on: "Preservation Hall means first-generation jazzmen from New Orleans to an awful lot of people. But every year there's a chance that one of the original links won't be there any more. It's a question of to what extent it's 'preservation' and to what extent it's allowing people who represent a style of music to work. Already, most bands, most nights, have somebody who'll be 'real' and somebody who'll be pretending to be people who've died, putting in parts for people who aren't there any more. But the Humphrey band is a very safe ticket. When I run concerts, I have a standing order for them. The agent rings up and says, 'They're back, do you want them? The fee's gone up another $500.' We say, 'Yeah, we'll have them.' And we can sell out every time."

Sue Coil, a New York editor and longtime friend of the Hall, was in Paris with Father Al and one of the bands. She avers that "Traveling with Father Al can be an experience. He brought with him a large plastic bag that had assorted food in it – crackers, cheese, little bits of this and that. He'd gather food from restaurants and add that to the collection. The day we were leaving, he spread it all around to inventory what he had, and he said, 'Oh, you poor little cracker, I guess I gonna keep you.' It was funny but also sad. Coming back from a trip to Sweden, he had a moldy piece of salami confiscated by the customs officials in New York.

"He is a huge man," continued Coil. "I said, 'Where have you been, Father Al?' He said, 'I've been all over and played for all kinds of people. I got a letter from the King.' He did; he got a letter from the King of Sweden, a personal letter saying how much his royal highness had enjoyed listening to Father Al play. He carries it in his banjo case. Their last night in Paris, the crowd kept stamping their feet for an encore. So Father Al gets up and says, 'This number we want to dedicate to my good friend, the Duchess.' He points at me. He'd been calling me 'Duchess' all week.

All these people are looking to see who is the Duchess, so I was a Duchess for five minutes."

NEW ORLEANS. Resa Lambert, who has frequently managed bands on the road, remembers once walking into one of the musicians' hotel rooms and finding the whole band there, sitting in a circle and discussing their teeth – while holding their teeth in their hands.

In Norway in 1986 Percy's band was invited into many private homes, in which the people sang to them.

This music is post-folk in the way that the USA is post-industrial. An important half-truth.

Bands in which there isn't much chance of anything going wrong are never very exciting. Risk is vital in jazz. The great majority of Blacks in our society are always at far greater risk than the great majority of Whites. Middle-class values involve buffering, reducing risk. Yet that experience of risk is psychologically important. Hence the fascination with life-and-death dramas. And with musics that make you move by staying continually off-balance.

Cornetist Charlie DeVore says: "The thing that makes the music so unique, you can't find it anywhere else, is that *beat*. It is so elusive. What is it about that New Orleans beat that is so different from other kinds of black music? It's that street band tradition that comes through. Frank Parker started out playing street music, and he played rhythm-and-blues, and did a lot of modern jazz and stuff, but he could always go back to his antecedents. That just doesn't exist for black musicians in other parts of the country. Frank tunes his drums a certain way, and gets that big New Orleans sound. It's strong, but it's not heavy. It's a lilt, it's a tremendous lift."

The American Geriatric Society is having a convention in New Orleans. A group of them show up at Preservation Hall. Chatting on the sidewalk, one says it's a kind of object lesson in how staying active and creative and appreciated can literally be a lifeline for our older citizens.

Jaffe says they've had so many negative experiences in their lives that, "To be a musician, you have to remember the good things." Recalling the great drummer Alfred Williams, who played briefly at the Hall in the early 60s: "He broke his hand putting money in a parking meter. He whacked it and broke his wrist, and it stopped him from playing, and so he really just died. It was strange. It so depressed him."

From the mountains of accumulated fan mail in the storerooms behind the Hall:

Christmas cards every year, for many years, from dozens of musicians and their wives to the Jaffes.

From Rudy and Mae Murray Baucom: "In case you don't remember us, we are the couple from North Carolina. We were there in June this year and went to Preservation Hall every night (9 nights). We would like to be in New Orleans all the time but our work is here, also our children and grand-children, so we have to be satisfied going there about once a year. . . . I am a Train Dispatcher and work with the N.S. Ry. here in Raleigh, have been railroading for 38 years now. I play trumpet some, have a lot of fun with it, we have a Jam Session about once a week here at home."

From David Lange, then Prime Minister of New Zealand: "Thank you and other members of the management of Preservation Hall for the special arrangements made for me and my delegation to visit and hear the band on Sunday last."

From Danny: "I am a good listener

of yours and for sentimental reasons am asking you now to play Happy Birthday for my girlfriend Karen. It's our one year anniversary. Please. Thank you very much."

From Janet and George, Toronto: "As promised we are sending you the copy of *Coda* with the writeup of the Royal York and the party that followed with George and Cliff's band. It was really wonderful seeing you all again. The concert was superb but the sessions after at the bar and then back at the house were just great. We can only hope that you enjoyed yourselves as much as we did."

From US Supreme Court Justice Harry A. Blackmun: "I write this little note to tell you again what a joy and pleasure it was for my entire group, including Mrs Blackmun and myself, to hear you all at the Kennedy Center on March 30. It was a warm and happy evening, and we need so much warmth and happiness these days."

From Jack McKenna of the Kinsey Machine Tool Company: "Two years ago I enjoyed hearing your band for the first time in Preservation Hall. What a thrill for me to visit New Orleans for the first time and visit where the music I love so much started.... Naturally I was thrilled by that sweet sound that DeDe Pierce plays on his trumpet. And the blending of all the instruments is perfect. To be part of a sell-out audience last night at our Culture Center, Clowes Hall, and enjoy again the original New Orleans music was wonderful. My hobby is 'Barbershop Harmony' and I am a member of The Speed Capitol Chorus here in Indianapolis.... Please come back again next year."

From Marty Adler at the US Embassy in Nicaragua: "Thanks for the tie and pins. I'm enclosing copies of a few shots from the band's performance and reception in Managua, along with a review that appeared in *La Prensa* the next day. Recognizing that the band incurred some inconvenience in coming to Managua, I want you all to know that your show was a major boost to Nicaraguan and American spirits here."

From the folks at New Antiques, Tulsa, Oklahoma: "We were recently in New Orleans and so enjoyed our experience with you that we wish to donate this chair in case you would like to add another musician."

From the New Orleans Superintendent of Schools: "Thank you for your kindness and special consideration during the recent visit of the Chinese Ambassador to our city."

Allan Jaffe tells me of the challenges they faced in getting the Hall established in the early 60s: "The racial issue was the most difficult thing to overcome. Like we could never get a parade permit for the parades that we started. I got dressed up and I went to see the Chief of Police and I told him I wanted to run these parades and what we were doing. And I told him we would hire a policeman. We hired this policeman who worked next door at Pat O'Brien's, and then we got a permit. We used to ask him to come out in plain clothes and just walk along with us. His name was O'Shaughnessy. He was a nice cop."

Wrote Curt Jerde, one of the curators of the Jazz Archive at Tulane University: "There had never been an organization, an institution, an agency of any kind in the city that took it upon itself to assert the interests of the black contingent in the jazz community. Preservation Hall has succeeded by interfacing imported, updated marketing techniques with an abiding appreciation for local, traditional lifeways. Its success rests also in large part upon the generous life support it has provided to an evanescent corpus of old jazz greats. That factor required a sensitive understanding of the paternalistic underpinnings which tie together the lives of people in the southern experience."

CALIFORNIA. Summer, 1985. A very quick college-age girl at the Concord Pavillion runs onto the stage, kisses Narvin on the cheek and scoots away almost before he can look up from his banjo. Seemingly outrageous things like this pass almost unnoticed at Preservation Hall concerts. Sing brags about his old dog who could say "Mama" and would sit on the porch, waiting for him to come home every night.

In the bland, perfect auditoriums, people half-twisting, half-dancing in their seats.

In San Francisco Airport, a woman comes up to Willie Humphrey with great respect and says, "I just wanted to thank you for many, many years of your beautiful music."

Frank Parker and Willie Humphrey jabbing, resisting, feinting at each other with words and gestures, building tension toward the release-in-laughter payoff. This happens a lot with New Orleans musicians. It happens in the music too. It's that dimensional quality, those ceaseless waves of emotion they cultivate, which separates this music from the stagnant lake of Dixieland. Dixie unrolls like a seismograph on a planet where earthquakes never happen. At the San Jose Historical Museum grounds, Sing arrives to find the following note: "Dear Pianist: I hope you can transpose up a major third with facility. I did the best I could under the circumstances. This piano should have been buried long ago. – Tuner." And it is literally true. Sing struggles through, transposing, with Narvin calling out the chords to him, and without a mike on the piano.

Fourth of July, 1984, Marin County Fairgrounds. Playing in a glowing blue and yellow striped tent. Sing's "I Sing Because I'm Free" seems appropriate, and after the fireworks he continues with "God Bless America" with the audience all joining in. Through most of the concert, the band appreciates an older man dancing with a younger woman in front. Willie points at them as they go off, and everyone claps. A little boy is dancing by himself during the second set; when he starts away Frank Demond tries to motion him to come up on stage, but he won't do it.

Then Willie starts to dance, and everyone shouts enthusiastically "Whooo!" He hands out pins saying "I Danced With Willie" during a little pause while Allan is trying to convince the sound people to turn down the amplification. Apparently deafened by rock music, and hopelessly tempted by being given so many knobs to twist, sound men have, since the 70s, become a nemesis. Percy takes an extra chorus because one of Narvin's banjo strings breaks. Afterwards, one of the many who come up to thank them says, "This is my sixth year. I just love it. But I can't come and hear you at Santa Rosa tomorrow because I'm showing sheep at the Calistoga Fair."

Sing establishes a record, in my hearing, by hitting four klunkers in a row on his descending notes in the introduction of "Amen." You can never be sure how many he'll hit; it sort of wakes you up and makes you pay attention. Such percussive shots define the man, with his sweet, hot roughness, total noncomformity, and endless complaints. At the end of the piece he slaps the wood of the piano, right in rhythm, an affectionate pat.

LOS ANGELES. Willie is a great family man. A dozen or more nieces, nephews, grandchildren and others I can't account for come backstage to greet Uncle Willie with lots of love and have their pictures taken with him. Back in New Orleans, so many people in his neighborhood know him; he stops his car to gossip with them and show me properties his grandfather owned around there. He has given encouragement and help to the young Michael White, who lives in the same neighborhood and now also plays at the Hall. Willie's wife, Ora, cooked me a meal of the best oyster gumbo I've ever eaten because a friend brought her some fresh filé from up-country. Willie gives generously of himself after concerts, signing autographs and chatting with people. He tells me, "People are very receptive, you know? And when people are enthusiastic, that makes me, too." A lady excitedly comes up to tell how she heard them in Fairbanks, Alaska, when it was 40 below outside.

At UCLA, Jaffe is scheduled to give a speech at intermission to 700 college presidents from the US and abroad. He doesn't want to. When the band gets a tremendous standing ovation after the first half, he convinces the authorities to cancel his talk.

One must realize that a certain professionalism is demanded in this concert market – a different professionalism from that demanded by the old dance halls and cornerstone layings on which many of the jazzmen cut their teeth. The more sophisticated players, like Willie, understand this.

SAN FRANCISCO. My heart leaps whenever I see them, hear them. Tonight they are playing for a big insurance company party at a sprawling old nightclub, with one of those snowflake light balls turning in the middle of the room. This is the vein Preservation Hall has somehow tapped, the major US market, with all its Anglo orderliness and discipline and conformity. Core-Americana wanting a bit of a lilt added to their lives, and loving white-haired Narvin's wide, proud smile. When Frank waves his handkerchief, many wave their napkins back.

At first, there is an unusually low-key feeling of a dance, with moderate tempos. Then, at some undefined point, for mysterious reasons, it shifts into more of a concert. Many seem to have heard the band before, and know the routines; as soon as the first notes of *The Saints* are sounded, they get up to dance. The middle-class American way of having a good time is to make uniform conga lines, rather than each dancing in his own way, as black Orleanians do. Preservation Hall musicians pay no mind to such differences. Says Frank Demond: "The music moves the people's feet, and then they start to smile. I call it the heart opening."

The band has been performing for over 20 seasons at San Francisco's mammoth Stern Grove Midsummer Music Festival. As described by the glossy program notes, some local traditions have developed:

"Octogenarian Gladie Sargent climbs atop a table, lifts her skirt, and boogies to the music of the Band and the delight of the crowd. And then there are the 'pink sheets.' It all began with the Band's former trombone player, Jim Robinson, who toured with Preservation Hall until he died a year or two shy of 90. Occasionally he'd take a white handkerchief out of his pocket and wave it at the crowd. After a couple of seasons, this became something the audience waited for, and some people took their paper napkins and waved back. But a lot of peole hadn't had picnics and didn't have napkins. The only distributive thing to wave that they could get their hands on was a page from the pink section of the Sunday paper. It grew, all during one musical number, to the thousands – thousands of people waving pink pages. It was a magical moment.

"Over the next few years, when Jim waved his handkerchief at the crowd, everyone waved back the pink section. Now Jim has been replaced by Frank Demond . . . but now the crowd at Stern grove anticipates what's going to happen. They don't wait for Frank to wave his white handkerchief. They have their pink section ready to go at the first upbeat number. When it starts, the pink sheets are already waving. It's one of the most endearing sights you can imagine."

In a press interview Percy says the band gets better and better as it plays together longer; you could have an all-star band but it wouldn't be as good. But he dislikes formal interviews, and waves off another question. Percy's wave seems to mean: you understand jazz by hanging around the scene, not by trying to make fine-tuned mental distinctions.

"Have a nice day," the hotel clerk tells Sing as he checks out. "How I'm gonna have a nice day?" snaps this bulbous little guy with his shirt tail hanging out. "You took all my money."

At concerts I can tell, by now, how each band member is feeling. Normally outgoing, Willie spends most of the first half of a concert looking glumly down at his feet. Then, as the evening goes on, he gradually warms up.

Spontaneously, a whole group in an upper balcony, with a lead soprano, joins in a churchy singing of *Closer Walk*. The rest of the audience is caught between surprise, embarrassment, enjoyment and wondering how to react. Sing makes it okay by saying gently into the mike, "Yeah – *sing* that song." Later, a

belly dancer in tight jeans does her thing off to one side of the stage. It all fits.

The reality of touring with a band is so different from what is usually written about jazz. No wonder jazz players have so much scorn for jazz criticism. This isn't some academic exercise; it is their life. So who are these experts, writing about something they have never been part of?

What will happen when that wonderful old generation of musicians is gone? Will their inner spirit be gone from the music, too? Or will it have reseeded itself?

And what will that little boy up in Michigan have done with Frank Parker's drumsticks?

In 1986 Stanford University presented a cake to the Preservation Hallers as a tribute to their 20 years of concerts there.

Index

Page Numbers in Boldface Denote Photographs.

Notes on the Sources

A primary source of information for this book is the author's collection of hundreds of hours of taped interviews with musicians, Preservation Hall personnel and others, made mainly between 1984 and 1987. A glance at the Acknowledgements shows something of the range of these conversations. Some quotes are mere jottings in pocket notebooks. Hopefully, the tapes of transcriptions will one day be available in a public archive. For the sake of clarity and flow, direct quotations in the text from these, and from personal letters and other documents, omit ellipses unless such an omission would distort the intended meaning.

A second important resource available to the author, but not to the public, is the large volume of letters, clippings, photographs and other memorabilia housed in the service wing of Preservation Hall. Such documentation is shown as *PH*.

An indispensable public source is the collection of taped interviews at Tulane University's William Ransom Hogan Jazz Archive. Nearly all of the transcriptions or summaries cited are by the competent staff there and are indicated as *JA*. General sourcebooks available there and elsewhere include Donald Kennington: *The Literature of Jazz* (American Library Association, 1971) and Barry Kernfeld (ed.): *The New Grove Dictionary of Jazz* (Macmillan, 1988).

Less well known, and not necessarily here specifically cited as a source of background knowledge, is the "Jambalaya Program (1977-1980)." Funded by the National Endowment of the Humanities, and housed at the New Orleans Public Library, it consisted of a series of lectures on aspects of New Orleans culture by experts in various fields. An index to the tapes made of the lectures is available from the library.

Other public sources of importance to New Orleans jazz scholars include the Historic New Orleans Collection and the Notarial Archives of the City of New Orleans.

Introduction: The story of Bill Russell's career, as given here and later in the book, is based largely on his own statements to the author. More detailed accounts can be found in Tom Bethell: *George Lewis* (University of California Press, 1977); Bethell: *The Electric Windmill* (Regnery Gateway, 1987); Jay Allison Stuart [in other editions aka Dorothy Tait and Ann Fairbairn]: *Call Him George* (Peter Davies, 1961); and Frederick Turner: *Remembering Song* (Viking, 1982). A seminal if slanted volume on traditional jazz which helped give impetus to the postwar "revival" is Rudi Blesh: *Shining Trumpets* (Knopf, 1946/1958; Da Capo, 1976). Other general sources on the history of New Orleans jazz include Al Rose and Edmund Souchon: *New Orleans Jazz: a Family Album* (Louisiana State University Press, 1984); Martin Williams: *Jazz Masters of New Orleans* (Da Capo, 1979); Marshall W. Stearns: *The Story of Jazz* (Oxford, 1956); Nat Shapiro and Nat Hentoff: *Hear Me Talkin' to Ya* (Dover, 1955); and Frank Driggs and Harris Lewine: *Black Beauty, White Heat* (Morrow, 1982). Russell's letter (page 9) is among Barbara Reid's papers in the possession of her daughter Kelley Edmiston in New Orleans. *The New York Times*'s account of DeDe Pierce's burial (page 22) appeared on November 29, 1973. **Music for all Occasions:** Courtesy *PH*.

Chapter One: For historical data on buildings in the French Quarter, consult the city's Notarial Archives and the Historic New Orleans Collection. Lomax's quotes, here and later in the book, are taken from an interview with the author conducted in New York City in the spring of 1984. Henry Arnold Kmen's research appears in various places, but the quoted passages are from his essay in Hodding Carter (ed.): *The Past as Prelude: New Orleans, 1718-1968* (Tulane University, 1968). Willie Humphrey's comments, here as later, are from the author's numerous interviews with him in the mid-80s. A history of the New Orleans brass bands is William J. Schafer: *Brass Bands and New Orleans Jazz* (Louisiana State University Press, 1977). On ragtime, see Rudi Blesh and Harriet Janis: *They All Played Ragtime* (Oak Publications, 4th edn, 1971) and William J. Schafer and Johannes Riedel: *The Art of Ragtime* (Da Capo, 1977). Ernest Borneman's essay (pages 45-7) is reprinted in various places, among them Nat Hentoff and Albert J. McCarthy: *Jazz* (Da Capo, 1975). The blues are explored in Robert Palmer: *Deep Blues* (Viking, 1981) and LeRoi Jones: *Blues People* (Morrow, 1963) and *Black Music* (Apollo, 1968). Dr Leonard Bechet's passage (page 50) is from Alan Lomax: *Mister Jelly Roll* (University of California Press, 1973). Lewis's (pages 50-51) is from Bethell: *George Lewis*. Guesnon's first quote (page 53) is from a taped interview by Bill Russell in his possession; the second (pages 53-4) is from an obscure magazine called *Jazz Report* (as quoted by Ralph J. Gleason, ellipses omitted). Johnny Wigg's material (page 57) is from taped interviews at *JA*. Louis Armstrong's (page 58) is from *Hear Me Talkin' to Ya* (ellipses omitted). Buddy Bolden's life is traced by D.M. Marquis: *In Search of Buddy Bolden,*

First Man of Jazz (Louisiana State University Press, 1978).
Sunburst of the Soul: Courtesy Alan Lomax, via Allan Jaffe.

Chapter Two: John Joyce's quote (page 66) is from *The Archivist* (May 1987), a periodical of *JA*. Percy Humphrey's quotes are from an interview with him by Lars Edegran on August 10, 1972. Ora Humphrey recounted her memories to the author in 1985. The remarks of the New Orleans psychiatrist and of Tom Dent are from the Jambalaya Project. The interview with Emanuel Paul was conducted by the author in 1986. A translation of the Ernest Ansermet article (page 82) appeared in Ralph de Toledano: *Frontiers of Jazz* (Frederick Ungar, 1962). Bechet's quote (pages 82–3) is from his autobiography, *Treat it Gentle* (Da Capo, 1978). Polo Barnes's statement (pages 88-9) is from Valerie Wilmer: *The Face of Black Music* (Da Capo, 1976). Richard B. Allen's words (page 91) are from an interview by the author in 1985. Charlie DeVore's (page 93) are from the English magazine *Footnote* (December 1985). Barry Martyn's comments came in a conversation with the author in 1986. The New Orleans jazz subculture is treated in various ways in the following books: Jason Berry, Jonathan Foose and Tad Jones: *Up From the Cradle of Jazz* (University of Georgia Press, 1986); Jack V. Buerkle and Danny Barker: *Bourbon Street Black* (Oxford, 1973); Danny Barker: *A Life in Jazz* (Macmillan, 1986); and S. Frederick Starr: *New Orleans Unmasked* (Dedeaux, 1985).
That Was a Wonderful Life: Courtesy *JA, PH,* Richard B. Allen and Alma Barnes.
Those Marvelous Dance Halls: By Barbara Reid, courtesy Kelley Edmiston; Luthjens Burns courtesy *Second Line* magazine; by Richard B. Allen, courtesy Clive Wilson (from liner notes to *Kid Thomas at Kohlman's Tavern,* New Orleans Records NOR 7201).

Chapter Three: Bethell's article (page 113) appeared in the local *Vieux Carré Courier* (February 9-15, 1973). Russell's statement is from an interview with the author in 1986. Borenstein's account (pages 115-17) is compended from articles by him in *Preservation Hall Portraits* (Louisiana State University Press, 1968), *Travel & Camera* (September 1970) and *The Outsider* (spring 1963). Gonzales's interview with the author took place in 1985, Ferguson's in 1986. Thomas's interview was conducted by Kelley Edmiston before 1985, when it was transcribed. Charlie DeVore gave his interviews to the author in 1984. The author interviewed Pat Davis and Sue Coil in 1984, and Nancy Collins, Severn Darden, Sally Smith (pages 134-5) and Sascha

Borenstein in 1985. Guesnon's letter is in Bill Russell's personal collection.
Kid Thomas's Boogie: Courtesy David R. Young.
The Enduring Louis Nelson: Courtesy the *Times Picayune.*

Chapter Four: Grayson "Ken" Mills corresponded and conversed with the author in 1985 and 1986. Information on Barbara Reid comes primarily from the author's interviews with her husband, Bill Edmiston, and her daughter, Kelley Edmiston, between 1984 and 1987. Quotations from Russell and DeVore are from the same period. Marty Kaelin's words are from a letter to the author in 1985. Allen's letter is from his own collection.
A World You Couldn't Expect: Courtesy Dr Henry Blackburn.
Play with Pride: From the author's interviews with Narvin Kimball, 1984.

Chapter Five: The author's discussions with Allan Jaffe extended from 1984 to 1987. Interviews with Martyn, Russell, DeVore and Willie Humphrey are referenced above. Allen's memo (page 179) is at *JA*. Copies of the flyers, schedules, etc., exist at both *JA* and *PH*. Jaffe's parents were interviewed by the author in 1984 and 1987. Percy Humphrey's quotation (pages 192-3) is from an interview with him by Steve Young broadcast on Vermont Public Radio (July 20, 1987).
Happy Inside: Courtesy Stanford University.

Chapter Six: Richard Knowles, Stella Webb, Dodie Smith Simmons, Lars Edegran, John Paddon, Lulu White and Barry Martyn were interviewed by the author in 1986. Allen's note (page 207) is at *JA*. Edegran was interviewed by the author, and Rimington by Kelley Edmiston, in 1985. Percy Humphrey's words are from Young's interview. Bethell's article (page 216) appeared in *New Orleans* (January 1974). The author interviewed the Botsfords numerous times between 1984 and 1989. The historical analysis of the role of solos draws heavily on correspondence with Richard B. Allen and on listening to taped interviews at *JA* of the musicians mentioned.
Before Anything Else: Courtesy *PH* and Robbie and Bunch Schlosser.

Chapter Seven: Blackburn, DeVore and Thompson sketched the Minnesota Twin Cities stories in joint interviews with the author in 1984. Stephen Baffrey's remarks came during a telephone conversation in 1986. The Botsfords' and Jaffe's interviews have already been mentioned. Here, as elsewhere, most of the clippings about the bands

are from *PH*. Lucianne B. Carmichael's account (pages 250-52) appeared in the New Orleans newspaper the *Times Picayune* (March 8, 1987).
A Night on Tour: Courtesy David R. Young.
Tales of Emma: Chiefly from interviews with and accounts by Bill Russell and Chris Botsford. Emma's beauty was mentioned in Larry Gara: *The Baby Dodds Story* (Contemporary Press, 1959).

Chapter Eight: Stanley Stephens, Wendell Brunious and Michael White were interviewed by the author in 1985. Philip Frazier's quotation (page 267) ap-peared in *Dixie* (March 16, 1986). Percy Humphrey's reminiscences are again from Young's interview. The piece from *Let's Go USA* (page 273) was in the 1987 edition (ed. Diane J. Klein; published by St Martin's Press). Marcel Joly's remarks (page 275) appeared in *Footnote* (October 1986). Daniel Boorstin's (page 277) were in his book *The Image: a Guide to Pseudo-Events in America* (Atheneum, 1961/1985). Jaffe's friend's observations (pages 279-80) came in private correspondence with the author in 1986). The account of Jaffe's funeral ceremonies is drawn from the reports of several eyewitnesses.

Illustration Acknowledgements

Unless otherwise stated, all photographs in the book are the copyright of William Carter. The author and publishers gratefully acknowledge the following for granting permission for the use of their material. Acknowledgements are listed alphabetically by source; references are to page numbers.

Borenstein Collection: 114, 117, 123

Leonard E. Brackett: 100

Jules Cahn: 140, 219

Betty Carter: 72, 216, 238

Bobby Coke: x, 34, 35, 44, 58, 108

Jerome Cushman: 33, 40, 80

Frank Demond: 18, 32, 90, 96, 112, 181, 198, 205, 222, 246, 260, 275 (top)

Kelley and Bill Edmiston: 148, 151, 152

George Fletcher: 177

Lee Friedlander: 23

Historic New Orleans Collection: 28, 173

Doggy Hund: 206

Marty Kaelin: 154

Grauman Marks: 285

Barry Martyn: 77

Charles Moore/Black Star: 59

George Olson: 195, 209

Dave Pfankuchen: 55, 92, 121

Preservation Hall Collection: front endsheet, i, ii, 4, 7, 24-5, 26, 29, 30, 37, 38, 39 (top), 45, 47 (bottom), 52, 56, 62, 75, 84, 95, 106-7, 110, 112, 118, 125, 127, 128, 131, 133, 137, 143, 157, 159, 161, 164, 166, 174, 185, 186, 196-7, 230, 234, 235, 254, 256, 258, 261, 262

William Ransom Hogan Jazz Archive: 47 (top), 66, 69, 76, 88, 193

Bob Schranck: 79

Michael Smith: 232

Gerry Spiegel: 48

Charles Stroud: 83, 103

Times Newspapers, London: 178